The Sinatra Celebrity Cookbook

Barbara, Frank & Friends

The Affiliates
Barbara Sinatra Children's Center
at Eisenhower Medical Center
Rancho Mirage, CA

Barbara Sinatra '99

The Affiliates is a volunteer organization of men and women dedicated to supporting the Barbara Sinatra Children's Center in its mission to break the cycle of child abuse. The Affiliates are the driving force behind many of the Center's fund-raising activities. Another primary emphasis is to raise public awareness about how to recognize and prevent child abuse and its devastating, long-term effects through Affiliate-sponsored educational forums, open houses, and community outreach programs.

Copyright © 1996 by
The Affiliates
Barbara Sinatra Children's Center at Eisenhower
39000 Bob Hope Drive
Rancho Mirage, California 92270

To order this cookbook call: 1-800-488-1000.
Cost: $24.95 plus tax and handling.

ISBN: 0-9646756-0-9

Library of Congress Catalog Card Number 96-92543

First Printing, January 1997

Printed in the USA by

WIMMER
The Wimmer Companies, Inc.
Memphis

Table of Contents

Introduction

Barbara and Frank Sinatra have had the pleasure of dining throughout the world with royalty, celebrities, government dignitaries, sports personalities and other notables at residences and fine restaurants. Their at-home get-togethers, whether formal or informal, are legendary for lively conversation, excellent food, and making guests feel welcome.

Despite hectic schedules, both Barbara and Frank find time to make good use of their own state-of-the-art kitchens. Sometimes entertainment is casual with colorful table pottery and western motif; at other times the settings are elegant, with Fabergé box centerpieces, delicate crystal and distinguished china.

For many years, the Sinatras have been urged by friends and fans to prepare a book of recipes – their own, and those of friends and favorite restaurants. With Barbara Sinatra's assistance, plans for this, *"The Sinatra Celebrity Cookbook... Barbara, Frank & Friends"* began.

Frank Sinatra, himself an excellent cook, enthusiastically supported the idea and became a willing "recipe-tester." A partner "all the way," Chef Sinatra selected a number of his favorite recipes, including "Eggplant Parmigiana," "Frank's Favorite Clam Sauce," and "Chicken, Potato and Onion Dish." Each Sinatra contribution is strongly Italiano, fine combinations of classic preparation and modern short cuts. Ol' Blue Eyes often commandeers the kitchen to prepare his famous "Fresh Marinara Sauce for Pasta," using the freshest basil, garlic, and tomatoes.

Whether it be kitchens in hotel suites or at home, Barbara Sinatra boasts she is an aficionada of "peasant food." Her "Pasta Fagioli" is a favorite of family and friends. Barbara is also a fan of food with a Mexican flavor... the hotter the better. Both Sinatras are health-conscious and rely on fresh, nutritious ingredients.

To collect celebrity recipes, letters were dispatched to the Sinatras' friends, and to hotels and restaurants visited during concert tours and vacations. With the quick receipt of the first half-dozen recipes, organizers knew they had tapped into a gold mine of friendship, humor, warmth and genuine culinary delight.

A look at the premier sextet: From songwriter Sammy Cahn and his wife, Tita, came "Chicken Paillards with Herbs," a simple but elegant entree... eight herbs in all with a splash of olive oil and grated fresh lemon zest. Whoopi Goldberg could not keep humor out of her instructions for "Jewish American Princess Fried Chicken," and that recipe is wonderful... cajun spice is the magic ingredient. We have an offbeat recipe for a "Potato Sandwich" from Gene Kelly that is so delicious you'll want it to be part of your everyday menu. Singer Neil Diamond entrusted us with "Beef Pot Roast," perfected by his mother, Rose. Neil's recipe is a combination of Old World cooking and New World shortcuts, such as onion soup mix and bottled catsup. Angie Dickinson, with perfect penmanship, sent us her delicious "Sweet Simple Cole Slaw." From funnyman Dom DeLuise came a triple windfall: three recipes in one envelope including "Dom's Mom's Meatballs," made with beef, pork, cheese, fresh parsley, pine nuts, and Mom's "secret" ingredients.

Favorite recipes kept pouring in neatly typed, scrawled in longhand, or copies of kitchen recipe cards. Presidents Clinton, Reagan, Bush and Ford, Charles Bronson, George Burns, Claudette Colbert, Hubert de Givenchy, Oscar de la Renta, Clint Eastwood and Sidney Poitier are just a few notables who provided favorite recipes. Except for the contributions of world-renowned professional chefs, every recipe in this collection has been double-tested. When major culinary stars such as Chef Bernard Dervieux and Chef Wolfgang Puck sent

recipes for "Veal Chop with Wild Mushrooms" and "Alaskan Salmon with Ginger/ Black Pepper," we knew those fine recipes had been tested and tasted by masters.

With *The Sinatra Celebrity Cookbook... Barbara, Frank & Friends,"* the reader is invited not only to try these recipes, but to share food memories, anecdotes and reminiscences of dining experiences made memorable by the most important ingredient of all... good friends. The Affiliates have tried to offer a cookbook that is both pleasurable and enduring.

All proceeds from this book benefit the Barbara Sinatra Children's Center at Eisenhower Medical Center in Rancho Mirage, California. The Center, founded by Frank and Barbara Sinatra in 1986, is held in esteem the world over for its programs to treat and counsel abused children.

From Barbara and Frank Sinatra, from The Affiliates of the Barbara Sinatra Children's Center... bueno appetito.

Who We Are and Why

Barbara Sinatra Children's Center at Eisenhower Medical Center

Barbara and Frank Sinatra are founders of the Barbara Sinatra Children's Center on the campus of Eisenhower Medical Center in Rancho Mirage, California. The facility, founded in 1986 to counsel and treat abused children, provides comprehensive programs to combat the problems of child abuse. Barbara Sinatra, the driving force behind the Children's Center's efforts to positively affect the lives of children, has vowed that no child who needs help will ever be turned away because of inability to pay for treatment. Her celebrated husband is 100% in support of his wife's ambitious efforts. Frank Sinatra has performed at numerous fund-raising events to maintain the Barbara Sinatra Children's Center's goals; many of his entertainment industry friends have joined him in raising funds for the Center. Both Barbara and Frank Sinatra are tireless in their fund-raising efforts on behalf of the Center.

The Barbara Sinatra Children's Center has the dedicated support of experienced and respected clinicians as it further develops successful methods of treatment of physical, emotional, and sexual abuse. The Center, supported by friends and admirers of the Sinatras, as well as anonymous individuals throughout the world, provides intervention and treatment services as part of an inter-agency team consisting of police, child protective services, district attorneys' offices, and the court system.

Communities of the Coachella Valley in Southern California, esteemed professionals, and community leaders are increasing their reliance on the Barbara Sinatra Children's Center as a source of healing for abused children and their families. To appreciate the Center's important work, one must understand the enormous scope of the problem of child abuse and its impact throughout our society.

Barbara and Frank Sinatra do not simply lend their names to a cause in which they believe – Mr. and Mrs. Sinatra devote time, care, energy, and love to children who are increasingly looking to the Barbara Sinatra Children's Center for help and hope.

How You Can Help

Become a member of the Uncles Club with a $1,000 annual contribution. This group of very special men supports the mission of the Barbara Sinatra Children's Center, that no child who needs help will be turned away because of lack of ability to pay for treatment. The group has a positive effect on the lives of physically, emotionally, and sexually abused young victims, who are able to receive treatment because of their Uncles' financial support.

Become a member of the Aunts Club with a $1,000 annual contribution. This group of special women is dedicated to the interests of the children at the Barbara Sinatra Children's Center. Like the Uncles, Aunts enrich the lives of young victims by ensuring that the care and support they need will always be there.

In appreciation, the children send remembrances to the Aunts and Uncles on birthdays and other special occasions. Annual contributions by Aunts and Uncles provide financial support that enables many child victims to receive treatment for their abuse.

Become a Friend of the Children with a minimum $200 annual contribution. As Friends of the Children, individuals, organizations, and businesses offer financial support to the Barbara Sinatra Children's Center's goal of breaking the cycle of child abuse. Their primary purpose is to ensure the growth of the Center's programs and services for the community.

Become a member of the Affiliates with a $150 annual contribution. This growing organization raises funds and helps to educate the community about problems of child abuse. Together with the Sinatras, this cookbook is a project of The Affiliates.

Make a Tribute or Memorial Gift. Gifts in memory of a loved one or friend, or gifts honoring a special occasion, may be made to the Barbara Sinatra Children's Center. All gifts contribute to the many vital activities of the Center, including purchasing equipment, providing community services, and assisting in child and family therapy.

Your generous participation is appreciated.

Before and After Treatment

The Effects of Treatment

Acknowledgements

Cookbook Committee 1994-1996

Chairperson . . . . *Sharon Spiegel*

Editor . . . . *Maureen Daly*

Recipe Collection . . . . *Judy Gelfand*

Production . . . . *Roberta Nyman*
Sloane Halloran Lewis

Testing . . . . *Lyn Burke*
Paul Woods
Helen Allen

Marketing . . . . *Marianne Hodgkins*
Lonna Wais
Joyce Weiss

Promotion/Consultation . . . . *Susan Reynolds*

Cookbook Committee 1993-1994

Chairpersons:
   Recipe Collection . . . . *Judy Gelfand*
   Production/Coordination . . . . *Sharon Spiegel*
Vice-Chairpersons:
   Recipe Collection . . . . *Galen Solomon*
   Production/Coordination . . . . *Roberta Nyman*

Editor . . . . *Maureen Daly*

Testing . . . . *Lyn Burke*
Paul Woods

Marketing . . . . *Joan Haimsohn*
Marianne Hodgkins

The Launch Committee 1992-1993

Judy Gelfand	*Sallie Manassah*	*Galen Solomon*
Cyma Cohen	*Pat Oygar*	*Leslie Gebhart*
Rose Narva	*Cydney Osterman*	*La Donna Keaton*

The Children's Center wishes to thank
the following for their help in making our dream a reality.

Barbara and Frank Sinatra

Inga Alexander
Michael Allen
Isabel Barnett
Andrew Beam
John Belonis
Ella Berkeley
Tricia Bothmer
Clare Bowen
Dee Boyer
Jim Boyer
Robin Ceriele
Jean Chapman
Patricia Charles
Tina Cohen
Caroline Brown-
  Crescenzi
Evelyn Cucchiarella
Carol Feinstein
Helene Galen
Peggy S. Greenbaum
Lovey Greenberg
Minnette Haber
Nancy Harris
Roberta Holland
Bobbe Horvitz
Mary Jane Jenkins
Ed Jieffer
Barbara Kaplan
Patrick Kenner

Nelda Linsk
Kalisa Maffeo
Lynn Mallotto
Lois Mauer
JoAnn McGrath
Susan Meyer
Margo Munro
Betty Lee Nelson
Patty Newman
Maxine Owens
Bill Pattis
Veronique Peck
Barbara Platt
Bill Porter
Chris Rasmussen
Rella Rifkin
Mary Rothschild
Sylvia Rotman
George Schlatter
John Shields
Lorely Shrivastava
Barb Smith
Robert Spiegel
Bob Street
Cal Vander Woude
Rita Wade
Diane Watt
Roland Young
Virginia Zamboni

Notables who provided recipes

Therapists and Staff of the Barbara Sinatra
Children's Center

Eisenhower Medical Center Foundation

Eisenhower Medical Center Auxiliary

Susan Reynolds, Scoop Marketing

Mary Kay Plock and Harlan Corenman,
  Eisenhower Medical Center Public Relations

Design and Production:
  Patty Lewis and Kelle Bates,
  Visual Communications, Annenberg Center
  for Health Sciences at Eisenhower

Division Page Art Work provided by the children
of the Barbara Sinatra Children's Center

Steven Uslan, Prestone Graphics

Photography:
  Front cover by Harry Langdon

  Back cover by Bradley K. Hansen,
  Visual Communications, Annenberg Center
  for Health Sciences at Eisenhower

Photographs on recipe pages provided by
the celebrities

Other photographs courtesy of Mr. and Mrs.
Frank Sinatra, Eisenhower Medical Center
Public Relations, and others.

Barbara Sinatra Children's Center
Eisenhower Medical Center, Rancho Mirage, California

Dedication

I love good food. When my lovely Barbara agreed to be my wife, my mom and dad naturally took time to teach her my favorite recipes. Many of those recipes and others that we use in our home are in this book. I guess I'm living proof you can eat all of the Italian foods – pastas, sauces, and breads, and still grow up to be thin.

My earliest childhood memories are of my father, Marty, in the kitchen. He did much of the cooking, as Dolly, my wonderful mother, was a powerful force and dedicated worker in the political arena. She was out there fighting for women's rights long before women even knew they should have them. My pop would stand at the stove cooking the greatest pasta sauce any young Italian boy could hope for. One time, I called at the last minute and my pop cooked an Italian meal for the entire Tommy Dorsey orchestra. Some of the sax players had to eat in the hallway, but they still loved the meal. Now that I'm an adult, two of my favorite things to do are to cook and to eat; occasionally, I do both... and always with a beverage! But, that's a subject for another book.

Fortunately, I met the love of my life, a gorgeous young woman by the name of Barbara Ann. That's when I really began to appreciate all the finer things in life, including those that came out of the kitchen. Barbara's talents as a good cook extend to her graciousness as a hostess by making guests feel completely comfortable and welcome.

The best recipe is a well-prepared meal, fine wine, and good conversation with people you know. With these ingredients, you can't miss. Barbara and I have had high tea with Anwar and Jehan Sadat in their Cairo home; sipped cocktails with Don Rickles and Bruce Springsteen at La Dolce Vita; gathered our road family after a concert for supper at an out-of-the-way Italian joint – these types of occasions are always quite special.

As you sample the recipes in this book, Barbara and I hope you experience the same warmth with your loved ones and friends that we do with ours.

A salute!

Frank Sinatra

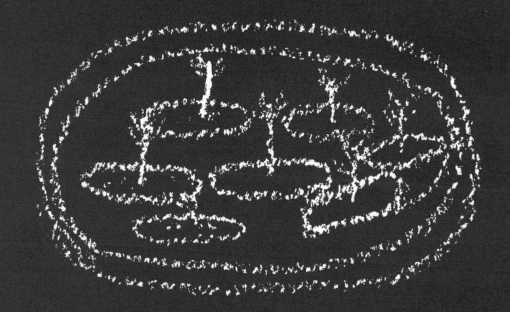

Appetizers & Starters

Joyce, age 7

LINDA EVANS

Artichoke Dip

- 1 (8 ounce) package cream cheese, softened
- ½ cup mayonnaise
- 1 teaspoon hot pepper sauce
- 1½ tablespoons minced green onion (white portion only)
- ½ cup (2 ounces) grated Parmesan cheese
- 1 cup finely chopped cooked artichoke bottoms

- Combine cream cheese, mayonnaise and hot pepper sauce, creaming until smooth.
- Add green onion and Parmesan cheese to cream cheese mixture. Using spatula, fold in artichoke bottoms.
- Spread mixture in 4-inch round soufflé dish.
- Bake at 350 degrees for 20 minutes; do not overcook or mixture will separate. Blot top of baked dip with paper towel to absorb excess grease.
- Serve warm with rice crackers. Makes 3 cups.

LORD JAMES HANSON, CBE

Caviar Canapés

- 4 hard cooked eggs
- mayonnaise
- salt
- grated onion
- 4 slices white sandwich bread
- 3 tablespoons caviar

- Using egg cutter, slice eggs crosswise. Remove yolk and reserve 4 center slices of white.
- Press yolk through sieve. Add just enough mayonnaise to form creamy consistency. Season with few grains salt and add a small amount of onion.
- Cut bread with 2-inch round cutter. Toast to brown on both sides.
- Place egg white round on each toasted bread round. Pipe egg mixture into center of white and spoon ½ teaspoon caviar on yolk mixture.
- Makes 16.

MRS. WALTER H. ANNENBERG (LEONORE)

Cheese Puffs

½ (8 ounce) package cream cheese, softened
1 cup (4 ounces) grated yellow Cheddar cheese
½ medium-sized onion, grated
1 egg yolk
salt and black pepper to taste
20 to 24 slices thin bread rounds
paprika for garnish

- Two hours before serving, combine cream cheese, Cheddar cheese, onion and egg yolk. Season with salt and black pepper. Chill until ready to assemble puffs.
- Toast bread slices.
- Spread cheese mixture on toasted rounds. Sprinkle with paprika. Place on baking sheet.
- Broil until lightly browned.
- Serve hot. Makes 20 to 24.

SENATOR ROBERT DOLE

Seville Shrimp

¾ cup margarine, softened
½ cup (2 ounces) grated Parmesan cheese
½ cup dry bread crumbs
¼ cup lemon juice
⅔ cup chopped green onion
1 clove garlic, minced
¼ teaspoon salt
1 pound cooked medium shrimp, peeled and deveined
parsley sprigs

- Combine margarine, cheese, bread crumbs, lemon juice, green onion, garlic, salt and shrimp, reserving a few shrimp for garnish.
- Spoon mixture into 8 individual casseroles.
- Bake at 350 degrees for 20 to 23 minutes.
- Garnish servings with parsley and reserved shrimp. Serves 8.

**GRANITA, MALIBU, CALIFORNIA
LEE HEFTER, EXECUTIVE CHEF
WOLFGANG PUCK, PROPRIETOR**

Crisp Potato Galette with Gravlax and Dill Creme Fraiche

3 potatoes, peeled and grated
1 cup clarified butter, divided
salt and freshly ground black pepper
1 pound gravlax or smoked salmon, thinly sliced
½ cup creme fraiche or sour cream
3 shallots, minced
5 sprigs dill, chopped
juice of 1 lemon
1 tablespoon olive oil
½ bunch chives, chopped
3 ounces salmon caviar

- Toss potatoes with half of butter. Season with salt and black pepper.
- Heat two 10-inch non-stick sauté pans over high heat until very hot. Divide remaining ½ cup butter between pans.
- Add potatoes to pans, dividing evenly. Shape each portion into thick pancake. Cook for 1 to 2 minutes, reduce heat and sauté until almost golden brown. Using spatula to check underside, turn and sauté other side until golden. Remove galettes from pans and keep warm in oven at 425 degrees for 10 minutes.
- Prepare dill cream by combining creme fraiche or sour cream, shallots, dill, and juice of ½ lemon. Season with salt and black pepper. Mix well.
- Remove galettes from oven. Spread with dill cream and arrange gravlax slices to cover each. Lightly brush gravlax with oil, sprinkle with black pepper and drizzle with juice of remaining ½ lemon.
- Cut galettes into serving portions. Garnish with chives and caviar.
- Serve immediately. Serves 4 to 6.

What we cannot put in these recipes is the importance of the ambiance and guests gathered around the table. Whether it's a fine cup of hot espresso and homemade cheesecake or tiramisu, a glass of Italian red with veal Milanese, who you're with can be as important as what is on the menu. You can talk with acquaintances, but you want to dine with friends. An enjoyable meal can create a bond between people that lasts forever. — Frank Sinatra

MARTY INGELS

Marty's Nutty Cheese Roll

1   (8 ounce) package cream cheese, softened
½   cup (2 ounces) crumbled Blue cheese
1   cup (4 ounces) shredded sharp Cheddar
      cheese
¼   teaspoon garlic powder
dash of white pepper
dash of Worcestershire sauce
1   tablespoon brandy
1   tablespoon sherry
1   cup chopped walnuts

- Combine cream cheese, Blue cheese and Cheddar cheese. Add garlic powder, white pepper, Worcestershire sauce, brandy and sherry, blending thoroughly.
- Shape cheese mixture into a ball. Roll in nuts.
- Cover cheese ball with plastic wrap and chill for 2 hours.
- Serve with snack crackers. Makes 1 pound.

JERRY BUSS

Seven Layer Dip

1   cup sour cream
1   packet taco seasoning mix
1   (8 ounce) can bean dip
2   avocados, peeled, pitted and mashed
1   cup (4 ounces) grated Cheddar cheese
1   cup (4 ounces) grated Monterey Jack cheese
1   tomato, chopped
3   or 4 green onions, chopped
¼   cup black olives, chopped
sour cream for garnish
tortilla chips

- Blend sour cream and taco seasoning.
- On serving plate, spread and layer ingredients in order listed: bean dip, seasoned sour cream, avocado, Cheddar cheese, Monterey Jack cheese, tomato, onion and black olives. Garnish with dollop of sour cream.
- Serve at room temperature with tortilla chips for dipping. Serves 8 to 10.
- Dip can be assembled a day in advance and stored in refrigerator.

CLAUDETTE COLBERT
"I first had these at Emily De Micheli's home in Barbados. It is an old recipe used by many Barbadian cooks."

Cheese and Olive Puffs

2 **cups (8 ounces) shredded sharp Cheddar cheese, softened**
⅓ **cup butter, softened**
1 **cup all-purpose flour**
¼ **teaspoon Tabasco**
dash of Worcestershire sauce
2 **(10 ounce) bottles pimento-stuffed green olives, drained and blotted dry**

- Using food processor, blend Cheddar cheese and butter together until smooth. Add flour, Tabasco and Worcestershire sauce.
- Wrap each olive with small amount of pastry, completely covering and shaping into balls. Place on ungreased baking sheet.
- Freeze, then transfer to plastic bag and store in freezer until ready to use.
- Place on baking sheet. Bake at 400 degrees for about 12 minutes or until crust is golden.
- Serve puffs hot. Makes 36 to 48.

Claudette was what everyone imagines a Star of the Silver Screen to be — beautiful, gracious, a generous friend, and hostess with a sensational sense of style and terrific sense of humor. Being with Claudette at her home in Barbados was like walking onto an elegant, but welcoming movie set. Frank and I remember wonderful cocktail parties overlooking the ocean, nibbling these delicious canapés passed by white-gloved waiters. I love to remember Claudette's exuberant laugh as she and Frank reminisced about their early days in Hollywood. She was a treasured confidante and good friend.
— Barbara Sinatra

HELEN GURLEY BROWN
"Sorry I don't have specific amounts for these ingredients but you really don't need them. A five-year-old child can make these hors d'oeuvres."

Very Satisfying Hors D'oeuvres

1 **red onion, minced**
mayonnaise
grated Parmesan cheese
thin party rye slices or crackers

- Combine onion with dollops of mayonnaise and generous amount of Parmesan cheese for a firm consistency.
- Spread mixture on rye slices or crackers.
- Broil until lightly browned.
- Serve hot.

TOM DREESEN

"This recipe is from one of my dearest friends, Clarisso Mancuso. It came from Italy with her grandmother in 1878. Whenever I visit Clarissa, she honors me with her cooking. This is one of my favorite recipes, too."

I WISH YOU LOTS OF LOVE AND LAUGHS ALL YOUR LIFE
Tom Dreesen

Stuffed Artichokes

4	medium-sized artichokes
1	large clove garlic, minced
¼	cup olive oil
1	cup dry bread crumbs
¼	cup chopped parsley

salt to taste
¼ teaspoon black pepper
oregano to taste
golden raisins to taste (optional)
4 slices lemon

- Remove chokes from artichokes. Steam in small amount of water for 15 minutes, adding water to pan as needed. Drain thoroughly.
- Combine garlic, oil, bread crumbs, parsley, salt, black pepper, oregano and raisins. Add small amount of artichoke cooking liquid if needed to moisten stuffing.
- Spoon stuffing between artichoke leaves. Place artichokes in small baking pan and top each with lemon slice. Cover.
- Bake at 350 degrees for 30 minutes. Serves 4.

MAIN STREET, NEW YORK, NEW YORK
JEFFERY KADISH, EXECUTIVE CHEF

Oven Roasted Chicken Wings with Orange Horseradish Marmalade

2 pounds chicken wings
salt and black pepper to taste
½ cup soy sauce
½ cup whole grain mustard
¼ cup freshly ground horseradish
¾ cup orange marmalade
¼ cup lemon juice

- Season wings with salt and black pepper.
- Combine soy sauce and mustard. Marinate wings in liquid for 30 minutes. Drain well and place on greased baking sheet.
- Bake at 375 degrees for 40 minutes. Remove from oven and cool.
- Place cooked wings on a hot sizzle pan. Roast until brown and crispy.
- Prepare sauce by combining horseradish, marmalade and lemon juice, mixing well.
- Serve hot wings with sauce. Serves 4.

CHERYL LADD

Spinach Dip

1 round loaf French bread
2 (10 ounce) packages frozen chopped spinach, thawed and well drained
1 bunch scallions, sliced
1 (8 ounce) can water chestnuts, drained and chopped
1 cup mayonnaise
2 tablespoons sour cream
¼ cup salad seasoning with dried vegetable bits
1½ teaspoons garlic powder

- Cut slice from top of bread loaf and set aside. Hollow loaf, removing bread in pieces and leaving sides and bottom about 1-inch thick. Cut bread pieces and top slice in chunks for dipping.
- Combine spinach, scallions, water chestnuts, mayonnaise, sour cream, salad seasoning and garlic powder. Mix thoroughly.
- Spoon spinach mixture into bread bowl.
- Serve with bread pieces or snack cracker. Serves 16.

RUTA LEE
"Cheers, Sweeties — who cares about the rest of the meal?"

"Jello" for Adults

consommé
vodka
sour cream
caviar
fresh lemon juice
green or white onion

- Pour consommé into saucepan. Heat to near boiling. Cool to room temperature and place in freezer to chill.
- Pour consommé gel into cocktail dishes or glasses. Pour jigger of vodka over consomme.
- Garnish each serving with dollop of sour cream, spoon of caviar, squeeze of lemon juice and a sprinkle of onion.
- Serve immediately.

JOE MANTEGNA

"Traditionally, you select the largest shell in your bowl to use as a spoon to pluck mussels from their shells...and to sip the juices. Take time and savor this...using crusty bread to mop up every last drop. If you're rushing off to see a movie, spoons are okay."

Mussels Mantegna

  2 to 3 pounds mussels
  1 small onion or 2 large shallots, minced
  2 tablespoons butter or margarine
  1 to 2 tablespoons olive oil
  ¼ pound fresh mushrooms, sliced
  2 or 3 cloves garlic, minced
handful of fresh parsley, chopped
  2 to 4 tablespoons white wine or dry vermouth
  1 (14½ ounce) can Italian-style stewed tomatoes
salt and black pepper to taste
fresh basil or oregano (optional)

* Scrub and debeard fresh, tightly closed mussels. Set aside.
* Sauté onion or shallots in butter or margarine and oil in heavy stock pot over medium heat until transparent.
* Add mushrooms and garlic to onion and sauté until golden, shaking frequently to stir.
* Stir in parsley and add wine to just cover bottom of stock pot.
* Add tomatoes to vegetables, cover and bring to a boil over high heat. Season with salt and black pepper.
* Add mussels, cover tightly to steam. Carefully shaking pot every 30 seconds, cook over high heat for 3 minutes. Mussels are done when all shells are opened; discard any mussels that do not open.
* Check broth and adjust seasonings, adding basil or oregano if desired.
* Divide mussels among deep individual serving bowls. Carefully pour cooking liquid over mussels; do not use last liquid in pot because it may contain shell fragments. Serves 4.

JOHN LUJACK

Pigs in Blanket

 2 **cups water**
⅓ **cup barley**
 1 **cup regular rice**
 2 **heads cabbage, cores removed**
2½ **pounds ground raw turkey**
 1 **onion, diced**
 2 **(10½ ounce) cans tomato soup**
 2 **soup cans water**
 1 **small onion, chopped**

- Bring 2 cups water in saucepan to boil. Add barley and cook, uncovered, for 15 minutes or until nearly tender.
- Stir rice into barley and cook, uncovered, for about 15 minutes or until rice is nearly done. All liquid will not be absorbed. Set aside.
- In large pot of boiling water, submerge cabbage heads. As leaves soften, separate and push to bottom of pot; remove when pliable and drain. Repeat until all large leaves are cooked, remove remaining cabbage and set aside.
- While cabbage leaves are cooking, brown turkey with onion in skillet, stirring to crumble. Drain excess fat.
- Add barley and rice mixture to turkey. Bring to a boil, then turn off heat.
- Blend soup and soup cans of water in saucepan. Heat thoroughly.
- Place 1 tablespoon meat mixture in each cabbage leaf. Roll tightly and secure with wooden pick. Place in baking pan.
- Chop remaining cabbage and mix with onion. Sprinkle on cabbage rolls. Pour tomato sauce over rolls.
- Bake, covered, at 375 degrees for 30 minutes. Turn oven off but do not remove rolls for 15 to 30 minutes.
- Serve cabbage rolls hot. Serves 6.

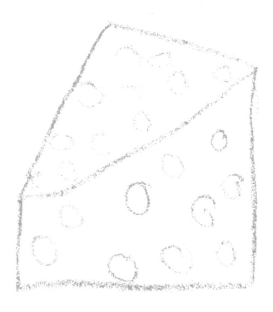

JAY LENO

Uncle Louie's Chicken Wings Marinara

2 to 3 dozen chicken wings
all-purpose flour
safflower or peanut oil for deep frying
crushed garlic to taste
olive oil
1 (29 ounce) can whole plum tomatoes
3 to 4 teaspoons chopped parsley
salt to taste
2 tablespoons hot sauce

- Broil wings or dredge in flour and deep fry in safflower or peanut oil. While wings cook, prepare sauce.
- Sauté garlic in ⅛-inch depth hot olive oil in skillet.
- Press tomatoes through sieve and add to garlic in oil.
- Add parsley and salt to tomatoes. Cook for about 20 minutes. Toward end of cooking time, stir in hot sauce to taste. Cook for additional 3 to 4 minutes.
- Toss wings with ½ cup sauce. Serve with remaining sauce for dipping. Serves 6 to 8.

COMME CHEZ SOI, BRUSSELS, BELGIUM
PIERRE WYNANTS,
PROPRIETOR AND EXECUTIVE CHEF
"For the wine: Something young, fruity and fresh, either burgundy or Pinot Noir."

Tomatoes and Snails with Fresh Basil

4 ripe tomatoes, peeled and diced
salt and black pepper
48 small gray snails, canned
2 shallots, finely chopped
1½ cloves garlic, pressed or chopped
2 tablespoons unsalted butter
5 tablespoons coarsely chopped basil
4 tablespoons coarsely chopped parsley
2 tablespoons bread crumbs

- Spoon tomatoes into 12x8x2-inch broiler-proof dish. Season lightly with salt and black pepper.
- Strain snails, reserving juice.
- Sauté shallots and garlic in butter in saucepan until tender.
- Add snails and ⅔ cup reserved snail liquid to vegetables. Stir in basil and parsley. Bring to a boil.
- Pour snail mixture over tomatoes. Sprinkle with bread crumbs.
- Broil until browned. Serve hot. Serves 4.

DEAN MARTIN

Caviar Potato Appetizers

6 small baking potatoes
½ cup sour cream
onion salt to taste
¼ cup caviar

- Bake potatoes at 400 degrees until done.
- Cut potatoes in halves. Scoop out pulp, leaving thin layer attached to shell. Mash pulp until smooth.
- Whip sour cream and onion salt into mashed potatoes. Spoon mixture into potato shells.
- Sprinkle 1 teaspoon caviar on each potato half.
- Makes 12.

I've heard you're never supposed to drink anything cold when eating. Well, that never went over too well with Dean. He used to say that drinking a cold beverage made blood rush to the stomach and that aided digestion. The only time Dean got indigestion was when he got hold of some bad ice... NOT.
— *Frank Sinatra*

THE HONORABLE HAZEL O'LEARY

Artichoke and Cheese Squares

2 (6½ ounce) jars marinated artichoke hearts
¾ cup minced onion
2 cups (8 ounces) grated sharp Cheddar cheese
4 eggs, lightly beaten
¼ cup bread crumbs
¼ teaspoon salt
black pepper to taste
1 teaspoon garlic powder
½ teaspoon parsley flakes
dash of hot pepper sauce

- Drain artichokes, reserving ½ of marinade. Chop artichokes and set aside.
- Sauté onion in reserved marinade in large skillet over moderate heat for 5 minutes.
- Add artichokes, cheese, eggs, bread crumbs, salt, black pepper, garlic powder, parsley and hot pepper sauce. Mix thoroughly. Spread mixture in well-buttered 11x7x1½-inch baking dish.
- Bake at 325 degrees for 30 minutes or until done. Cool in dish for 5 minutes before cutting into squares.
- Serve warm or at room temperature. Makes 36.

ROBERT AND MARION MERRILL

Gravlax

2 tablespoons sugar
2 tablespoons coarse or kosher salt
2 pounds center cut fresh salmon, cut in 2 large
  fillets (scaled but skin intact)
1 large bunch dill

- Combine sugar and salt. Rub mixture on cut surfaces of salmon, using as much as needed to cover both pieces.
- Place bed of dill on bottom of glass baking dish large enough to contain salmon. Lay salmon fillet, skin side down, on dill. Arrange additional dill on cut surface. Top with second fillet, cut side down. Add additional dill on top of stacked fillets.
- Cover with wax paper, then cover with aluminum foil. Place heavy object (such as rocks or bricks) on foil-covered salmon. Pressure will help create a brine to marinate and process the salmon.
- Chill for 48 to 72 hours, turning entire salmon about every 12 hours.
- Scrape dill and seasonings away from salmon. Slice diagonally away from the skin, as for smoked salmon.
- Serve with mustard sauce. Serves 8.

MUSTARD SAUCE
1 tablespoon Dijon mustard
1 tablespoon prepared yellow mustard
1 tablespoon sugar
2 tablespoons wine vinegar
½ cup olive oil
3 tablespoons chopped dill

- Combine Dijon and yellow mustards, sugar and wine vinegar in small bowl.
- Gradually add oil, whisking to blend. Stir in dill.
- Chill sauce before serving.

VERONIQUE PECK

Quesadillas Carolwood
Cheese Stuffed Tortillas

  3 green chiles, minced
  1 large onion, minced
  2 tomatoes, peeled and chopped
  1 bunch coriander, chopped
  1 (16 ounce) package Monterey Jack cheese
  ¾ cup light olive oil or peanut oil
16 tortillas
coarse salt and freshly ground black pepper to
    taste

- Combine chiles, onion, tomatoes and coriander in small serving bowl. Mix thoroughly and set aside.
- Cut cheese in thin 2-inch slices.
- Pour oil into shallow pan or bowl large enough for dipping tortillas.
- Heat grill coals to glowing. Dip tortilla into oil, lightly coating, and fold over slice of cheese. Place on rack over coals; do not break tortilla. Using fork tines to hold tortilla in place, grill for 1 or 2 minutes on each side or until golden.
- Serve immediately, topping each quesadilla with small amount of salsa. Makes 16.
- For indoor cooking, fry tortillas in oil in skillet.

ITZHAK PERLMAN
"If you want more tang, add raw chopped onions. That's the way my mother used to make it. Make sure you have plenty of antacids — but it's worth it!"

Itzhak Perlman's Very Fattening Chopped Chicken Livers

1 pound chicken fat
1 pound chicken livers
1 medium-sized onion, finely chopped
3 hard-cooked eggs
salt to taste

- Render chicken fat in large skillet.
- Add livers to rendered fat, turn off heat and let livers stew in hot fat for 6 minutes.
- Stir onion into fat. When onion is slightly browned and livers are cooked, remove livers and onions, place in sieve. Drain briefly.
- Chop livers with eggs.
- Serve with matzo or rye bread.

DIANE SAWYER

"Not only are these potato skins sinfully delicious, but they're loaded with vitamins and minerals."

Roasted Potato Skins with Scallion Dip

4 pounds baking potatoes
coarse salt to taste

- One to three days in advance of serving, prepare dip.
- Using paring knife, peel skin from potatoes lengthwise in ¼-inch wide strips, removing a thin layer of potato with skin. Reserve potatoes for another use, submerging in cold water.
- Place strips, skin side up, in single layer in well-buttered 15x10x1-inch jelly roll pans.
- Bake at 450 degrees for 15 to 20 minutes or until crisp and golden.
- Toss skins with salt, place on wire racks and let stand until cool. Potato skins can be prepared a day in advance, stored in an air-tight container and served at room temperature or reheated at 450 degrees for 5 minutes or until they are hot.
- Serve skins with dip. Serves 6.

SCALLION DIP
1 small clove garlic
¼ cup chopped scallions
½ cup chopped parsley
½ cup sour cream
½ cup mayonnaise
1 teaspoon Worcestershire sauce or to taste
salt and black pepper to taste

- Using food processor or blender, mince garlic, scallions and parsley.
- Add sour cream and mayonnaise to vegetables. Blend until smooth.
- Stir in Worcestershire sauce, salt and black pepper.
- Chill, covered, overnight or up to 3 days.

JO (JOSIE) STAFFORD

Crab "Amy"

2 **(7 ounce) cans crab meat or 2 cups fresh or frozen crab meat**
1 **cup mayonnaise**
2 **(8 ounce) packages cream cheese, softened**
2 **tablespoons dry vermouth or sherry**
6 **tablespoons horseradish**
2 **teaspoons lemon juice**
1 **onion, chopped**

* Break crab meat into small chunks.
* Blend mayonnaise, cream cheese, vermouth or sherry, horseradish, lemon juice and onion together. Stir crab meat into mixture. Spoon into 1-quart casserole.
* Bake at 350 degrees for ½ hour.
* Serve spread hot with snack crackers.
* Serves 12 to 16.

Years ago, when the band traveled from town to town by bus, we'd sometimes get to a gig just minutes before it was time to go on. The guys looked like we slept in our clothes and in most cases we had. However, Josie always looked lovely — all fresh and frilly — whenever she went on. The way Josie sang, she could have been wearing burlap sacks with army boots and still thrilled the crowds.
— Frank Sinatra

KATHLEEN SULLIVAN

Sweet Pea Guacamole

2 **cups cooked peas**
¼ **cup chopped onion**
1 **teaspoon lemon juice**
2 **cloves garlic, minced**
4 **or 5 drops hot pepper sauce**
¼ **teaspoon white pepper**
2 **tablespoons chopped cilantro**
2 **tablespoons chopped tomato**

* Using food processor with metal blade or blender, combine peas, onion, lemon juice, garlic, hot pepper sauce, white pepper and cilantro. Process or blend until smooth.
* Spoon mixture into serving dish. Chill, covered, for 1 to 2 hours.
* Garnish with tomato. Serve with tortilla chips or snack crackers. Makes 2½ cups.

Breakfast & Brunch

Bonnie, age 10

CLINT BLACK
"Lisa and I love this drink and we hope you do, too."

Skinny Chocolate Banana

  1   **cup ice**
1½ **tablespoons sugar-free hot chocolate mix**
 ½ **cup non-fat milk**
 ½ **cup decaffeinated coffee**
  1   **banana**
  1   **packet sugar substitute**

- Combine ice, chocolate mix, milk, coffee, banana and sugar substitute in blender container.
- Blend until smooth.
- Serve cold. Serves 1.

MONTEL WILLIAMS
"We Marylanders believer that we're the only ones in the world who really know how to cook crab. And everyone else is just an imitator."

Montel's Maryland Crab Cakes

  1   **pound fresh crab meat (no substitute),**
      drained and diced
24 **salt-free or low-salt saltine crackers, finely**
      crushed
 ¼ **teaspoon crushed red pepper flakes**
  3   **tablespoons dried parsley**
 ½ **cup mayonnaise**
  1   **egg**
  1   **tablespoon Worcestershire sauce**
  3   **shakes hot pepper sauce**
  1   **teaspoon dry or 1 tablespoon prepared Dijon**
      mustard
vegetable oil for frying

- Combine crab meat, cracker crumbs, red pepper and parsley.
- Blend mayonnaise, egg, Worcestershire sauce, hot pepper sauce and mustard. Add to crab mixture and mix well. Chill for about 20 minutes.
- Using about 3 tablespoons mixture, shape into patties. Fry in ¼-inch hot oil in large skillet for 3 minutes on each side or until golden brown. Drain on paper towel.
- Serves 4.

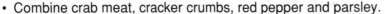

BONO

Smoked Haddock Hash Browns and Poached Eggs

⅓ **pound smoked haddock or cod, boned**
1 **cup milk**
¾ **pound Idaho potatoes, peeled and cubed**
1 **very small onion, minced**
1 **clove garlic, crushed**
½ **cup butter, divided**
1 **bunch parsley**
1 **egg yolk**
½ **cup all-purpose flour**
¼ **cup white wine**
½ **cup cream**
1 **teaspoon chopped chives**
1 **large bunch fresh baby spinach**
⅓ **cup olive oil, divided**
salt and black pepper to taste
1 **teaspoon vinegar**
4 **large duck eggs or chicken eggs**

- Simmer fish in milk for 5 minutes. Drain, let stand to cool and flake into coarse pieces.
- While fish cooks and cools, prepare vegetables. Cook potatoes in boiling salted water.
- Heat onion and garlic in 2 tablespoons butter until softened.
- Drain potatoes and mash; consistency should not be too smooth. Fold onion and garlic, parsley, fish and egg yolk into potatoes. Chill for 1 hour.
- Divide potato mixture in 4 portions and mold each with flour into 3x1-inch cake. Flour generously.
- Prepare dressing. Cook wine to reduce by half. Stir in cream and cook to reduce. Whisk in ¼ cup butter and cook to smooth consistency but not too thickened. Stir in chives. Keep warm.
- Cook spinach in small amount of water and 2 tablespoons butter for 1 minute.
- Lightly brown potato cakes in 1 tablespoon oil, turning once. Bake at 350 degrees for 5 minutes.
- Bring 4 cups water to a boil, season with salt and pepper and add vinegar. Reduce heat to simmer liquid.
- Break eggs, 1 at a time, into cup and carefully pour each into simmering water. Cook for 3 minutes.
- Arrange spinach in ring on each of 4 warmed plates. Place potato cake in center and top with poached egg. Drizzle sauce over spinach and brush eggs with oil.
- Serve immediately. Serves 4.

Bono and Edge's visit to our home in Rancho Mirage to shoot the "Duets" video with Frank was the beginning of a special friendship. In addition to their love of music, Frank and Bono both paint. Here were these two music icons sitting at our bar talking about oils versus acrylics, color, and interpretation of abstract shapes. Frank and I value Bono's gifts to the youngsters at the Children's Center and his continued courtesies. — Barbara Sinatra

---

GREGORY PECK

"When ready to eat, heap on the salsa and hot pepper sauce as hot as you can stand it. Children may not favor the chives or the hot stuff. This is really a grown-up recipe. It will serve four adults with or without hangovers. For those with hangovers, add a generous helping of home-fried potatoes, black-eyed peas or chili and beans."

Sunday Morning Happy Pappy Eggs

8 **eggs**
⅓ **cup whipping cream**
2 **to 3 teaspoons butter**
⅓ **cup chopped chives**
4 **slices baked ham, cut in ½-inch squares**
salsa
hot pepper sauce

- Blend eggs with cream. Scramble eggs in butter in large skillet over low-medium heat to soft consistency, add chives and ham, and continue cooking, stirring constantly and gently with long handled fork; do not overcook.
- Serve eggs with salsa and hot pepper sauce. Serves 4.

Greg and Veronique were part of a sensational dinner that George and Jolene Schlatter hosted for Frank's 80th birthday at their home — Kirk and Anne Douglas were also guests. It was a particularly memorable evening because Frank, Kirk, and Greg regaled us with stories about their early days in Hollywood... they've been friends for so long and it was wonderful seeing them so happy and in such high spirits. Greg has been very generous with his time in helping the Center. He appeared in and narrated "A Safe Place," a moving video about the work done at the Center. — Barbara Sinatra

---

CLIFFORD PERLMAN

Lielo's Special

2 **eggs, beaten**
2 **teaspoons cream cheese or grated Parmesan cheese**
2 **teaspoons minced shallots**
2 **teaspoons finely chopped parsley**
1 **teaspoon butter**

- Combine eggs, cheese, shallots and parsley. Scramble egg mixture in butter in skillet over low-medium heat to soft consistency.
- Serve hot. Serves 1.

NORM CROSBY
"To derive the maximum pleasure from this easy-to-prepare and healthful treat, you should hold the sandwich in your left hand, have a Bud Light in your right hand...put your toes in some sand and pretend that you're at the beach."

Old Fashioned Pepper Steak Sandwich

1½ pounds New York sirloin steak, slightly
       frozen
  2 green bell peppers, sliced
  1 large sweet onion, sliced
vegetable oil
  4 small French, Italian or sourdough rolls
salt and black pepper to taste
mustard or ketchup

- Slice steak into thin strips and set aside.
- Stir-fry bell pepper and onion in oil in large skillet or wok until crisp-tender. Add steak and cook to preferred doneness.
- Split rolls, hollow slightly and warm in microwave or toaster oven.
- Spoon beef and vegetable mixture into rolls. Season with salt, black pepper and mustard or ketchup. Serves 4.

JOSE CARRERAS
"The best sandwich in the world."

Jose Carreras' Sandwich Recipe

½ fresh tomato
Italian ciabatta (bread)
salt
olive oil
carpaccio beef
aceto balsamico (2 drops balsamic vinegar*)
  2 slices Parmesan cheese

- Rub cut side of tomato on surface of bread. Sprinkle lightly with salt and brush with small amount of oil.
- Layer beef (thin shavings of raw beef filet) on bread. Top with 2 drops of balsamic vinegar.
- Place cheese slices on beef. Serves 1.
- * Can be purchased at a specialty store.

CAROL LAWRENCE

Carol's Calzone

DOUGH
4 cups all-purpose flour
1 tablespoon sugar
1½ teaspoons salt
coarsely ground black pepper
¾ cup margarine or vegetable shortening
1 egg
½ cup warm water

- Sift flour, sugar and salt together. Using pastry blender or knives, cut margarine or shortening into dry ingredients until consistency of corn meal.
- Blend generous sprinkle of black pepper, egg and water. Add to dry mixture and beat until smooth.
- On lightly-floured surface, knead dough gently. Divide in 2 portions. Roll out 1 portion to thickness greater than pastry crust. Fit in greased 13x9x2-inch glass baking dish, extending dough up sides and on top edge of dish.

FILLING
5 links medium Italian sausage
5 or 6 hard-cooked eggs
3 (16 ounce) containers Ricotta cheese
3 eggs
2 tablespoons sugar
salt and black pepper to taste
½ cup sugar
2 tablespoons vegetable shortening
egg yolk, beaten
¼ cup water

- Sausage should be dried in refrigerator for 3 days before using. Broil until browned. Cut in halves lengthwise, then dice or slice in small pieces. Set aside to cool.
- Cut eggs in thin slices. Discard slices without portion of yolk.
- Beat 3 eggs, sugar, salt and black pepper together.
- Combine Ricotta and egg mixture. Chill until ready to use.
- Spread half of sausage in dough-lined dish. Spoon half of Ricotta mixture on sausage. Layer egg slices on Ricotta. Repeat sausage and Ricotta layers. Sprinkle with generous amount of sugar.
- Roll remaining dough to rectangle shape. Place over layered ingredients, leaving a fold in center to allow for expansion of filling, and crimp edges to seal. Prick dough with fork tines at 1-inch intervals.
- Brush with shortening. Using ravioli crimper, cut out thick leaves from extra dough and roll "ropes" of dough. Arrange on top crust. Brush with egg yolk mixed with water.
- Bake at 375 degrees on lower rack for 10 minutes or until bottom is golden brown. Move to center rack and bake for 30 to 50 minutes or until crust is golden brown, brushing occasionally with yolk liquid. When golden and rising, sprinkle sugar on top and bake for 5 to 10 additional minutes; crust should be crunchy and golden.
- Cool on wire rack. Serve lukewarm. Serves 6.

RON MASAK

Artichoke Pie

2 (9 ounce) packages frozen artichoke hearts
½ cup chopped onion
¼ cup butter or margarine
1 tablespoon all-purpose flour
½ cup half and half
½ cup sour cream
4 eggs, beaten
salt and black pepper to taste
¼ teaspoon nutmeg
2 teaspoons minced parsley
1 baked 9-inch pastry shell
½ cup (2 ounces) shredded Cheddar cheese
½ cup (2 ounces) shredded Swiss cheese
¼ cup (1 ounce) grated Parmesan cheese

- Prepare artichoke hearts according to package directions. Drain and set aside.
- Sauté onion in butter in large skillet until tender but not browned.
- Blend flour with onion. Stir in half and half and cook, stirring often, until thickened.
- Combine sour cream, eggs, salt, black pepper, nutmeg and parsley. Add to sauce.
- Layer half of artichokes in pastry shell. Sprinkle with Cheddar cheese, add remaining artichokes and top with Swiss cheese.
- Pour egg mixture over layered ingredients. Sprinkle with Parmesan cheese.
- Bake at 350 degrees for 45 minutes.
- Serve hot. Serves 4 to 6.

GEORGE BURNS

Scrambled Scrambled Eggs

"I haven't cooked in the last 70 years, but I think I still remember how to make scrambled eggs. I'm pretty sure you use eggs, put them in a pan (and it's better if you break them first). Make sure you move the shells to one side, then let them cook for about three minutes. When it's done, forget the eggs and eat the shells."

DON MEREDITH

Susan and Don's Favorite Baked Eggs

4 scallions, sliced
2 cloves garlic, minced
½ green bell pepper, chopped
2 (10 ounce) packages frozen chopped spinach, thawed
½ cup half and half
salt and black pepper
12 eggs
2 cups (8 ounces) shredded Mozzarella cheese
1 tablespoon extra virgin olive oil
1 (14½ ounce) can crushed tomatoes
½ teaspoon cayenne pepper
½ cup hot salsa (optional)

- Combine scallions, garlic, bell pepper and spinach in large skillet. Cook over medium heat, stirring frequently, until fresh vegetables are tender.
- Stir half and half into vegetables. Season with salt and black pepper.
- Spoon spinach mixture into 13x9x2-inch baking dish.
- Break eggs, 1 at a time, into cup (without breaking yolks). Carefully pour each on spinach mixture.
- Sprinkle cheese on eggs.
- Combine oil, tomatoes, salt, black pepper, cayenne pepper and salsa in saucepan. Warm thoroughly. Pour sauce over cheese layer.
- Bake at 350 degrees for 10 to 15 minutes or until eggs are set.
- Serve hot with sausage or bacon. Serves 6 to 8.

DON MEREDITH

Baked Breakfast Grapefruit

2 grapefruits, peeled and pith removed
1 teaspoon thyme
2 tablespoons honey
2 tablespoons brown sugar

- Separate grapefruit into segments. Place in 8x8x2-inch baking dish.
- Sprinkle grapefruit with thyme, honey and brown sugar.
- Bake at 350 degrees for 30 minutes.
- Serve warm. Serves 4.

RICARDO MONTALBAN

Huevos Rancheros

- 4 medium tomatoes, peeled and diced
- 4 green onions, minced
- 6 sprigs cilantro, finely chopped
- 2 Serrano chiles, seeded and finely chopped
- 1 teaspoon lemon juice
- 1 teaspoon olive oil
- 8 corn tortillas
vegetable shortening or lard
- 2 (16 ounce) cans refried beans
- 8 eggs
butter or margarine

- Combine tomatoes, green onion, cilantro and chiles. Stir in lemon juice and oil. Set aside.
- Heat tortillas in shortening or lard in skillet to soften. Keep warm.
- Cook beans in shortening or lard in skillet, turning with spatula, until somewhat crisp on surface. Keep warm in oven.
- Fry eggs in butter or margarine until white is firm but yolk is still soft, basting with butter.
- Place 1 egg on each tortilla and spoon salsa on egg.
- Serve with beans. Serves 4.

DALE ROBERTSON
This recipe originated with Varvel Robertson, Dale's mom.

Grease Gravy

- 1 (12 ounce) package hot pork sausage patties
- ¼ cup all-purpose flour
- 4 cups whole milk
salt and black pepper to taste
- 12 biscuits

- Brown sausage in large skillet. Remove with slotted spoon, drain on paper towel and set aside. Or crumble sausage as it cooks and leave in skillet while preparing gravy.
- Blend flour into hot sausage drippings.
- Add milk, increasing amount as desired. Cook for a few minutes. Gravy will be thin consistency. Season with salt and generous amount of black pepper.
- Serve gravy over hot biscuits, with sausage as side dish. Serves 6.

ROGER MOORE

"My dear Barbara, please correct the spelling mistakes. Quayle is with a Y of course and the reason for all the errors is that deep in the heart of deepest Phuket in Thailand I am using a machine that is completely unfamiliar and half of the time it types out the letters in Thai. Apart from that, it is around a hundred degrees Fahrenheit and I am in the midst of shooting what we call a fillum, namely, 'The Quest' and my Quest is to try and make my contribution to your cookbook of which the proceeds go to what is the most worthwhile cause of all, namely THE CHILDREN.

"I trust you are all having a wonderful time in PALM SPRINGS whilst I sweat and slave away in this infernal heat which also happens to be a holiday here, a sort of Water Festival, so no one is working except the crazy movie people."

Bachelor's Egg Mess

　3　tablespoons grated Parmesan or sharp Cheddar cheese
salt and white pepper to taste
　2　or 3 green onions, chopped
　1　large tomato (with an E if your name is Quale, where is the I?), sliced
　3　eggs
　2　slices toast

- Melt cheese in skillet over very low heat. Season with salt and white pepper.
- Add green onion and tomato to cheese and stir for 1 or 2 minutes.
- Break eggs, 1 at a time, into cup. Carefully add to skillet to avoid breaking yolks. When egg white begins to set, stir through mixture until consistency is satisfactory to you.
- Slide egg mixture onto toast slices.
- Serves 1.

CAROL BURNETT
"Hope you enjoy it as much as I have!"

Potassium Drink

1 **(46 ounce) can low-sodium vegetable cocktail juice**
1 **carrot, cut in 2-inch pieces**
2 **stalks celery, cut in 2-inch pieces**
2 **green or red bell peppers, seeded and cubed**
1 **onion, chopped**
½ **cup water**
½ **teaspoon chili flakes (optional)**

- Combine juice, carrot, celery, bell pepper, onion, water and chili flakes in saucepan.
- Simmer, uncovered, for 25 minutes. Strain through sieve, pressing to extract juice.
- Serve hot or over ice. Makes 5 cups.

BUDDY ROGERS

Omelette with Ricotta

2 **tablespoons all-purpose flour**
1 **tablespoon milk or water**
4 **eggs, lightly beaten with fork**
¼ **teaspoon salt**
2 **tablespoons butter**
1 **(8 ounce) carton Ricotta cheese**
2 **tablespoons warm water**
1 **teaspoon grated Parmesan cheese**
pinch of salt
1 **cup tomato sauce (optional)**

- Blend flour with milk or water. Mix with eggs and ¼ teaspoon salt.
- Using 2 tablespoons egg liquid for each, cook omelettes in small amount of butter in small skillet, cooking for 3 minutes on each side.
- Combine Ricotta cheese, warm water, Parmesan cheese and salt. Spoon portion of Ricotta mixture on each omelette and roll to enclose.
- Serve omelettes with tomato sauce. Serves 4.

CLAUDIA SCHIFFER
"For the French version of this pancake, add a little calvados on top. Bon Appetit."

Apple Pancake á la Claudia

  4 or 5 apples
lemon juice
  3 eggs
  2 tablespoons sugar
  2 cups milk
1¾ cups all-purpose flour
pinch of salt
vegetable oil
cinnamon
sugar

- Peel apples and slice thinly. Squeeze lemon juice over apples to prevent discoloration.
- Beat eggs with sugar until foamy. Alternately add milk and flour, beating thoroughly until batter consistency. Stir in salt.
- Using a ladle of batter at a time, pour batter to form pancake in heated oil in large skillet or on griddle. Immediately place apple slices in circle on batter. When pancake is firm, turn, cook briefly and turn again.
- Sprinkle cinnamon and sugar on hot pancake. Serves 4.

KENNY ROGERS
"This is a delicious recipe for luncheons and light suppers. I enjoy it often and my guests love it as well."

Chicken Salad á la Rogers

  3 regular dill pickles
  2 cups pulled (not chopped) cooked chicken breast
½ cup chopped walnuts
¼ cup slivered or chopped almonds
chopped scallions (optional)
salad dressing
lettuce leaves

- Using potato peeler, remove skin from pickles. Chop pickles.
- Combine pickles, chicken, walnuts, almonds and scallions.
- Stir in salad dressing of choice.
- Serve individual portions on lettuce leaves. Serves 4.

WAYNE M. RODGERS

Hunter's Eggs

1 green bell pepper, chopped
½ onion, minced
2 shallots, minced
2 tablespoons butter, divided
1 tablespoon tomato paste
2 (14½ ounce) cans peeled tomatoes, crushed
1 clove garlic, minced
3 cups chicken livers
¼ cup red wine
½ teaspoon dried or 2 sprigs oregano
2 tablespoons chopped basil
½ cup chopped black olives
2 tablespoons chopped anchovies
6 to 10 eggs

- Sauté bell pepper, onion and shallots in 1 tablespoon butter in skillet until tender. Stir in tomato paste and tomatoes. Cook until thickened and set aside.
- Sauté garlic and livers in 1 tablespoon butter, cooking for 5 minutes. Add wine and cook for additional 2 minutes. Using slotted spoon, remove livers and set aside.
- Stir oregano and basil into wine. Cook for 1 minute. Add mixture to tomato sauce.
- Spread livers in large skillet. Spoon marinara sauce over livers and sprinkle with olives and anchovies.
- Break eggs, 1 at a time, into cup and carefully add to sauce in skillet; eggs should be covered with sauce. Cover until eggs are poached. Serves 6 to 8.

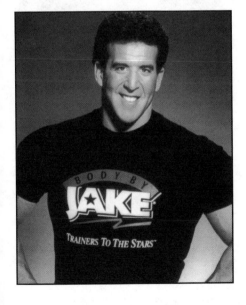

JAKE OF BODY BY JAKE

Jake's Shake

2 cups orange juice
1 cup crushed ice
½ cup strawberries
1 medium-sized banana

- Combine orange juice, ice, strawberries and banana in blender container. Blend until smooth.
- Serves 1.

CONNIE STEVENS

Leek and Zucchini Flan

  3 **tablespoons unsalted butter, softened**
  2 **leeks**
boiling salted water
  1 **pound zucchini, coarsely grated**
  2 **eggs**
  1 **cup half and half**
  3 **tablespoons finely grated Parmesan cheese**
1½ **teaspoons chopped chervil**
1½ **teaspoons chopped chives**
salt and black pepper to taste

- Grease 6 ramekins or soufflé cups with 1 tablespoon butter. Place in roasting pan.
- Thinly slice leeks, using white and light-green portions only. Cook in boiling salted water for 6 minutes. Drain well, blot dry with paper towel and place in mixing bowl.
- Cook zucchini in remaining 2 tablespoons butter in skillet, stirring frequently, for about 5 minutes or until softened. Add zucchini to leeks.
- Beat eggs, half and half, Parmesan cheese, chervil, chives, salt and black pepper together. Stir into vegetables.
- Divide mixture among ramekins or soufflé cups. Add boiling water to pan to half the depth of individual dishes.
- Bake at 350 degrees for 30 to 35 minutes or until firm.
- Serve hot. Serves 6.

BEVERLY SILLS

Dutch Babies

  3 **eggs**
½ **cup all-purpose flour**
½ **cup milk**
½ **teaspoon salt**
½ **teaspoon vanilla**
  2 **tablespoons melted butter**

- Place 8-inch iron skillet in freezer. Preheat oven to 450 degrees.
- Combine eggs, flour, milk, salt and vanilla in blender container. Blend at low speed until smooth.
- Pour melted butter into cold skillet. Pour batter into skillet.
- Bake at 450 degrees until browned. Eggs will puff like a soufflé.
- Serve immediately with jam, stewed fruit, maple syrup or butter. Serves 2 to 4.

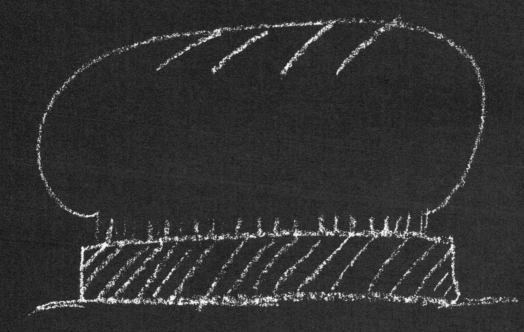

Soups, Salads & Breads

Sally, age 8

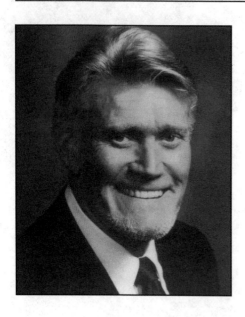

CHUCK CONNORS

Manhattan Clam Chowder

12 to 18 large chopped chowder clams with juice
    or 2 (12 ounce) cans chopped clams plus ¾
    cup clam juice
 2 (28 ounce) cans tomatoes, crushed
 1 (12 ounce) can tomato paste
 4 large potatoes, peeled and diced
 3 or 4 stalks celery, sliced
 2 large onions, diced
 3 cloves garlic, diced
 6 large carrots, sliced
 1 teaspoon oregano
 1 bay leaf
 1 cup chopped parsley
16 cups water
black pepper to taste
 ½ cup olive oil

- In stock pot, combine clams with juice, tomatoes, tomato paste, potatoes, celery, onion, garlic, carrots, oregano, bay leaf, parsley, water, black pepper and oil.
- Simmer for 3 to 4 hours. Remove bay leaf.
- Serve hot. Serves 8 to 10.

LEONARD AND WENDY GOLDBERG

Wendy's Watercress and Pea Soup

 1 cup sliced green onion (white and green tops)
 ½ cup butter
 3 cups hot chicken broth
 1 teaspoon chervil
 ½ teaspoon sugar
dash of white pepper
2½ cups frozen small peas
 1 bunch watercress, torn and stems discarded
 1 cup half and half

- Sauté onion in butter in large saucepan for 3 minutes.
- Add chicken broth, chervil, sugar, white pepper and peas to onion. Simmer for about 20 minutes.
- Stir in watercress and immediately turn heat off.
- Pour portion of vegetables and liquid into blender container. Blend to liquefy. Repeat with remaining portions. Chill thoroughly.
- Stir half and half into purée before serving. Serves 4.

JOHN AND CONSTANCE TOWERS GAVIN

Asparagus Soup

  1 **pound frozen or 1½ pounds fresh asparagus**
  1 **medium-sized onion**
  3 **cups non-fat chicken broth, divided**
boiling water
  2 **tablespoons all-purpose flour**
  2 **teaspoons lemon juice**
  ½ **teaspoon celery seeds**
salt and black pepper to taste
sour cream (optional)
curry powder (optional)

- Cut tips from 6 stalks asparagus and set aside. If using fresh asparagus, snap and discard woody bottom portions. Rinse well.
- Place asparagus in skillet with onion and ½ cup chicken broth. Bring to a boil, reduce heat and simmer, covered, for about 7 minutes. If using fresh asparagus, increase broth to 1 cup and simmer for about 15 minutes or until tender.
- While asparagus cooks, poach reserved tips in boiling water until just tender (about 2 minutes for frozen and 5 minutes for fresh). Quickly drain and plunge in cold water to cool. Set aside.
- Using blender, purée cooked asparagus with liquid.
- Heat 2¼ cups broth (1¾ cups for fresh asparagus version) in saucepan.
- Blend remaining ¼ cup broth with flour until smooth. Whisk into simmering broth until smooth. Simmer, covered, for 5 minutes.
- Add puréed asparagus, lemon juice, celery seeds, salt and black pepper to broth. Check seasoning. Flavor will be milder if soup is served chilled. Additional broth or milk can be added to thin soup if preferred.
- Serve hot or cold. Garnish individual servings of soup with asparagus tip, dollop of sour cream and sprinkle of curry powder. Serves 6.
- Soup can be prepared a day in advance and stored in refrigerator.

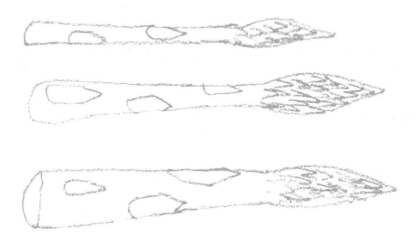

GREGORY HARRISON

Seafood Chowder

36 to 48 clams in shells or 2 (7 ounce) cans clams
 1 onion, sliced
 2 tablespoons finely chopped green bell pepper
 2 stalks celery with leaves, chopped
 ¼ cup diced carrots
 ¼ cup butter, divided
 2 potatoes, peeled and sliced
pinch of thyme
 1 bay leaf
sprig of parsley
water
 2 (6 ounce) cans shrimp or 1 pint oysters
 2 cups milk or half and half

- If using fresh clams, wash carefully, soak in water a few minutes to allow any dead clams to surface and discard any dead or broken clams. Place clams in large steamer in stock pot with water to cover bottom of pot; do not submerge clams. Steam until done. Remove shells, reserving liquid. Discard coarse covering from clams and cut away black necks with scissors.
- Sauté onion, bell pepper, celery and carrots in 2 tablespoons butter in stock pot until tender.
- Add clams, potatoes, thyme, parsley and bay leaf. Add water to reserved clam liquid to measure 4 cups (or use 4 cups water with canned clams) and pour into stock pot. Simmer for 30 minutes or until potatoes begin to soften.
- Stir shrimp or oysters and milk or half and half into clam mixture. Simmer until oysters begin to curl. Season well with black pepper. Remove bay leaf.
- Serves 6 to 8.

EYDIE GORME AND STEVE LAWRENCE

Easy Vegetable Soup

3 green onions, chopped
1 head cabbage, chopped
2 green bell peppers, chopped
4 to 6 stalks celery, chopped
4 to 6 carrots, chopped
1 leek, chopped
1 packet vegetable soup mix
1 bunch parsley, stems
   discarded
1 bunch dill
water
2 (28 ounce) cans tomatoes,
   crushed

- Combine onion, cabbage, bell pepper, celery, carrots, leek, soup mix, parsley and dill in stock pot.
- Add water to cover. Stir in tomatoes.
- Bring to a boil, reduce heat and simmer until vegetables are tender.
- Serves 8 to 10.

OSCAR DE LA RENTA

Pumpkin and Crab Soup

1 **pumpkin**
10 **scallions, minced**
½ **teaspoon coriander**
6 **cups chicken stock**
½ **teaspoon brown sugar**
½ **teaspoon cinnamon**
2 **tablespoons curry powder**
olive oil
salt and black pepper to taste
2 **ears fresh corn**
1 **pound lump crab meat**
2 **cups plain yogurt**

- Slice top from pumpkin. Scoop pulp from pumpkin, remove seeds and set aside. Place top on pumpkin shell. Bake at 225 degrees for 2 hours. Shell will be used as soup tureen.
- Using food processor or blender, purée pumpkin pulp, scallions and coriander.
- Combine purée and chicken stock in saucepan. Bring to a simmer.
- Stir brown sugar, cinnamon, curry powder and oil into hot liquid. Season with salt and black pepper.
- Cut corn from cobs. Add with crab meat to soup. Simmer until corn is cooked.
- Before serving, stir yogurt into soup. Pour into pumpkin tureen. Serves 8.

When I did "Concert for the Americas," Barbara and I stayed at Oscar's magnificent estate on the coast of the Dominican Republic. It was a long way from the days when my aunts, uncles, cousins and my parents and I spent summers on the Jersey Shore. — *Frank Sinatra*

JOANNA BARNES

J.B.'s Soup

6 **carrots, sliced**
4 **medium zucchini, sliced**
½ **cup butter**
1 **medium-sized onion, chopped**
3 **potatoes, peeled and sliced**
⅔ **cup chopped parsley**
8 **cups chicken broth**
¾ **cup half and half**
½ **cup chopped dill**
salt and black pepper to taste

- Sauté carrots, zucchini and onion in butter in stock pot for 5 minutes or until onion is softened and translucent but not browned.
- Add potatoes, parsley and broth to sautéed vegetables. Bring to a boil, reduce heat and simmer, covered, for 45 minutes.
- Using a portion of the vegetables and liquid at a time, purée in food processor or blender until smooth.
- Stir dill and half and half into purée. Season with salt and black pepper.
- Serve cold or hot. If reheating, do not boil.
- Serves 8.

DENNIS JAMES

"This soup makes a lovely first course for four people. If the meat is added and warm sourdough bread served, it makes a very hearty dinner for two. Incidentally, the garlic cloves become very tender and sweet."

Escarole and Bean Soup

¾ **to 1 pound head escarole**
1 **medium-sized white onion, halved and sliced**
¼ **cup olive oil**
2 **chicken bouillon cubes**
3½ **cups hot water**
10 **cloves garlic, peeled**
½ **pound smoked turkey sausage, cut in ½-inch chunks (optional)**
1 **(15 ounce) can Great Northern white beans, drained and rinsed**
¼ **teaspoon red pepper flakes (optional)**
salt and black pepper to taste
freshly grated Parmesan cheese

- Detach escarole leaves from head, wash thoroughly, tear into pieces and drain.
- Sauté onion in oil in stock pot until lightly browned.
- Dissolve bouillon in hot water. Add broth, whole garlic cloves and sausage to onion. Simmer for 20 minutes.
- Stir escarole and red pepper into broth. Simmer, covered for 25 minutes or until tender.
- Add white beans to vegetables and broth. Simmer, covered for 15 minutes. Season with salt and black pepper.
- Sprinkle Parmesan cheese on individual servings of soup. Serves 4.

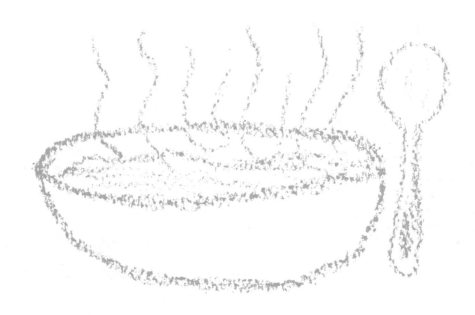

LEE IACOCCA

Antoinette Iacocca's Italian Meatball Soup

1 (4 pound) stewing chicken or fryer
1 medium-sized onion, quartered
1 large carrot, cut in chunks
1 stalk celery, cut in chunks
cold water
salt and freshly ground black pepper to taste
1 pound finely-ground lean veal
1 large egg
1½ tablespoons grated Parmesan cheese
1 tablespoon minced parsley
½ pound small pasta squares
grated Parmesan cheese

- Combine chicken, onion, carrot and celery in stock pot. Add water to cover. Bring to a boil, season with salt and black pepper, reduce heat and simmer for about 2 hours or until broth is reduced and chicken is very tender.
- Remove chicken and strain broth. Skim excess fat from broth or chill broth, then skim.
- Separate meat from bones. Shred chicken to measure 1 cup and add to broth. Reserve remaining chicken for another recipe.
- Combine veal, egg, Parmesan cheese and parsley. Mix thoroughly and shape into meatballs about the size of a large marble.
- Pour broth into stock pot and bring to a boil. Drop meatballs and pasta into broth and simmer for 20 minutes.
- Sprinkle individual servings of soup with Parmesan cheese. Serves 8 to 10.

**DRIMCONG HOUSE, GALWAY, IRELAND
GERRY GALVIN, EXECUTIVE CHEF AND PROPRIETOR**

Colcannon Cream Soup

½ pound curly kale, finely chopped
1½ pounds potatoes, peeled and diced
2 leeks, chopped
5 cups chicken or vegetable stock
¼ cup plus 2 tablespoons butter
1 cup half and half
salt and white pepper to taste
nutmeg to taste

- Simmer kale, potatoes and leeks in butter in large saucepan for 10 minutes; do not brown vegetables.
- Add stock to vegetables. Simmer for 20 minutes.
- Season with salt, white pepper and nutmeg.
- Whip to liquefy vegetables, then strain for smooth consistency.
- Whisk cream into soup. Reheat before serving.
- Serves 6.

SENATOR EDWARD KENNEDY

Cape Cod Fish Chowder

2 **pounds fresh haddock**
2 **cups water**
2 **ounces salt pork, diced**
2 **medium-sized onions, sliced**
1 **cup chopped celery**
4 **large potatoes, diced**
1 **bay leaf, crumbled**
boiling water
4 **cups milk**
2 **tablespoons butter or margarine**
1 **teaspoon salt**
freshly ground black pepper to taste

- Simmer haddock in water for 15 minutes. Drain, reserving broth. Remove skin and bones from fish.
- Sauté salt pork in stock pot until crisp. Remove pork. Sauté onion in pork fat until golden brown.
- Add fish, celery, potatoes and bay leaf to onion.
- Measure reserved fish broth and add enough boiling water to measure 3 cups liquid. Add to fish and vegetables. Simmer for 20 to 30 minutes.
- Stir milk and butter or margarine into soup. Simmer until thoroughly heated. Season with salt and black pepper. Serves 8.

HARRY CONNICK, SR.

Tortellini Soup

4 **cloves garlic, chopped**
¼ **cup chopped green onion**
2 **tablespoons butter**
2 **(15 ounce) cans chicken broth**
1 **(14½ ounce) can Italian-style stewed tomatoes**
1 **(8 ounce) package cheese-stuffed tortellini**
½ **bunch spinach, coarsely chopped**
6 **basil leaves**
½ **cup (2 ounces) grated Parmesan cheese**
freshly ground black pepper to taste

- Sauté garlic and green onion in butter in large saucepan until tender; do not overbrown.
- Add broth and tomatoes to garlic and onion.
- Bring to a boil, add tortellini and cook according to package directions, adding spinach and basil for final minute of cooking time.
- Sprinkle individual servings with Parmesan cheese. Serves 4.

VINCENT KICKERILLO

Potato and Artichoke Soup

4 **large leeks**
2 **teaspoons kosher salt**
¼ **cup unsalted butter, divided**
1 **teaspoon white pepper**
3 **stalks celery, finely diced**
1½ **pounds Idaho potatoes, peeled and cut in
     1-inch cubes**
4 **cups chicken broth**
1 **bay leaf**
1 **(14 ounce) can artichoke bottoms, drained
     and cut in 1-inch pieces**
2½ **cups half and half**
minced scallions or chives for garnish

- Trim ½ of green stalk from leeks, cut leeks in ½ lengthwise and cut crosswise in ½-inch pieces. Place in colander, rinse well and drain.
- Sauté leeks with kosher salt in 3 tablespoons butter in stock pot over low heat until leeks are wilted.
- Add white pepper, celery, potatoes, chicken broth and bay leaf. Simmer, uncovered for 15 to 20 minutes or until potatoes are tender.
- Strain vegetables, reserving broth. Using food processor, pulse vegetables to form chunky purée.
- Combine purée and reserved broth in stock pot. Add artichokes and half and half. Warm over low heat.
- Strain in remaining 1 tablespoon butter.
- Garnish individual servings of soup with scallions or chives. Serves 6.

When I started out as the boy singer with the Harry James orchestra, and later with the Dorsey organization, we ate in every greasy spoon, roadside diner, and rib joint that lined the highways along which our buses would travel. I became quite an authority on the various cuisines of America, and did notice that some of these joints had better food than others. Of course, back then we didn't call them cuisines, we just grabbed something to eat to keep us warm on cold long nights when the bus went from one gig to another. Then my interest in cooking was not so much a desire for fine dining as a passionate hope to stay alive. As time went on, I became even more discerning in my culinary pursuits. You see, at that point I only weighed about 100 lbs. and if I lost any weight they couldn't see me from behind the microphone, so it was important that I maintained my frame, even though I was quite skinny. — Frank Sinatra

---

TOMMY AND JO LASORDA

"If I didn't have Dodger-blue blood running through my veins, I'd want my wife Jo's chicken soup inside me. For years, this elixir has sustained me through cold winters and breakneck schedules."

Tommy Lasorda's Favorite Chicken Soup

6 **large chicken breast halves**
water
salt to taste
lemon pepper to taste
bay leaf
8 **medium carrots, cut in 1-inch pieces**
5 **stalks celery, cut in 1-inch pieces**
1 **large onion, minced**
½ **cup chopped parsley**
1 **cup orzo pasta**
black pepper to taste
dill weed to taste

- A day before serving, place chicken, bay leaf, salt and lemon pepper in stock pot. Add water to cover. Simmer for 45 minutes to 1 hour or until chicken is tender.
- Drain chicken in colander, reserving broth. Chill broth overnight to allow excess fat to rise to top for removal.
- Discard skin and bones from chicken, cut into chunks and store overnight in refrigerator.
- Pour broth into stock pot. Add carrots, celery, onion and parsley. Simmer until vegetables are tender; do not boil.
- While vegetables cook, prepare orzo according to package directions, undercooking slightly.
- Add chicken and orzo to vegetables and broth. Season with salt, black pepper and dill weed.
- Serves 6 to 8.

"I try to always have a big pot of this wonderful fat-free chicken soup ready for lunch or dinner for Tommy before or after a game, or if he brings home some of the guys — Tommy never liked to eat too heavy a meal before games. Everyone sits down and they love it — the soup is great served with fresh Italian bread." — Jo Lasorda

RAY MANCINI

"I find this a delicious healthful dish, to be enjoyed at any meal or as a snack in between meals. There is no way to make a mistake or ruin it."

Super Soup

1   head cabbage, chopped
1   stalk celery, chopped
3   green bell peppers, chopped
5   onions, chopped
6   tomatoes, chopped, or 1 (28 ounce) can whole
    tomatoes, crushed
several cloves garlic (optional)
1   packet onion soup mix or 3 to 5 bouillon
    cubes
water
black pepper

- Combine cabbage, celery, bell pepper, onion, tomatoes, garlic and soup mix or bouillon in stock pot. Add water to cover vegetables.
- Simmer until vegetables are tender. Season with black pepper.
- Serves 6.

SUZANNE SOMERS

Chunky Tomato Soup

4   or 5 medium leeks, cut in ½-inch slices
10 cloves garlic, minced
½   cup unsalted butter
2   (14½ ounce) cans tomatoes, seeded and
    chopped, with juice
2   cups dry white wine
1   tablespoon brown sugar
salt and white pepper to taste
pinch of cinnamon
pinch of cayenne pepper
whipping cream (optional)
baby yellow plum tomatoes, sliced, for garnish

- Sauté leeks and garlic in butter in large saucepan over medium heat for 5 minutes or until leeks are soft.
- Add tomatoes, wine, brown sugar, salt, white pepper, cinnamon and cayenne pepper to leeks and garlic. Simmer for 30 minutes.
- Stir 1 tablespoon cream into individual servings of soup and garnish with tomatoes.
- Serves 6.

DINA MERRILL

Curried Zucchini Soup

2 **medium-sized onions, chopped**
1 **large stalk celery, chopped**
3 **tablespoons unsalted butter**
1 **teaspoon curry powder or more to taste**
6 **medium zucchini, diced**
4 **cups chicken broth**
3 **tablespoons chopped Italian parsley**
juice of ½ lime
salt and freshly ground black pepper to taste
1 **cup buttermilk**

- Sauté onion and celery in butter in stock pot over low heat for about 5 minutes or until vegetables are softened.
- Stir curry powder into vegetables and cook, stirring often, for 3 minutes.
- Add zucchini and cook for about 5 minutes or until zucchini just begins to soften.
- Pour chicken broth into stock pot. Bring to a boil, reduce heat and simmer for about 15 minutes or until zucchini is very soft.
- Add parsley, lime juice, salt and black pepper to vegetables and broth.
- Using a portion at a time, purée soup in food blender. Pour purée into stock pot, stir in buttermilk, check seasoning and simmer; do not boil.
- Serves 8 to 10.

SENATOR HOWARD METZENBAUM
"Below is a favorite recipe of mine that is both 'heart smart' and fun."

Gazpacho

3 **(12 ounce) cans tomato juice**
1 **cucumber, diced**
1 **green bell pepper, diced**
6 **cloves garlic, mashed**
2 **tablespoons olive oil**
1 **tablespoon white wine vinegar**
¼ **teaspoon hot pepper sauce**
dash of lemon juice
½ **cup ice water**
salt and black pepper to taste

- Combine tomato juice, cucumber, bell pepper, garlic, oil, vinegar, hot pepper sauce, lemon juice and ice water.
- Chill overnight for best blending of flavors. Season with salt and black pepper.
- Serve cold with sprinkling of croutons or chopped eggs. Serves 4.

CHARLES PASSARELL, JR.

Puerto Rican Black Bean Soup

1	(16 ounce) package dried black beans
8 to 10	cups water
⅔	cup olive oil
6	cloves garlic, minced or ground
2	onions, minced or ground
6	sweet chili peppers, seeded, minced or ground
4 to 5	teaspoons salt
¼	teaspoon black pepper
¼	teaspoon dried oregano, crushed
2	tablespoons sugar
2	bay leaves
¼	teaspoon ground cumin
2	tablespoons dry wine
1½	tablespoons vinegar
½	cup chopped onion

cooked rice
sour cream

- Wash beans, place in stock pot, add water 1 to 2 inches above beans and soak overnight.
- Drain, rinse in fresh water and drain again. Place in stock pot and add 8 cups water. Bring quickly to a boil, reduce heat to medium and cook, covered for 15 minutes.
- Sauté garlic, onion and chili peppers in oil in skillet over low heat for 10 minutes, stirring occasionally.
- With slotted spoon, transfer 1 cup boiled beans to skillet and mash with vegetables.
- Add mashed mixture, salt, black pepper, oregano, sugar, bay leaves and cumin to beans in stock pot. Cook, covered, over moderate heat for 1 hour. Add remaining 2 cups water if needed to cook beans.
- Stir wine and vinegar into beans and liquid. Simmer for 1 hour.
- Remove cover and cook until sauce thickens.
- Sprinkle individual servings with onion, rice and sour cream. Serves 8.

LIZA MINNELLI

Avocado Soup

3	ripe avocados, peeled and pitted
2	(15 ounce) cans vichyssoise
2	cups half and half
1	cup chicken broth
¼	cup lemon juice

avocado slices for garnish

- Using ½ of ingredients, place avocado, vichyssoise, half and half, broth and lemon juice in blender container. Blend until smooth. Repeat with remaining ingredients.
- Chill until ready to serve. Garnish with avocado slices.
- Serves 4 to 6.

NEHEMIAH PERSOFF

Cold Yogurt Vegetable Soup

1 medium-sized tart apple
1 large avocado, peeled and pitted
1 clove garlic
3 green onions, white and green separated
3 cucumbers, peeled
6 cups plain yogurt
2 cups finely diced tomatoes
1 tablespoon minced dill
1 teaspoon minced basil
4 radishes, thinly sliced
salt and black pepper to taste
chopped walnuts for garnish

- Using food processor, process apple, avocado, white portion of green onion and 2½ cucumbers until liquefied. Pour into mixing bowl.
- Beat yogurt to liquefy. Add to vegetable liquid.
- In order listed, add tomatoes, dill, basil, thinly sliced green portion of green onion, radishes and remaining cucumber, thinly sliced and halved.
- Season with salt and black pepper.
- Chill, covered, for at least 2 hours.
- Sprinkle individual servings of soup with chopped nuts. Serves 8.

JOANNA POITIER

Butternut Squash Soup
or Broccoli Soup

1 large butternut squash or 2 bunches broccoli
4 (14½ ounce) cans chicken broth
salt and black pepper to taste

- For squash soup, peel squash, remove seeds and cut into medium cubes. For broccoli soup, chop broccoli. Place vegetable in large saucepan and add chicken broth. Liquid should cover vegetable by ½-inch.
- Cook over medium to medium high heat for about 20 minutes or until tender. Remove from heat and let stand for 10 minutes.
- Pour vegetable and liquid into blender container. Blend for 1 to 2 minutes or until smooth. Return soup to saucepan, season with salt and black pepper and reheat.
- Serves 8.

SIDNEY AND ALEXANDRA SHELDON

"Alexandra and I are constantly traveling around the globe, for I won't write about a place — or a meal — unless I've been to that place or had that meal. Consequently, we are quite lucky to be able to sample food from around the world. While there are so many types of food that we enjoy tremendously, such as Chinese, French, Thai, Mexican, Indian, etc., I would have to admit that the cooking of Italy is one of our favorites. And from there, if I had to isolate my favorite recipe, it would have to be the hale and hearty soup, Pasta E Fagioli."

Pasta E Fagioli

Pasta and Bean Soup

1 (8 ounce) package dried borlotti, pinto,
  cannellini or Great Northern beans
4 cups water
4 to 6 cups hot chicken broth or water
½ cup salt pork or bacon
1 large onion, minced
2 cloves garlic, minced
2 tablespoons lard
1 tablespoon all-purpose flour
salt to taste
crushed red pepper flakes to taste
2 tablespoons minced fresh sage or 1 tablespoon dried sage
1 (8 ounce) package ditalini or elbow macaroni
hot chili oil
extra virgin olive oil
1 (4 to 6 ounce) piece Pecorino Romano
  cheese, freshly grated
1 (4 to 6 ounce) piece Grana Padano or
  Parmigiano-Reggiano cheese, freshly grated

- Place beans in stock pot, add water and soak overnight. For faster method, pour boiling water over beans and let stand for 1 hour.
- Cook beans in same water until half-tender.
- Add broth to bean liquid and continue to cook.
- Sauté salt pork or bacon, onion and garlic in lard in skillet over low heat, stirring constantly, until onion is soft.
- Stir flour and 1 cup bean liquid into pork and vegetables, then add mixture to beans in stock pot. Season with salt, red pepper and sage. Simmer until beans are almost done.
- Add ditalini or macaroni to beans and cook until tender.
- When serving soup, offer chili oil and olive oil in cruets and grated cheeses separately in small bowls for seasoning and garnish.
- Serves 6 to 8.

PETER YARROW

Puff the Magic Dragon's Luncheon Feast

SALAD
1 head Boston lettuce, torn in medium pieces
2 Belgian endives, leaves separated
1 cucumber, peeled and sliced
1 (6¼ ounce) can tuna in water, drained
8 radishes, sliced
2 tomatoes, each cut in 8 wedges
½ cup (2 ounces) grated Parmesan cheese

• Prepare dressing.
• Combine lettuce, endive, cucumber, tuna and radishes in salad bowl, mixing well.
• Add tomatoes, drizzle dressing over salad and toss gently.
• Sprinkle cheese on salad.
• Serves 6 to 8.

DRESSING
1 large clove garlic, crushed
¾ cup extra virgin olive oil
¼ cup balsamic vinegar
2 tablespoons Dijon mustard
4 drops hot pepper sauce
1 teaspoon Worcestershire sauce
1 teaspoon fresh lemon juice

• Soak garlic in oil for 30 minutes. Remove garlic and discard.
• Combine vinegar and mustard. Add oil, whisking to blend. Stir in hot pepper sauce, Worcestershire sauce and lemon juice.

PAUL ANKA
"This is my favorite salad. There are many variations of this dish but this is the one I grew up with."

Tabbouleh

Middle East Parsley Salad

½ **cup bourghol (wheat germ)**
water
3 **bunches parsley**
2 **medium-sized ripe tomatoes, diced**
4 **green onions**
1 **clove garlic, minced**
juice of 1 fresh lemon or to taste
2 **tablespoons pure olive oil or to taste**
salt and black pepper to taste

- Pour bourghol into bowl, add water to cover and let stand for 2 hours. Drain, pressing to remove all water.
- While bourghol soaks, wash parsley thoroughly, discard stems and finely chop leaves. Add tomatoes to parsley.
- Dice onion, using white section and part of green tops.
- Mix bourghol, onion and garlic with tomatoes and parsley.
- Squeeze lemon juice on salad and add olive oil. Using 2 spoons, toss to mix thoroughly. Season with salt and black pepper.
- Serve with pita bread quarters or romaine lettuce leaves. Serves 6 to 8.

CHARLES AZNAVOUR
"Hope that my broken English will be clear enough for the readers of your cookbook, and also that they will like my simple recipe."

Armenian Chicken Salad

SALAD
1⅓ pounds chicken breast, skin removed and boned
1 teaspoon salt
⅓ cup margarine or butter or pure olive oil
water
⅔ pound tomatoes
⅔ pound tart apples
3 hard-cooked eggs, sliced
2 bunches lettuce, shredded

- Season chicken with salt. Sauté in butter, margarine or olive oil for a few minutes. Add small amount of water and cook, covered, until tender. Let stand until cool. Cut into thin strips.
- Peel tomatoes, cut in halves, remove seeds and dice. Peel apples, cut in quarters, then slice diagonally.
- Prepare dressing.
- Combine tomatoes, apples, eggs, lettuce and ½ of chicken. Add dressing and toss lightly to coat. Arrange salad in serving dish. Place remaining chicken on top of salad.
- Serves 6 to 8.

DRESSING
⅓ cup mayonnaise
⅓ cup ketchup
1 tablespoon onion salt
pinch of celery salt
bunch of parsley, finely chopped
juice of 1 lemon
1 teaspoon cognac

- Blend mayonnaise, ketchup, onion salt, celery salt, parsley, lemon and cognac, mixing well.

CONRAD BAIN

"This is a superb complement to poached salmon or any light fish dish."

Cherry Tomato Surprise

With Vegetable Vinaigrette

SALAD
- 1 pint cherry tomatoes
- ⅔ cup chopped parsley
- 2 medium-sized scallions, cut in 1-inch pieces
- 2 stalks celery with tips, chopped

- Combine tomatoes, parsley, scallions and celery.
- Prepare dressing. Add to vegetables and toss lightly to coat. Serves 6.

DRESSING
- 3 tablespoons vegetable oil
- 2 tablespoons light brown sugar
- 4 teaspoons red wine vinegar
- ¾ teaspoon dried oregano
- ¾ teaspoon salt
- ½ teaspoon freshly ground celery seeds

black pepper to taste

- Blend oil, brown sugar, vinegar, oregano, salt, celery seeds and black pepper.

CHER

Cher's Tuna Pasta

1 (8 ounce) package shell pasta
2 medium tomatoes
boiling water
1 (12 ounce) can white tuna, drained
¼ cup low-fat or regular mayonnaise
2 stalks celery, finely chopped
1 (4 ounce) can black olives, drained and sliced
3 tablespoons minced parsley
3 tablespoons minced dill
Beau Monde seasoning to taste
salt and black pepper to taste

- Prepare pasta according to package directions. Drain and set aside to cool.
- Stem tomatoes. On opposite side, cut shallow X in skin. Blanch in boiling water for 1 minute, rinse under cold running water to cool and peel. Cut in halves, remove seeds and dice.
- Combine tuna and mayonnaise, mixing thoroughly.
- Add tomatoes, celery, olives, parsley and dill to tuna. Season with Beau Monde, salt and black pepper.
- Serve cold. Serves 4 to 6.

ANN MEYERS DRYSDALE

Oriental Cole Slaw

3 (3 ounce) packages Chinese noodles mix, with seasoning packets
1 head cabbage, chopped
8 to 10 green onions, chopped
¾ to 1 cup sliced almonds
¼ cup sesame seeds
olive oil
¾ cup seasoned rice vinegar
sugar to taste

- Lightly crush packages to break up noodles.
- Combine noodles, seasoning packets, cabbage and onion.
- Sauté almonds and sesame seeds in olive oil to cover until browned. Pour over cabbage mixture.
- Add vinegar to cabbage mixture and toss to mix. Sweeten to taste with sugar.
- Serves 8 to 10.
- Cooked chicken or shrimp can be added for main course salad.

ANGIE DICKINSON

Sweet Simple Cole Slaw

SALAD
1 **head cabbage, shredded**
1 **onion, chopped**
1 **green bell pepper, chopped**
¾ **cup sugar**

- Layer cabbage, onion and bell pepper in bowl. Pour sugar over vegetables.
- Prepare dressing. Pour over vegetables.
- Chill for 3 to 4 hours.
- Stir slaw before serving. Serves 6 to 8.

DRESSING
1 **cup vinegar**
¾ **cup vegetable oil**
1 **tablespoon sugar**
1 **tablespoon salt**
1 **teaspoon dry mustard**
1 **teaspoon celery seed**

- Combine vinegar, oil, sugar, salt, dry mustard and celery seed in saucepan.
- Bring mixture to a boil, stirring to dissolve sugar. Remove from heat and let cool before using.

OLYMPIA DUKAKIS

Olympia Dukakis' Greek Salad

SALAD
- 1   cucumber, chopped
- ½   small onion, minced
- 4   cups shredded iceberg lettuce
- ½   cup chopped celery
- 3   sprigs parsley, chopped
- ½   cup fresh small peas
- ½   cup chopped artichokes
- 2   tablespoons Feta cheese
- 2   tablespoons finely chopped anchovies

- Combine cucumber, onion, lettuce, celery, parsley, peas and artichokes. Add cheese and anchovies.
- Prepare dressing. Drizzle over vegetables and toss lightly to coat. Serves 2.

DRESSING
- 1   clove garlic, grated
- 2   teaspoons olive oil
- 4   teaspoons vinegar
- salt and black pepper to taste

- Combine garlic, oil, vinegar, salt and black pepper, blending well.

MARILYN HORN

Chilled Dilled Peas

- 1   cup sour cream
- 1   bunch chives, chopped
- ¼   cup chopped dill
- 1   teaspoon curry powder or to taste
- salt and freshly ground black pepper
- 1   (16 ounce) can tiny French peas, drained
- dill for garnish

- Blend sour cream, chives, chopped dill, curry powder, salt and black pepper.
- Add peas to sour cream mixture and mix lightly to coat.
- Garnish salad in serving bowl with dill.
- Chill thoroughly before serving. Serves 4.

**LE LOUIS IV, HOTEL DE PARIS,
MONTE CARLO, MONACO
ALAIN DUCASSE, EXECUTIVE CHEF**

Santa Barbara Shrimp Salad

Crunchy Marinade with Vegetables

20	shrimp
½	pound string beans
	salted boiling water
⅔	pound large tomatoes
6	purple artichokes
½	pound small wax beans
12	stalks green or purple asparagus, cut diagonally
⅓	pound mushrooms, thinly sliced
⅔	cup olive oil
2½	tablespoons truffle juice
	juice of 2 lemons
	salt and freshly ground black pepper
	olive oil
1	bunch chervil

- Pierce each shrimp lengthwise with small skewer, such as a kabob, and set aside.
- Trim ends from beans, cook in salted boiling water, drain and chill. Cut to uniform bite-sized lengths.
- Blanch tomatoes in boiling water for 15 seconds. Drain, peel and dice.
- Cut artichokes round, slice in halves, then slice thinly.
- Combine string beans, tomatoes, artichokes, wax beans, asparagus and mushrooms.
- Blend olive oil, truffle juice and lemon juice. Drizzle 3 tablespoons of mixture over vegetables and let stand for about 10 minutes. Season with salt and black pepper.
- Cook shrimp in small amount of olive oil. Drain well and season with black pepper.
- Spoon portion of marinated vegetables into individual serving bowls. Top each with 5 shrimp. Drizzle lightly with olive oil mixture and sprinkle with chervil. Serves 4.

BILLY JOEL
"This is one of my favorite recipes and should be started a day ahead of time."

Grilled Tuna and Marinated Cucumber Salad

1 **cup olive oil**
¼ **cup teriyaki sauce**
¼ **cup lemon juice**
salt and black pepper
chopped parsley
4 **tuna steaks**
½ **cup white wine vinegar**
½ **teaspoon coriander**
olive oil
1 **packet sugar substitute**
2 **cucumbers, peeled and thinly sliced**
chopped white onions (optional)

- A day in advance of serving, prepare marinade by blending oil, teriyaki sauce, lemon juice, salt, black pepper and parsley.
- Marinate tuna steaks overnight in refrigerator. Marinade should completely cover the steaks.
- A day in advance of serving, combine vinegar, coriander, a dash of olive oil and sugar substitute.
- Marinate cucumbers and onion in dressing overnight.
- Drain tuna. Using barbecue grill or open flame, grill tuna just until done; interior should be pink. Break into chunks.
- Drain liquid from cucumber. Combine tuna and cucumber.
- Serves 4.

CHUCK KNOX
"Great for lunch with 'piping' hot bread."

Exotic Turkey Salad

SALAD
- 8 **cups coarsely chopped cooked chicken or turkey**
- 1 **(20 ounce) can water chestnuts, drained and sliced**
- 2 **pounds seedless grapes**
- 1 **cup sliced celery**
- ⅔ **cup toasted slivered almonds**
- 3 **cups pineapple chunks, drained**
- 8 **Boston or Butter lettuce leaves**

- Combine chicken or turkey, water chestnuts, grapes, celery, almonds and pineapple.
- Prepare dressing.
- Add dressing to chicken or turkey mixture, tossing to coat.
- Chill for several hours before serving.
- Serve on lettuce leaves. Serves 8 to 12.
- Salad can be prepared a day in advance and stored in refrigerator.

DRESSING
- 3 **cups mayonnaise**
- 2 **tablespoons lemon juice**
- 2 **tablespoons soy sauce**
- 1 **tablespoon curry powder**

- Blend mayonnaise, lemon juice, soy sauce and curry powder, mixing until smooth.

STEVE LARGENT

Fruited Chicken Salad

SALAD
4 cups diced cooked chicken breast
2 cups seedless green grapes or 1 (16 ounce) can pineapple chunks, drained
1 cup chopped celery
1 (11 ounce) can mandarin oranges, drained
2 tablespoons grated onion or onion powder to taste
1 (5 ounce) can chow mein noodles
lettuce leaves

- Combine chicken, grapes or pineapple, celery, oranges and onion.
- Prepare dressing.
- Add dressing to chicken mixture, tossing to coat.
- Chill, covered, for several hours.
- Just before serving, add chow mein noodles. Arrange salad in lettuce-lined serving bowl.
- Serves 8.

DRESSING
1 cup mayonnaise or salad dressing
1 tablespoon prepared grain mustard

- Blend mayonnaise or salad dressing with mustard, mixing until smooth.

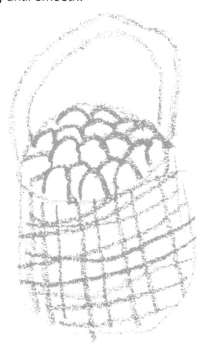

MISS PEGGY LEE

"I hope this recipe is sufficient. Most of my other cooking is done without measuring."

Jade Salad

 2 **heads Romaine lettuce**
 2 **bunches green onions, cut in ¼-inch pieces**
1⅓ **cups light olive oil**
 ⅔ **cup red wine vinegar**
 2 **teaspoons Dijon mustard**
 ½ **teaspoon garlic powder**
 ½ **teaspoon black pepper**
 2 **tablespoons sugar or equivalent sugar substitute**
 ¼ **cup toasted sesame seed**
 ¼ **cup (1 ounce) freshly grated Parmesan cheese**
 ½ **cup sliced almonds**

- Rinse lettuce and blot with paper towel to dry thoroughly. Cut lettuce julienne (strips should be width of linguine). Place in salad bowl.
- Combine green onion, oil, vinegar, mustard, garlic powder, black pepper, sugar or substitute, sesame seed and Parmesan cheese.
- Pour green onion mixture over lettuce and toss to coat and mix thoroughly. Sprinkle with almonds. Serves 4 to 8.

LIZA MINNELLI

Liza's Salade de Provence

 2 **cups cooked yellow corn**
 1 **pink grapefruit, peeled and sectioned, cut in bite-sized pieces**
 1 **cup cut hearts of palm**
thinly sliced fresh mushrooms
vinaigrette dressing (made with safflower oil)

- Combine corn, grapefruit, hearts of palm and mushrooms.
- Drizzle dressing over vegetables and mix lightly to coat.
- Serves 3 or 4.

I like to call Liza my daughter because I was with her father, Vincent, when she was born. Her first cries sounded like an Italian opera coming from the nursery — a Star had been born.
— Frank Sinatra

JIM OTTO

Caesar Salad

SALAD
1½ heads Romaine lettuce
1½ cups croutons
 1 avocado, peeled, pitted and diced (optional)
 ¼ cup (1 ounce) grated Parmesan cheese

- Tear Romaine into 2-inch pieces, place in salad bowl and set aside.
- Prepare dressing.
- Add croutons and avocado to lettuce. Spoon dressing over salad, sprinkle with cheese and toss lightly.
- Serve on chilled individual salad plates. Serves 4.

DRESSING
 3 large strips anchovies
 2 large cloves garlic, chopped
 2 hard-cooked egg yolks, mashed
juice of ½ lemon
 1 tablespoon Worcestershire sauce
 2 dashes hot pepper sauce (optional)
 1 teaspoon Dijon mustard
 2 tablespoons red wine vinegar
 ¾ cup olive oil

- Mash anchovies into paste and add garlic and egg yolk. Blend in lemon juice, Worcestershire sauce, hot pepper sauce, mustard and vinegar.
- Gradually add oil, stirring with fork or whisk to blend well.

THE PALMS AT PALM SPRINGS, CALIFORNIA
DON AND SHEILA CLUFF, OWNERS

Spinach and Gingered Rice Salad

SALAD
1½ pounds spinach, torn in small pieces
 1 cup thinly sliced red cabbage
 ¼ pound radish sprouts
 2 shallots, thinly sliced
 ½ cup sliced mushrooms
mandarin orange sections
anise seed

- Prepare dressing and rice.
- Combine spinach, cabbage, sprouts, shallots and
  mushrooms, tossing to mix. Chill while dressing and rice cool.
- Toss salad, rice and dressing together in large bowl.
- Serve on individual salad plates, garnishing with oranges and anise seed. Serves 6.

RICE
 ½ cup long grain brown rice
 ½ cup wild rice
 ½ ounce ginger root
 3 cups water
 ½ teaspoon fresh mint
pinch of nutmeg

- Combine brown rice, wild rice and whole piece of ginger in saucepan with water. Simmer
  until rice is tender. Drain and dry.
- Discard ginger from rice. Add mint and nutmeg.
- Cover with cloth and let stand until cool.

DRESSING
 1 cup unseasoned rice vinegar
 1 tablespoon fresh lemon juice
 ½ teaspoon red wine vinegar
 ¼ teaspoon freshly ground black pepper
 ½ teaspoon fresh dill
 ½ teaspoon fresh tarragon
 ½ teaspoon fresh thyme
 ¼ teaspoon whole anise seeds
 1 clove garlic, minced
 1 teaspoon olive oil

- Combine rice vinegar, lemon juice, wine vinegar, black pepper, dill, tarragon, thyme, anise
  seeds and garlic in heat-proof glass bowl, whisking to blend.
- Place bowl, covered, in saucepan. Add 1 inch water to saucepan.
- Over low heat, gradually bring water to boil. Remove bowl, place in warm area to cool, then
  chill until ready to use.
- Just before serving, blend in olive oil.

**MARIA SHRIVER
FROM MARIA AND ARNOLD'S RESTAURANT
SCHTAZI ON MAIN
CREATED BY CHEF MICHAEL ROSEN**

Maria's Oriental Chicken Salad

CHICKEN
- 2 pounds boneless chicken breasts
- 1 cup low-sodium soy sauce
- 3 ounces green onion, cleaned and chopped
- 1½ ounces ginger root, peeled and cut julienne
- ¼ to ⅓ cup dark sesame oil

salt and black pepper to taste

- A day or at least several hours in advance of serving salad, prepare chicken.
- Combine soy sauce, onion, ginger and oil, blending well. Season with salt and pepper.
- Pour mixture over chicken and marinate for several hours or overnight.
- Bake chicken, skin side up, at 350 degrees for about 30 minutes or until done.
- Let stand until cool, remove skin and shred.

SALAD
- ¼ to ½ pound mixed greens, torn in bite-sized pieces
- 1 head iceberg lettuce, torn in bite-sized pieces
- 1 bunch watercress tops
- 1 bunch cilantro
- 1 bunch mint leaves
- 1 large carrot, cut julienne
- 1 small cucumber, peeled and cut julienne
- 3 large oranges, peeled and sectioned
- ½ cup toasted slivered almonds

pinch of pickled ginger
fried won ton skins

- Prepare dressing.
- Wash and spin dry greens and lettuce. Chill for crispness.
- Combine greens, lettuce, watercress, cilantro, mint, carrots, cucumber, oranges, almond and ginger in salad bowl.
- Add shredded chicken and toss to mix.
- Lightly drizzle dressing over salad, tossing to coat; add more dressing as necessary. Garnish with won ton skins.
- Serves 4.

DRESSING FOR MARIA'S ORIENTAL CHICKEN SALAD

   1 **cup rice wine vinegar**
   1 **tablespoon low-sodium soy sauce**
   2 **tablespoons dark sesame oil**
   ½ **cup peanut oil**
   ¼ **cup sugar or to taste**
   1½ **teaspoons coarsely ground black pepper or to taste**
   ½ **teaspoon crushed red pepper flakes**
salt to taste

• Combine vinegar, soy sauce, sesame oil and peanut oil. Add sugar, black pepper, red pepper and salt. Whisk until well blended.

GEORGE AND JOLENE SCHLATTER
"Henry Mancini loved this recipe for his steamed artichokes. Just pour into the center and enjoy."

Speedy, Fresh and Zesty Beverly Hills Italian Dressing

   1 **(8 ounce) bottle regular or low-fat Italian dressing**
   1 **to 2 tablespoons fresh lemon juice**
   1 **clove garlic, crushed**

• Discard 1 tablespoon Italian dressing. Add lemon juice and garlic to dressing and shake well.
• Serve dressing on steamed fresh broccoli, green beans or raw vegetables or on green salads. Store in refrigerator.
• Makes 2 cups.

The only thing I don't like about George Schlatter is that he keeps me up too late. I've always called George "CFG," and the "F" was always dealer's choice. He is funny, friendly, foolish... there's not that many "F's" left to choose from. — Frank Sinatra

---

ROD AND PAULA STEIGER

Oriental Chicken Pasta

4   chicken breast halves
1   (12 ounce) package rotini pasta
2   tablespoons olive oil
½   cup sesame seeds
¼   cup vegetable oil
½   cup sliced green onion

- Prepare salad a day in advance or at least several hours before serving.
- Cook chicken, cool, cut into cubes and set aside.
- Prepare pasta according to package directions, adding olive oil to water. Cook until al dente. Drain, rinse with cold water and drain again.
- Sauté sesame seeds in oil in small skillet over medium heat, stirring occasionally and cooking until golden brown.
- Prepare dressing.
- Pour dressing over pasta. Add chicken, sesame seeds and green onion. Toss gently to coat with dressing.
- Chill, covered, for at least 2 hours or overnight.
- Serves 8.

DRESSING
½   cup vegetable oil
⅓   cup soy sauce
⅓   cup white wine vinegar
¼   cup sugar
½   teaspoon salt
¼   teaspoon black pepper

- Combine oil, soy sauce, vinegar, sugar, salt and black pepper. Whisk to blend.

NANCY CHAFFEE WHITAKER

Spinach Salad
with Chutney Dressing

SALAD
- 6 slices bacon
- 1 pound spinach, torn in bite-sized pieces
- 6 fresh mushrooms, sliced
- 1 cup sliced water chestnuts
- ⅓ to ½ cup (1 to 2 ounces) shredded Gruyere cheese

- Cook bacon until crisp. Drain well and crumble.
- Prepare dressing.
- Combine bacon, spinach, mushrooms, water chestnuts and cheese.
- Drizzle dressing over salad and toss to mix.
- Serves 6.

DRESSING
- 1¼ cups wine vinegar
- 1 clove garlic, minced
- 2 to 3 tablespoons sweet chutney
- 2 teaspoons sugar
- 2 tablespoons Dijon mustard
- ⅓ to ½ cup vegetable oil

salt and freshly ground black pepper to taste

- Combine vinegar, garlic, chutney, sugar and mustard in blender. Blend until smooth.
- Add oil and season with salt and black pepper.
- Chill, then bring to room temperature before serving.

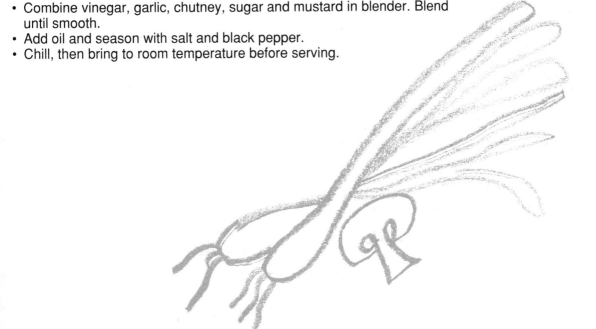

WYNONNA JUDD

Mexican Corn Bread

    3 cups cornmeal
    ¼ cup sugar
    1 large onion, chopped
   1½ cups (6 ounces) grated sharp Cheddar
       cheese
    1 (12 ounce) can Mexicorn, drained
    ¼ cup chopped jalapeño peppers
   2½ cups buttermilk
    3 eggs
    ¼ pound bacon, cooked and crumbled
       (optional)

- Combine cornmeal, sugar, onion, cheese, corn and jalapeño peppers.
- Add buttermilk and eggs to dry ingredients and mix well. Stir in bacon.
- Pour batter into 13x9x2-inch baking pan.
- Bake at 375 degrees for 35 to 40 minutes.
- Serves 10.

THE HONORABLE JACK KEMP

Mexican Corn Bread

    1 cup cornmeal
    1 cup all-purpose flour
    1 cup sugar
    1 tablespoon plus 1 teaspoon baking powder
    ¼ teaspoon salt
    1 cup margarine, softened
    4 eggs
    1 (16 ounce) can creamed corn
    1 (4 ounce) can chopped green chiles, drained
    ½ cup (2 ounces) shredded Monterey Jack
       cheese
    ½ cup (2 ounces) shredded Cheddar cheese

- Combine cornmeal, flour, sugar, baking powder and salt.
- Add margarine, eggs and corn to dry ingredients and mix well. Stir chiles, Monterey Jack cheese and Cheddar cheese into batter.
- Pour batter into greased 12x8x2-inch baking pan.
- Bake at 350 degrees for 55 minutes.
- Serves 8 to 10.

CARRIE FISHER

Gloria Crayton's Corn Bread Muffins

> 1 **cup cornmeal**
> 1 **cup all-purpose flour**
> 2 **tablespoons baking powder**
> 1½ **teaspoons salt**
> ¼ **cup sugar**
> ¼ **cup vegetable oil**
> 2 **eggs**
> 1 **cup milk**

- Combine cornmeal, flour, baking powder, salt and sugar.
- Add oil, eggs and milk to dry ingredients, blending well. Let batter stand for 30 minutes.
- Spoon batter into greased or paper-lined muffin pan.
- Bake at 450 degrees for 18 minutes.
- Makes 12.
- For variety, add 1 jalapeño pepper, seeded and finely chopped, to batter.

**THE HONORABLE LLOYD AND B.A. BENTSEN
DEPARTMENT OF TREASURY**

Mexican Corn Bread

> 2 **eggs**
> ⅔ **cup vegetable oil**
> 1 **cup sour cream**
> 1 **cup yellow cornmeal**
> 1 **cup creamed yellow corn**
> 1 **tablespoon baking powder**
> 1½ **teaspoons salt**
> 4 **jalapeño peppers, seeded and finely chopped, or 1 (2 ounce) can diced green chiles**
> 1 **cup (4 ounces) grated sharp Cheddar cheese, divided**

- Combine eggs, oil, sour cream, cornmeal, corn, baking powder and salt, blending well.
- Stir in jalapeño peppers or chiles and ½ cup cheese.
- Pour batter into well-greased 12x8x2-inch baking pan. Sprinkle remaining ½ cup cheese over batter.
- Bake at 425 degrees for 30 to 35 minutes.
- Serves 8 to 10.

BOB BARKER

Bruschetta

6 large ripe tomatoes (about 2½ pounds)
salt and black pepper to taste
½ cup tightly-packed basil leaves
8 cloves garlic, peeled and halved
1 cup extra-virgin olive oil
6 (1 inch thick) slices sourdough or coarse Italian bread

- Peel tomatoes, remove seeds and cut into ½-inch cubes. Place in large bowl and season with salt and black pepper.
- Reserving 6 large basil leaves, stack remaining leaves, roll up and thinly slice. Sprinkle over tomatoes.
- Set aside 2 garlic halves and add remainder to tomatoes. Stir in olive oil.
- Marinate vegetables at room temperature for 1 to 2 hours.
- Grill or toast bread slices until well browned. Rub each hot slice with 2 pieces garlic; garlic should nearly melt into toast.
- Discard garlic cloves from vegetable mixture. Generously spoon mixture on toast, including some oil with each spoonful.
- Garnish each slice bruschetta with a reserved basil leaf. Serve immediately.
- Serves 6.

**AL DENTE RESTAURANT,
PALM SPRINGS, CALIFORNIA
KENDRA RICCIO,
PROPRIETOR AND EXECUTIVE CHEF**

Bruschetta

8 Roma tomatoes, diced
4 cloves garlic, minced
12 basil leaves, chopped
2 tablespoons extra virgin olive oil
salt and black pepper to taste
1 loaf Italian bread, sliced and toasted

- Combine tomatoes, garlic, basil, oil, salt and black pepper.
- Spoon mixture on bread slices.
- Serves 8 to 10.

ANGELA LANSBURY

"This (dough rising) takes about an hour to an hour and a quarter, so I sometimes start the dough, then go out to the garden while it's rising."

Angela Lansbury's Famous Power Loaf

      2 **cups boiling water**
  1½ **cups cracked wheat cereal**
      3 **tablespoons vegetable shortening, softened**
      2 **tablespoons honey**
      1 **tablespoon salt**
      2 **packets active dry yeast**
   ⅔ **cup warm (105 to 115 degrees) water**
      4 **cups stone-ground whole wheat flour, divided**
      1 **cup bran flakes**
      1 **cup quick-cooking oats**
   ½ **cup wheat germ**

- Pour boiling water over wheat cereal and stir to combine. Add shortening, honey and salt. Let stand until lukewarm.
- Dissolve yeast in warm water. Add to cereal mixture.
- Gradually add 4 cups wheat flour to cereal mixture. Stir in bran flakes, oats and wheat germ, mixing well.
- Cover dough bowl with damp cloth and let rise for 1 to 1¼ hours or until double in bulk.
- Shape dough into loaves, place in greased 9x5x3-inch loaf pans and let rise again.
- Bake at 350 degrees for 45 minutes or until browned. Makes 2.

DAN LAURIA

Carmela's Pizza Bread

4 cups all-purpose flour
3 tablespoons olive oil
2 teaspoons baking powder
¼ teaspoon black pepper
2 eggs
water
2½ pounds smoked ham butt, cubed
½ teaspoon oregano
8 cups (32 ounces) shredded Mozzarella cheese
1 (3 ounce) stick pepperoni, cubed
1 cup (4 ounces) grated Parmesan cheese

- Stir oil into flour until beads form. Add baking powder and black pepper.
- Reserving 1 egg yolk, pour egg white and other egg into measuring cup. Add water to measure 1 cup.
- Gradually add egg liquid to flour mixture, mixing to form dough. Divide dough in halves.
- On lightly-floured surface, roll each portion of dough as thin as possible.
- Sauté ham with oregano in skillet over low heat. Reserving ham liquid, remove ham and set aside.
- Pour ham liquid on rolled dough, patting to spread evenly.
- In order listed, layer ½ of ingredients on each piece of dough: ham, Mozzarella cheese, pepperoni and Parmesan cheese.
- Carefully bring edges of dough together and roll to resemble bread loaf. Pierce dough with fork tines to vent steam during baking. Place rolls in 13x9x2-inch baking pan.
- Bake, uncovered, at 275 degrees for 1½ hours, brushing top of loaves occasionally with beaten egg yolk.
- Cut into ¾-inch slices to serve. Serves 8 to 12.

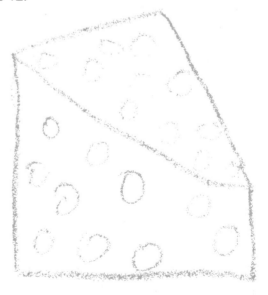

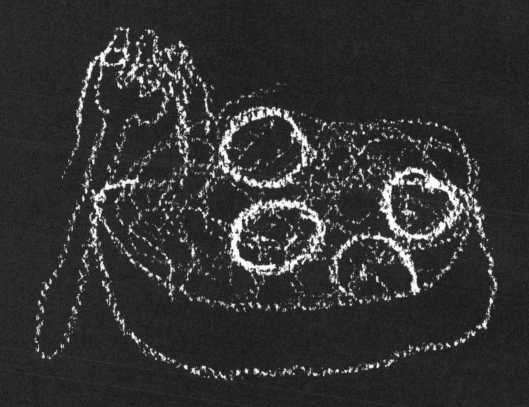

Pasta

Dustin, age 8

JOAN COLLINS

Pasta Primavera

1 **(16 ounce) package penne pasta**
1 **bunch broccoli, broken in flowerets**
2 **medium-sized onions, coarsely chopped**
1 **tablespoon butter**
2 **medium zucchini, cut in 2-inch strips**
8 **large mushrooms**
2 **large tomatoes**
2 **cloves garlic, crushed**
salt and black pepper to taste
grated Parmesan cheese (optional)

- Prepare pasta according to package directions, cooking until al dente. While pasta is cooking, prepare vegetables. Drain pasta, rinse with hot water, drain and keep warm until ready to use.
- Steam broccoli for 7 minutes or until broccoli is cooked but still firm.
- Sauté onion in butter until tender. Drain and add to broccoli.
- Steam zucchini for about 5 minutes or until cooked but not softened.
- Grill mushrooms for a few minutes. Drain, cool and cut in large chunks.
- Blanch tomatoes in boiling water for 10 seconds, drain and plunge in cold water. Peel, quarter, cut in halves again, and remove seeds.
- Combine zucchini, mushrooms, tomatoes and garlic. Season with salt and black pepper.
- Add vegetable mixture to pasta in saucepan. Warm over very low heat.
- Reheat broccoli in steamer for 1 minute, add to pasta mixture and mix gently to avoid breaking flowerets.
- Sprinkle with cheese.
- Serve warm but not too hot. Serves 4.

TIM ALLEN

Tim's Favorite Manly Man Mixed Vegetable Lasagna

  1 (8 ounce) package lasagna noodles or
      ¾ pound fresh lasagna noodles
  1 large onion, chopped
  2 tablespoons olive oil
  2 cloves garlic, minced
1½ pounds carrots, diced
1½ pounds leeks, sliced
  1 pound zucchini or sweated eggplant, diced
  1 green bell pepper, chopped
  2 (16 ounce) cartons Ricotta cheese
salt and freshly ground black pepper
  7 to 8 cups Italian style tomato sauce
  1 (8 ounce) package thinly sliced Mozzarella
      cheese
grated Parmesan cheese

- Prepare lasagna according to package directions. While noodles are cooking, prepare sauce. Rinse and drain noodles well before using.

- Sauté onion in oil in Dutch oven for about 10 minutes; do not brown.

- Add garlic, carrots, leeks, zucchini or eggplant and bell pepper to onion. Sauté vegetables, covered, for 10 to 20 minutes or until tender.

- Stir Ricotta cheese into vegetables. Season with salt and black pepper.

- Spread thin layer of tomato sauce in greased 14x10x2-inch baking dish. Add layer of lasagna noodles, vegetable mixture, cheese slices and tomato sauce. Repeat layers to use all ingredients, finishing with tomato sauce.

- Sprinkle any remaining Mozzarella cheese and Parmesan cheese.

- Bake at 400 degrees for 1 hour. If browning too quickly, cover with aluminum foil.

- Serves 6 to 8.

CAROL ALT

"I also cut up the finished pie into squares and place individually on paper plates and wrap in plastic freezer bags to place in the freezer to make 'ready-meals' for the household when I am away on location."

Vegetable Lasagna

1 (16 ounce) package lasagna noodles
1 (32 ounce) jar spaghetti sauce, divided
1 cup chopped carrots
1 cup chopped broccoli
1 cup sliced mushrooms
1 cup spinach
2 tablespoons garlic powder or 4 cloves garlic, sliced
salt and black pepper to taste
oregano or other Italian herbs to taste
1 (16 ounce) package sliced regular or low-fat Mozzarella cheese
1 (15 ounce) carton Ricotta or low-fat cottage cheese
½ cup (2 ounces) grated Parmesan cheese

• Prepare noodles according to package directions, cooking al dente. While noodles are cooking, prepare sauce. Drain noodles well before using.
• Combine spaghetti sauce, carrots, broccoli, mushrooms, spinach and garlic in saucepan. Season with salt, black pepper, oregano and other herbs. Simmer to heat thoroughly.
• Pour thin layer of sauce in 14x10x2-inch baking pan. In order listed, layer portion of noodles, Mozzarella, sauce, noodles, Ricotta and sauce; repeat layers until all noodles are used. Spread remaining Mozzarella and Ricotta cheeses and sauce on the layered ingredients and sprinkle with Parmesan cheese.
• Bake at 350 degrees for 45 minutes or until cheese is melted and top is browned.
• Cut into squares. Lasagna squares can be frozen in plastic bags; to reheat, microwave for about 3 minutes.
• Serves 5 or 6.

JAYNI AND CHEVY CHASE

Vegetable Lasagna

1 (16 ounce) package lasagna noodles
2 pounds broccoli, chopped
4 medium zucchini, chopped
1 medium-sized onion, chopped
2 cloves garlic, minced
1 (28 ounce) can whole tomatoes, drained
3 cups low-fat Ricotta cheese
3 cups (12 ounces) grated Mozzarella cheese
1 teaspoon oregano
1 (16 ounce) jar spaghetti sauce
½ cup (2 ounces) grated Parmesan cheese

- Prepare noodles according to package directions. While noodles are cooking, prepare sauce. Drain noodles well before using.
- Steam broccoli for 2 minutes.
- Combine broccoli, zucchini, onion, garlic, tomatoes and salt in skillet. Sauté for about 5 minutes over high heat.
- Mix Ricotta, Mozzarella and oregano together.
- Warm spaghetti sauce in saucepan.
- In 13x9x2-inch glass baking dish, in order listed, layer: ½ spaghetti sauce, ⅓ noodles, ½ tomato sauce, ½ cheese mixture, ⅓ noodles, ½ tomato sauce, ½ cheese mixture, ⅓ noodles and ½ spaghetti sauce. Sprinkle top with Parmesan cheese.
- Bake at 350 degrees for 45 minutes. Let stand for 10 minutes before cutting and serving.
- Serves 8.

FARRAH FAWCETT

"I was able to get this recipe by literally going down to the kitchen and watching (and helping) this lovely French woman prepare it. We were staying in the south of France and whenever I have this dish, it brings back the loveliest memories of Ryan and me with our friends in Cap Ferrat, France."

Fresh Tomato Sauce

3 cloves garlic, pressed
3 sprigs rosemary
2 basil leaves, sliced
3 tablespoons olive oil
¾ cup white wine
2 large tomatoes, peeled and chopped
3 tablespoons capers

- Sauté garlic, rosemary and basil in oil in small skillet over low heat until softened.
- Add white wine to garlic and herbs. Increase heat to high.
- Stir in tomato and capers. Sauté for just 2 minutes; do not overcook tomatoes.
- Serve over fish or pasta. Serves 4.
- If desired, cook away alcohol in wine by simmering wine for 1 minute before serving.

SONNY BONO, MEMBER OF CONGRESS
"Spaghetti al Filetto di Pomodor — this was the dish served Sophia Loren in the Bono home during her visit to Palm Springs as the star of our International Film Festival."

Spaghetti al Filetto di Pomodor

Spaghetti with Fresh Tomato Sauce

1 (16 ounce) package spaghetti
5 large ripe tomatoes
boiling water
1 clove garlic, minced
¼ cup olive oil
1 bunch basil, chopped
salt and black pepper to taste
crushed red pepper (optional)
grated Parmesan cheese (optional)

- Prepare pasta according to package directions. While pasta is cooking, prepare sauce. Drain cooked pasta well.
- Blanch tomatoes in boiling water for 1 minute, drain, peel and cut into bite-sized pieces.
- Sauté garlic in oil in skillet over medium heat until tender. Add tomatoes and sauté for 1 minute. Stir in basil and remove from heat.
- Toss pasta with tomato sauce. Season with salt and black pepper.
- Sprinkle individual servings with red pepper and Parmesan cheese.
- Serves 4.

DOM DE LUISE

Lucy's Pasta

5 cloves garlic, minced
⅓ cup olive oil
3 onions, thinly sliced in crescents
½ cup finely chopped parsley
1 (16 ounce) package spaghetti or linguine
3 or 4 eggs
¼ cup plus 2 tablespoons freshly grated Parmesan cheese
½ cup finely torn basil
freshly ground black pepper to taste

- Sauté garlic in oil until browned. Add onion and sauté until onions are crunchy and browned; just before onions are cooked, stir in parsley and sauté until parsley is softened.
- Prepare pasta according to package directions, cooking until al dente.
- While pasta is cooking, beat eggs, cheese and basil together.
- Drain pasta and immediately add egg mixture, folding and mixing to allow heat of pasta to cook egg.
- Add sautéed vegetables to pasta mixture and mix well.
- Sprinkle with black pepper and season with additional parsley, basil and cheese as desired.
- Serves 4 to 6.

TONY BENNETT

Anna Benedetto's Lasagna

1¼ pounds ground beef
  2 medium-sized onions, chopped
  ½ pound hot Italian sausage
  4 or 5 cloves garlic, minced
  1 (28 ounce) can Italian plum tomatoes, drained
  1 (28 ounce) can Italian tomato purée
  2 (6 ounce) cans tomato paste
  ¼ cup minced basil
  ¼ teaspoon cinnamon
  1 teaspoon salt or to taste
  ½ teaspoon freshly ground black pepper
  1 (16 ounce) package lasagna noodles
  1 tablespoon olive oil
  1 tablespoon salt
  2 (15 ounce) cartons Ricotta cheese
  3 eggs, lightly beaten
  2 cups (8 ounces) grated Romano Pecorino cheese

- Brown ground beef and onions together. Drain excess fat and set aside.
- Remove sausage from casing, crumble and place in large saucepan with garlic. Cook for a few minutes.
- Add tomatoes, purée and paste to sausage. Stir in basil, cinnamon, 1 teaspoon salt and black pepper. Add ground beef and onion, mixing well. Simmer, stirring occasionally, for 20 minutes.
- While sauce is cooking, prepare noodles according to package directions, adding olive oil and salt to water (if not included in package directions). Cook until al dente and drain well.
- Combine Ricotta cheese and eggs.
- In 14x10x2-inch baking pan, layer ingredients in order listed: small amount of sauce, ¼ noodles, ⅓ Ricotta mixture, ⅓ Romano cheese and ¼ sauce; repeat layers twice. Top with remaining noodles and sauce.
- Bake at 350 degrees for 45 minutes or until browned and bubbly. Let stand 10 minutes before cutting to serve.
- Serves 6 to 8.

MICHAEL DANTE

Michael Dante's Penne Puttanesca

- 3 cloves garlic, chopped
- light olive oil
- 1 small bunch fresh basil, chopped
- ¼ cup chopped parsley
- 1 (2 ounce) can anchovies, chopped
- 12 Italian Roma tomatoes, diced
- 1 (2 ounce) can chopped ripe olives, undrained
- 1 (2 ounce) jar chopped green olives, undrained
- 1½ ounces capers
- crushed red pepper to taste
- 1 (16 ounce) package penne pasta

- Sauté garlic in small amount of oil in deep skillet until tender; do not brown.
- Add small amount more of oil to skillet. Then add, in order listed: basil, parsley, anchovies, tomatoes, ripe olives, green olives, capers with small amount of liquid, and red pepper.
- Simmer for about 30 minutes, stirring frequently and adding small amount of caper liquid if needed.
- While sauce is cooking, prepare pasta according to package directions. Drain well.
- Serve sauce on pasta. Serves 4.

ERNIE'S, SAN FRANCISCO, CALIFORNIA
VICTOR AND ROLAND GOTTI, PROPRIETORS

Rigatoni alla Norcina

- 1 (16 ounce) package rigatoni
- 2 slices bacon, diced
- 3 lean sausages, casings removed
- ¼ cup olive oil
- ½ cup whipping cream
- black pepper to taste
- ½ cup (2 ounces) grated Parmesan cheese

- Prepare pasta according to package directions. While pasta is cooking, prepare sauce. Drain pasta well before using.
- In oil in skillet over low flame, sauté bacon and sausage, stirring to crumble until meat is cooked.
- Stir cream and black pepper into meat mixture.
- Pour pasta into serving bowl, add sauce and sprinkle with cheese.
- Serves 4 to 6.

CLINT EASTWOOD

Spaghetti Western

½ cup chopped shallots
½ cup finely chopped celery
½ cup thinly sliced red bell pepper
½ cup thinly sliced yellow or green bell pepper
2 large cloves garlic, crushed
3 tablespoons vegetable oil
1 (14½ ounce) can whole tomatoes, undrained
½ cup tomato purée
½ cup fish stock or bottled clam juice
1 bay leaf
1 teaspoon anchovy paste
1½ teaspoons saffron threads or ground turmeric
salt and freshly ground black pepper to taste
12 large mussels in shells, scrubbed and beards removed
1 (10 ounce) package frozen artichoke hearts, thawed and drained
4 fresh jumbo shrimp, peeled and deveined
4 (1 ounce) sea scallops, quartered
1 (8 ounce) package spaghetti
½ cup whipping cream
2 tablespoons Pernod liqueur (optional)
1 (6½ ounce) can clams, drained and chopped
celery leaves (optional)

- Sauté shallots, celery, red and yellow or green bell pepper and garlic in oil for about 10 minutes or until tender, stirring frequently.
- Add tomatoes and liquid, purée, fish stock or clam juice, bay leaf, anchovy paste, saffron, salt and black pepper to sautéed vegetables. Simmer, covered, for 10 minutes.
- While vegetable mixture is cooking, pour 1 inch water into 3-quart saucepan. Bring to a boil. Add mussels in shells and cook, covered, for 4 minutes or just until shells open. Drain.
- Using sharp knife, cut mussels away from shells. Reserve 12 shells and discard remainder. Rinse mussels under cold running water and set aside.
- Add artichoke hearts, shrimp and scallops to vegetable mixture. Cook, stirring frequently, over medium-high heat for 5 minutes or just until shrimp turn pink.
- Prepare pasta according to package directions. While pasta cooks, continue with preparation of sauce. Drain pasta well before using.
- Stir cream and liqueur into seafood mixture. Simmer, covered, for 10 minutes.
- Add clams and mussels to sauce. Cook for 1 minute or until thoroughly heated.
- To serve, divide spaghetti among 4 large shallow bowls. Discard bay leaf from sauce. Remove shrimp, mussels and artichoke hearts from sauce; return mussels to reserved shells and set shrimp and artichoke hearts aside.
- Spoon sauce over pasta and garnish each serving with 1 shrimp, 3 mussels, 3 artichoke hearts and celery leaves.
- Serves 4.

JAMIE FARR
"If you wish to substitute tub margarine for butter, it is okay — and if you wish not to garnish plate with salami slices, that is okay."

Jamie's Artichoke Pasta

- 1 (16 ounce) package spaghetti
- ¼ cup butter
- ¼ cup olive oil
- 2 tablespoons all-purpose flour
- 1 cup chicken stock
- 3 cloves garlic, minced
- 1 tablespoon parsley flakes
- salt and black pepper to taste
- 1 (14 ounce) can artichoke hearts, drained and cut in halves
- ¼ cup (1 ounce) grated Parmesan cheese
- ⅔ cup sliced ripe olives
- 3 tablespoons butter
- ¼ pound salami, thinly sliced

- Prepare pasta according to package directions. While pasta is cooking, prepare sauce. Drain pasta well before using.
- Melt butter in small saucepan. Blend in oil and flour, stirring until smooth. Gradually add stock and cook for about 1 minute or until thickened.
- Add garlic, parsley, salt and black pepper to sauce. Simmer, stirring constantly, for 5 minutes.
- Add artichoke hearts, olives and cheese to sauce. Simmer, covered, for 5 minutes.
- Melt 3 tablespoons butter and toss with hot pasta. Pour into serving dish, spoon sauce over pasta and arrange salami slices around edge. Serves 4.

JANE WYMAN

Magnificent Pasta with Tomato Basil Sauce

- 3 pounds plum tomatoes, cut in medium chunks
- 2 yellow onions, cut in medium chunks
- 8 cloves garlic, peeled and minced
- ¼ cup olive oil or vegetable cooking spray
- salt to taste
- fresh basil leaves to taste
- 1 (16 ounce) package angel hair, spaghettini or penne pasta
- grated Parmesan cheese

- Combine tomatoes, onion and garlic in 2-quart casserole. Add oil or spray with olive oil cooking spray and toss to coat vegetables thoroughly.
- Bake at 325 degrees for 40 minutes or until tomatoes are darkened at edges.
- While vegetables are baking, prepare pasta according to package directions. Drain well.
- Remove vegetables from oven and let stand to cool slightly. Using blender or food processor, purée mixture. Season with salt and basil and process to smooth sauce consistency.
- Serve sauce over pasta and sprinkle with cheese.
- Sauce can be prepared in advance and stored in refrigerator. To reheat, microwave for 3 minutes.
- Serves 4.

NINA FOCH

Capellini with Caviar

1 **(12 ounce) package capellini pasta**
butter or olive oil
1 **(4 ounce) jar American golden caviar**
1 **lemon, cut in 8 wedges**

- Prepare pasta according to package directions. Drain well, return to pot, add butter or olive oil and toss to coat pasta strands.
- Divide pasta among 4 warmed plates. Sprinkle 2 teaspoons caviar in center of each serving and arrange 2 lemon wedges (1 at "nine o'clock" and the other at "three o'clock") at edges of plate.
- Serve immediately, offering pepper mill for individual use.
- Serves 4.

LE DOME RESTAURANT,
HOLLYWOOD, CALIFORNIA
EDDIE KERKHOFS, PROPRIETOR

Pasta and Caviar in a Vodka Sauce

1 **(8 ounce) package spaghetti**
½ **medium-sized onion, chopped**
¼ **cup plus 2 tablespoons butter**
1 **cup clear chicken broth**
¼ **cup plus 2 tablespoons vodka**
2 **cups whipping cream**
2 **bunches chives, chopped**
dash of salt and black pepper
2 **ounces Sevruga caviar**

- Prepare pasta according to package directions. While pasta is cooking, prepare sauce. Drain pasta well before using.
- Sauté onion in butter in skillet over low heat for about 45 seconds.
- Add chicken broth to onion and simmer to reduce liquid by ½.
- Stir vodka and cream into broth and cook until thickened.
- Add chives, salt and pepper to sauce.
- Using large kitchen fork, roll pasta into a cigar-shaped form on individual plate, spoon sauce over pasta and top each serving with ¼ of caviar.
- Serves 4.

ROBERT WAGNER

Pasta Alla B.J.

1 (16 ounce) package spaghetti or linguine
4 cloves garlic, minced
¼ cup olive oil
½ cup coarsely chopped green olives
½ cup coarsely chopped black olives
3 or 4 small tomatoes, coarsely chopped
1 green bell pepper, coarsely chopped
1 red bell pepper, coarsely chopped
1 yellow bell pepper, coarsely chopped
grated Parmesan cheese (optional)

- Prepare pasta according to package directions. Drain well before using.
- While pasta is cooking, combine garlic and oil in small saucepan. Warm over low heat until garlic is softened. Remove from heat.
- Place each vegetable in a separate small serving bowl on dining table.
- Pour pasta into warmed large bowl. Drizzle oil and garlic over pasta and toss to coat.
- Serve pasta on warmed dinner plates and offer vegetables and cheese for individual servings. Serves 6.

Jill and R.J. have done wonderful things for the Children's Center. Frank and I adore their good humor and friendship. A few years ago, R.J. befriended a youngster who was being counseled at the Center and has been personally supportive of the child's progress ever since — no fanfare or accolades, just simple caring and concern. — Barbara Sinatra

---

BINNIE B. FRANKOVICH

Fettucine Dolce

1 (8 ounce) package fettuccine
6 to 10 fresh mushrooms, diced
olive oil
¼ cup unsalted butter
2 to 4 tablespoons whipping cream
pinch of nutmeg
pinch of granulated garlic
½ cup (2 ounces) grated Parmesan or Romano cheese
2 tablespoons wine

- Prepare pasta according to package directions, cooking until al dente. While pasta is cooking, prepare sauce. Drain pasta well and return to pan.
- Sauté mushrooms in small amount of oil in skillet over medium heat until cooked. Reduce heat.
- Add butter and cream to mushrooms and cook until melted but not too hot.
- When butter and cream are blended, stir in nutmeg, garlic and cheese. Cook over low heat until cheese is absorbed.
- Add wine to sauce, stir and remove from heat. If sauce is thin, add more cheese.
- Pour sauce over pasta and toss to coat thoroughly. Serves 4.

BRUCE JENNER

High Jump Pasta Primavera

  5 cloves garlic, sliced
olive oil
  4 or 5 carrots, sliced
  1 bunch broccoli, chopped
  6 zucchini, unpeeled and sliced
  2 green bell peppers, sliced
  1 red bell pepper, sliced
  1 yellow bell pepper, sliced
seasoned salt to taste
seasoned black pepper to taste
garlic salt
garlic powder
  1 (12 ounce) package bow-tie pasta
  1 cup (4 ounces) grated Parmesan cheese
  1 bunch basil, chopped
basil sprigs

- Sauté garlic in small amount of oil in large skillet over medium heat until tender.
- Add carrots and sauté for 8 to 10 minutes. Add broccoli and cook, stirring constantly, for 5 to 6 minutes. Add zucchini and green, red and yellow bell pepper and cook until tender. As vegetables cook, season with seasoned salt, seasoned black pepper, garlic salt, and garlic powder. Add small amount of oil if necessary.
- While vegetables are cooking, prepare pasta according to package directions. Drain well and pour into serving dish.
- Spoon vegetables over pasta, add cheese and chopped basil and toss to mix. Garnish with basil sprigs.
- Serves 4 to 6.

JERRY VALE

Pasta Puttanesca

10 mushrooms, chopped
 2 cloves garlic, minced
 2 tablespoons olive oil
basil leaves to taste
 ½ (4 ounce) can sliced ripe olives, drained
20 fresh Roma, plum or Italian tomatoes, chopped
salt and black pepper to taste
pinch of crushed red pepper
 1 (16 ounce) package fusilli pasta
grated Parmesan cheese to taste

- Sauté mushrooms and garlic in oil in large skillet until softened.
- Stir basil, olives, tomatoes, salt, black pepper and red pepper into mushroom mixture. Simmer for 20 to 25 minutes or until tomatoes are tender.
- While sauce is cooking, prepare pasta according to package directions, adding drop of oil to salted water to prevent sticking. Cook until al dente. Drain well.
- Pour pasta into sauce and mix well. Sprinkle with cheese.
- Serves 4 to 6.

JOAN VAN ARK

Angel Hair Pasta with Garlic, Tomato and Spinach

 1 clove garlic, minced
 ¼ cup olive oil
 8 to 10 mushrooms, sliced
 4 or 5 large plum or Roma tomatoes, diced
 2 cups shredded fresh spinach or frozen chopped spinach, thawed and undrained
 1 teaspoon cracked black pepper
 1 teaspoon parsley flakes
 1 tablespoon oregano
 1 teaspoon Herbs du Provence
 1 (16 ounce) package angel hair pasta
grated Parmesan cheese (optional)

- Sauté garlic in oil in large skillet over low heat until translucent. Add mushrooms and sauté until tender.
- Add tomatoes and simmer until softened.
- Stir in spinach, black pepper, parsley, oregano and herbs. Simmer for 10 minutes.
- While sauce is cooking, prepare pasta according to package directions. Drain well.
- Combine sauce and pasta, sprinkle with cheese and toss to mix. Serves 4.

JERRY LEWIS
"We like this with an Italian dry white wine and a hearty Italian bread!"

Pasta with Vegetables and Pesto

PASTA
    4 cups chopped vegetables (broccoli, zucchini
        or others in combination)
    1 (8 or 12 ounce) package penne pasta
    1 cup low-fat chicken broth
freshly grated Pecorino, Romano or Parmesan
        cheese

- Prepare pesto.
- Steam vegetables until tender. Keep warm while preparing pasta.
- Prepare pasta according to package directions, cooking until al dente. Drain pasta.
- Combine vegetables, pasta, about ¼ cup pesto and chicken broth. Stir and toss until pasta is well coated.
- Spoon mixture into individual pasta bowls and serve with grated cheese.
- Serves 4.

PESTO
    1 cup basil leaves (stems discarded)
    2 cloves garlic
    ½ cup Italian parsley
    ½ to 1 cup extra virgin olive oil
    ½ cup pine nuts
salt and black pepper
ground red pepper to taste
olive oil

- Combine basil, garlic, parsley, oil, pine nuts, salt, black pepper and red pepper in blender. Blend until smooth.
- Store extra pesto in jar, covered with 1 inch olive oil, in refrigerator for up to 3 weeks.

People say you shouldn't go swimming until one hour after you eat. If you can even get up from the table an hour after one of my pasta meals you deserve the swim... but you might sink.
— Frank Sinatra

ROBERT LOGGIA

Pasta al Pesto

PASTA
1 (16 ounce) package linguine
grated Parmesan cheese
freshly ground black pepper

- Cook pasta in rapidly boiling salted water for 7 minutes or until al dente. Drain but leave pasta very moist. Pour into bowl.
- Add pesto to pasta and toss to completely coat. Sprinkle with cheese and a liberal amount of black pepper.
- Serves 6 to 8.

PESTO
5 cups basil leaves (stems discarded)
1 cup Italian parsley
1 cup arugula
1 medium-sized Spanish onion
3 large cloves garlic
1 cup pignoli nuts, divided
1 cup extra virgin olive oil
1 cup (4 ounces) grated Parmesan cheese
½ cup (2 ounces) grated Pecorino cheese
½ cup (2 ounces) grated Romano cheese
olive oil

- Combine basil, parsley, arugula, onion, garlic, ½ cup pignoli nuts and oil in blender. Blend until coarsely smooth. Pour into large bowl.
- Add remaining ½ cup whole pignoli nuts, Parmesan cheese, Pecorino cheese and Romano cheese to basil mixture, mixing with spoon. Drizzle surface with oil.

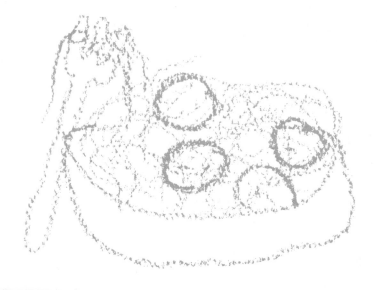

**LE CIRQUE, NEW YORK, NEW YORK
SIRIO MACCIONI,
PROPRIETOR AND EXECUTIVE CHEF**

Spaghetti Primavera

- 2 small zucchini
- 1 bunch broccoli
- 4 spears asparagus
- 1½ cups green beans
- ½ cup fresh or frozen peas
- 2 cups thinly sliced mushrooms
- salt and black pepper to taste
- 1 tablespoon peanut, vegetable or corn oil
- 1 teaspoon red or green chiles, chopped
- ¼ cup finely chopped parsley
- 1 teaspoon minced garlic, divided
- 3 cups ripe tomatoes (in 1-inch cubes)
- 6 tablespoons olive oil, divided
- 6 basil leaves, chopped
- 1 (16 ounce) package spaghetti or spaghettini
- ¼ cup butter
- 2 tablespoons chicken broth
- ½ cup whipping cream
- ⅔ cup (2½ ounces) grated Parmesan cheese
- ⅓ cup toasted pine nuts

- Prepare vegetables: trim ends from zucchini but do not peel, cut in quarters lengthwise, then in 1-inch lengths; trim broccoli and break in bite-sized pieces; cut asparagus spears in thirds, and trim green beans and cut to 1-inch lengths.
- Separately cook each vegetable in boiling water for about 5 minutes or until crisp-tender, drain well, rinse with cold water to chill, drain and combine in mixing bowl.
- Cook peas (fresh for 1 minute or 30 seconds if frozen). Drain and add to vegetable mixture.
- Cook mushrooms with salt and pepper in oil in skillet for about 2 minutes, shaking skillet to avoid sticking. Add mushrooms, chiles and parsley to vegetable mixture.
- Cook ½ teaspoon garlic and tomatoes, seasoned with salt and black pepper, in 3 tablespoons olive oil in saucepan for 4 minutes, stirring gently to avoid breaking tomatoes. Stir in basil and set aside.
- Pour remaining 3 tablespoons olive oil in skillet. Add remaining ½ teaspoon garlic and vegetable mixture. Cook, stirring carefully, until thoroughly heated.
- Prepare pasta according to package directions, cooking until al dente; do not overcook. Drain and return pasta to pot.
- Melt butter in stock pot. Stir in broth, cream and cheese. Cook, stirring constantly and moving on and off the heat, until smooth.
- Add pasta to sauce and toss quickly to coat. Add ½ the vegetables and the liquid from the tomatoes, stirring and tossing over very low heat. Add remaining vegetables.
- If sauce appears too dry, add up to ¼ cup whipping cream; sauce should not be soupy.
- Add pine nuts and toss to mix.
- Spoon tomatoes over individual servings. Serves 6 to 8.

**RISTORANTE GUALTIERO MARCHESI,
MILANO, ITALY
GUALTIERO MARCHESI,
PROPRIETOR AND EXECUTIVE CHEF**

Raviolo Aperto

  1 **ounce fresh egg pasta**
  4 **spinach lasagna noodles**
  4 **large parsley leaves**
14 **ounces scallops, cut in halves**
salt and freshly ground black pepper
  1 **piece ginger root, peeled and finely grated**
  ½ **cup butter**
  2 **tablespoons white wine**
  1 **tablespoon olive oil**

- Roll egg pasta very thinly and cut in 8 squares.
- Place parsley leaf in center of 4 pasta squares, cover each with another square and flatten with rolling pin.
- Cut scallops in halves and season with salt and black pepper.
- Press grated ginger to extract 1 tablespoon juice.
- Briefly sauté scallops in 2 tablespoons butter in skillet. Add wine and simmer for 2 minutes. Remove scallops. Boil cooking liquid to reduce. Lightly whisk in remaining 3 tablespoons butter and ginger juice.
- Cook pasta squares and spinach lasagna noodles in boiling salted water with olive oil for 3 to 5 minutes. Drain well.
- Place 1 lasagna noodle on individual plate. Return scallops to skillet, reheat and pour over lasagna. Cover with pasta squares and serve immediately. Serves 4.

ROBERT MARX

Linguine Alla Puttanesca
(Hooker's Sauce)

1 tin anchovies in olive oil (from Sicily or
  Portugal)
2 to 4 cloves crushed garlic
1 jar tiny "fine" capers
1 pint "Moroccan" olives with pits (salt-cured
  black olives)
crushed red hot pepper flakes
dry oregano
fresh Italian flat parsley
2 whole peeled carrots
1 (2 pound, 3 ounce) can San Marzano
  tomatoes
1 (1 pound) box linguine (De Cecco or
  equivalent)
Optional: 1 slivered green bell pepper, fresh
  grated Parmigiano Reggiano or Pecorino
  Romano cheese

- Sauté 3-5 anchovies in 2-3 tablespoons olive oil until liquefied in large sauté pan.
- Add crushed garlic and a pinch of crushed red hot pepper flakes to taste.
- Sauté until garlic is golden, but not brown. Crush tomatoes and add to anchovy garlic
  mixture. Add pinch of oregano, the whole carrots, 3-4 teaspoons capers, and the olives.
- Bring sauce to boil and simmer uncovered 30-45 minutes to thicken.
- Bring water to boil; salt after boiling, add pasta and cook al dente. Drain pasta.
- Remove carrots and pour sauce over pasta. Optional: top with bell pepper slivers and fresh
  grated Parmigiano Reggiano or Pecorino Romano cheese.
- Garnish with fresh chopped Italian parsley and crushed red hot pepper flakes to taste.
  Beware of olive pits when eating!

*Bob is a fabulous cook. When Frank worked in New York, Bob often joined us at our apartment in the
Waldorf after the concert where he would cook a dish of this wonderful pasta accompanied by a fine red
wine and a light salad. — Barbara Sinatra*

BOB NEWHART

Chicken Lasagna

> 4 **links turkey spicy Italian sausage, casings removed**
> 1 **pound ground chicken**
> 2 **tablespoons olive oil**
> 3½ **cups spaghetti sauce**
> 1 **(8 ounce) package lasagna noodles**
> 2 **cups (8 ounces) shredded low-fat Mozzarella cheese**
> 2 **cups (8 ounces) shredded low-fat Cheddar cheese**
> 4 **cups Ricotta or low-fat cottage cheese**
> **grated Parmesan cheese**

- Cook sausage and chicken, stirring to crumble, in oil in large skillet until browned. Drain excess oil.
- Stir spaghetti sauce into meat mixture. Simmer while preparing noodles.
- Prepare pasta according to package directions. Drain and place on flat surface.
- Spread ½ cup meat sauce in 13x9x2-inch baking dish. In order listed, layer: ½ pasta, ⅓ each of Mozzarella, Cheddar, Ricotta or cottage and Parmesan cheeses, and ½ sauce; repeat layers.
- Sprinkle remaining cheese on sauce layer.
- Bake, covered with aluminum foil, at 375 degrees for 30 minutes, remove foil and bake for additional 5 minutes. Let stand for 10 minutes before cutting into squares to serve.
- Serves 8.

JOANNA POITIER

Pasta Alla Olio

> 1 **(16 ounce) package penne pasta**
> **salt**
> **olive oil**
> 8 **cloves garlic, chopped**
> 1 **cup olive oil**
> 1 **cup chicken stock**
> 2 **large ripe tomatoes, peeled and chopped**
> 5 **large basil leaves, chopped**
> **salt and black pepper to taste**
> **grated Parmesan cheese to taste**

- Cook pasta in boiling salted water with small amount of oil in stock pot until chewy (less tender than al dente). Remove from heat, strain and rinse with cold water. Return to pot and toss with small amount of oil to prevent sticking. Keep warm.
- Sauté garlic in 1 cup oil in sauce pan until golden brown. Remove from heat and let stand for 5 minutes.
- Add broth to garlic, return to heat and bring to a boil. Season with salt and black pepper.
- Stir pasta, tomato, and basil into garlic sauce. Cook until pasta is al dente.
- Serve with cheese. Serves 3 or 4.
- For variety, add sundried tomato, 1 to 2 tablespoons capers, dried olives or anchovies to sauce.

MAD. 61, NEW YORK, NEW YORK
MARTA PULINI, EXECUTIVE CHEF

Smoked Mozzarella Ravioli in Fresh Tomato Fondue

PASTA
½ **cup semolina flour**
2 **cups all-purpose flour**
3 **eggs**
2 **egg yolks and 1 yolk for egg wash**

- Prepare filling and fondue. Set aside until ready to assemble ravioli.
- Combine semolina and flour. Mound on work surface and make a well in center.
- Place whole eggs and 2 egg yolks in well and mix, a small amount at a time, with fork into flour.
- Knead dough by hand until smooth and even consistency. Roll dough with lightly-floured rolling pin.
- Using pasta machine, run dough through on progressively finer settings until ¹⁄₁₀-inch thickness.
- Spread ½ of pasta sheets on work surface. Combine remaining egg yolk with small amount of water to form egg wash. Brush sheets with egg wash.
- Place 1 tablespoon filling at 1 inch intervals on pasta sheets. Cover with remaining sheets and press with fingertips around filling to remove air and seal. Using pasta cutter, cut in 2-inch squares. Dust with additional semolina and store in refrigerator until ready to cook.
- Cook ravioli in boiling water in large stock pot for a few minutes or until they float to surface.
- Warm fondue in small skillet; do not boil or sauce will separate.
- Drain ravioli. Place on individual plates and top with tomato sauce.
- Serves 6.

FILLING
1 **(16 ounce) package smoked Mozzarella, finely diced**
½ **cup walnut halves, coarsely chopped**
1 **egg**
¼ **cup plus 2 tablespoons grated Parmesan cheese**

- Grind Mozzarella cheese in grinder or food processor.
- Combine Mozzarella cheese, walnuts, egg and Parmesan cheese, blending well.

FONDUE
2 **pounds ripe plum tomatoes, peeled and seeded**
¾ **cup extra virgin olive oil**
10 **basil leaves**

- Combine tomatoes, oil and basil in blender. Process until smooth and thick.

BARBARA SINATRA

Pasta Fagioli

- 1 **cup dry macaroni or other pasta**
- 1 **clove garlic, chopped**
- 1 **tablespoon olive oil**
- 1 **(19 ounce) can cannellini beans, undrained**
- ½ **cup chicken broth**

salt and black pepper to taste
- 1 **tomato**

- Prepare pasta according to package directions. While pasta is cooking, prepare soup. Drain pasta before adding to soup.
- Sauté garlic in oil in skillet until browned.
- Add beans and broth to garlic and simmer for a few minutes.
- Season with salt and black pepper. Squeeze tomato into bean mixture.
- Add cooked pasta to soup and simmer for a few minutes to absorb flavor. Serves 2.

RICCIO'S, PALM SPRINGS, CALIFORNIA
TONY RICCIO, PROPRIETOR AND EXECUTIVE CHEF

Linguine Pescatore

- 4 **large cloves garlic, chopped**
- ¼ **cup plus 2 tablespoons olive oil**
- 8 **fresh medium clams**
- ½ **pound swordfish, cut in quarters**
- 8 **fresh green mussels**
- 8 **fresh black mussels**
- ½ **pound squid, peeled and cleaned**
- 12 **large shrimp, peeled and deveined**
- ½ **cup white wine**
- 1 **(28 ounce) can peeled Italian tomatoes**
- 1 **tablespoon finely chopped parsley**

salt and black pepper to taste
red pepper to taste
- 1 **(16 ounce) package linguine**

- Sauté garlic in oil in large skillet over medium heat until browned.
- Add clams, shrimp, swordfish, green and black mussels and squid. Sauté for a few minutes.
- Stir in white wine, tomatoes, parsley, salt, black pepper and red pepper. Simmer for 15 to 17 minutes.
- While seafood is cooking, prepare pasta by cooking in large pot of salted boiling water for 6 to 8 minutes; do not overcook. Drain and place in large serving platter.
- Ladle seafood over pasta. Serves 6.

FRANK AND BARBARA SINATRA

Sinatra Marinara Sauce

olive oil
3 cloves garlic
1 medium-sized onion, chopped
2 (28 ounce) cans tomatoes, undrained
basil to taste
salt and black pepper to taste
½ teaspoon oregano
1 (16 ounce) package pasta

- Pour oil into skillet to cover bottom. Sauté garlic in oil until very lightly browned. Remove garlic and discard.
- Sauté onion in garlic oil until very lightly browned.
- Using blender, separately purée each can of tomatoes with basil; turn blender on, then off immediately.
- Add purée to onion. Season with salt, black pepper and oregano. Simmer for 20 minutes, skimming top as the sauce cooks.
- While sauce is cooking, prepare pasta. Bring large pot of salted water to a boil, add 1 teaspoon oil and then add pasta. Begin checking after 7 minutes and cook until firm but neither hard nor sticky.
- Drain in colander, return to pan and add small amount of sauce to coat pasta to keep from clumping.
- Serve pasta with sauce on the side.
- Serves 4 to 6.

FRANK AND BARBARA SINATRA

Frank's Favorite Clam Sauce

4 cloves garlic, peeled
½ cup light olive oil
6 (6½ ounce) cans minced or whole clams, undrained
2 (16 ounce) packages angel hair or linguine pasta
chopped parsley
freshly grated Romano cheese

- Sauté garlic in oil in large skillet just until light golden brown. Remove cloves and discard.
- Add clams to garlic-flavored oil and heat thoroughly.
- Prepare pasta by cooking in large pot of salted boiling water until al dente; do not overcook. Drain in colander and place in serving dish.
- Pour clam sauce over pasta. Sprinkle with parsley and cheese. Serves 8 to 12.

ISAAC STERN

Lasagna

1 (16 ounce) package lasagna noodles
2 onions, chopped
2 to 4 cloves garlic, chopped
¼ cup olive oil
½ pound chopped veal
½ pound chopped beef
2 (14½ ounce) cans stewed tomatoes,
  undrained and crushed
2 (16 ounce) jars spaghetti sauce
freshly ground black pepper
chopped parsley
4 cups (16 ounces) grated Mozzarella cheese

- Prepare pasta according to package directions. While pasta is cooking, prepare sauce. Drain pasta before using.
- Sauté onion and garlic in oil in large skillet until lightly browned. Add veal and beef and sauté until meat is browned.
- Add tomatoes and spaghetti sauce to meat mixture. Simmer for 10 minutes. Season with black pepper and parsley.
- In 14x10x2-inch baking pan, in order listed, layer: ¼ sauce, ¼ noodles and 1 cup cheese. Repeat layers 3 times, alternating the direction of the noodles with each layer.
- Bake at 350 degrees for 30 minutes or until cheese is browned. Serves 8.

MICHAEL ANTHONY ERVZIONE

Paglia e Fieno

¾ pound mushrooms, diced
6 tablespoons butter, divided
½ cup tiny fresh or frozen peas, thawed
1 cup whipping cream, divided
½ cup slivered cooked ham
1 (6 ounce) package fresh spinach fettucine
1 (6 ounce) package fresh fettucine
salt and coarsely ground black pepper to taste
grated Parmesan cheese to taste

- Sauté mushrooms in 3 tablespoons butter in skillet over medium heat for about 5 minutes or until tender and edges are lightly browned.
- Add peas to mushrooms. Simmer, covered, for 2 minutes.
- Stir ½ cup cream into vegetables. Bring to a boil, reduce heat and simmer, stirring often, until slightly thickened.
- While sauce is cooking, prepare pasta according to package directions, cooking for about 2 minutes or until al dente. Drain well.
- Combine ½ cup cream and 3 tablespoons butter in pasta pan. Bring to a boil. Add pasta and cook, stirring frequently, until cream begins to thicken. Add ½ vegetable sauce and Parmesan cheese, tossing to mix.
- Pour pasta mixture into serving bowl, spoon remaining vegetable sauce over pasta and sprinkle with cheese. Serve hot. Serves 6.

FRANK AND BARBARA SINATRA

Fettucine á la Sinatra

1 **(8 ounce) package fettucine**
¼ **cup butter**
½ **cup whipping cream**
¼ **cup plus 2 tablespoons grated Parmesan cheese**
salt and black pepper
chopped parsley for garnish
grated Parmesan cheese for garnish

- Prepare fettucine according to package directions, cooking until al dente. While pasta is cooking, prepare sauce. Drain pasta well before using.
- Melt butter in small saucepan. Remove from heat.
- Blend cream and cheese into melted butter. Return to heat, season with salt and black pepper, and heat thoroughly but do not boil.
- Add sauce to pasta and let stand, covered, for 2 minutes. Place on serving plate and garnish with parsley and cheese.
- Serves 3 or 4.

FRANK AND BARBARA SINATRA

Tony O's Recipe for Peas and Macaroni

1 **medium-sized onion, diced**
olive oil
2 **(16 ounce) cans sweet peas, undrained**
1 **(8 ounce) can tomato sauce**
1 **teaspoon sugar**
salt and black pepper to taste
crushed red pepper to taste
1 **(8 ounce) package small elbow macaroni or tubettini**
grated Parmesan cheese

- Sauté onion in small amount of oil in large skillet over medium heat until golden to light brown, stirring occasionally to prevent burning.
- Add peas to onion. Stir in tomato sauce, sugar, salt, black pepper and red pepper.
- Simmer, covered, for 30 to 45 minutes. Mixture should be fluid but not watery; add small amounts of water if needed.
- Prepare pasta according to package directions. Drain well and add to pea sauce. Consistency should be loose but not soupy.
- Sprinkle servings with cheese.
- Serves 4 to 6.

**LA DOLCE VITA, BEVERLY HILLS, CALIFORNIA
JIMMY ULLO,
PROPRIETOR AND EXECUTIVE CHEF**

Salmon Ravioli with Tomato Vodka Sauce

RAVIOLI
- 3 tablespoons minced onion
- 3 tablespoons olive oil
- 1 pound fresh salmon, skin removed, boned and cut in large pieces
- ¼ cup plus 2 tablespoons white wine
- 2 tablespoons minced parsley
- ¼ cup (1 ounce) grated Parmesan cheese
- 2 egg yolks
- salt and black pepper to taste
- 1 recipe basic egg dough

- Sauté onion in oil in heavy medium-sized skillet over medium heat until translucent.
- Add salmon, wine and parsley to onion. Cook until exterior of fish is opaque but interior remains pink.
- In food processor bowl, combine fish mixture, cheese and egg yolks. Pulse to form purée. Season with salt and black pepper.
- Cool at room temperature, then cover and chill.
- Prepare sauce.
- On lightly-floured surface, roll dough to form sheets. Place 1 tablespoon filling at 2½-inch intervals on sheet. Cover with second sheet and press with fingertips to remove air and seal dough. Cut into ravioli shapes.
- Cook ravioli in large pot of boiling salted water for about 4 minutes or just until tender, yet firm to bite.
- Serve ravioli with sauce. Serves 4 to 6.

SAUCE
- 1 small onion, chopped
- ¼ cup butter
- ⅓ cup vodka
- 1 pound ripe tomatoes, peeled and chopped
- 1 tablespoon tomato paste
- 2 cups whipping cream
- salt and black pepper to taste

- Sauté onion in butter in heavy skillet over medium heat until translucent.
- Add vodka to onion and cook until evaporated.
- Blend tomatoes, tomato paste and cream with onion and simmer until thickened. Season with salt and black pepper.
- For smooth consistency, force sauce through sieve or purée in food processor or blender.

Poultry

Jack, age 5

CLAUDE AKINS

Claude Akins' Barbecued Honeyed Orange Chicken

1 (3 pound) broiler-fryer, cut in quarters
2 teaspoons grated orange peel
1 teaspoon grated lemon peel
1 cup fresh orange juice
½ cup fresh lemon juice
½ cup honey
2 tablespoons Worcestershire sauce (optional)
2 cloves garlic, minced (optional)
1 teaspoon dry mustard
½ cup melted margarine, butter or olive oil
salt and freshly ground black pepper to taste

- Place chicken in ceramic bowl.
- Combine orange peel, lemon peel, orange juice, lemon juice, honey, Worcestershire sauce, garlic, mustard and melted margarine or butter or oil. Pour over chicken in dish.
- Marinate at room temperature for 2 hours, turning at 30-minute intervals.
- Remove chicken from marinade, reserving marinade. Place chicken on grill, 6 inches from glowing coals. Brushing with marinade several times, cook chicken for 20 minutes, turn with tongs and cook for additional 20 minutes or until tender.
- Or to prepare indoors, place chicken skin side down in baking dish and brush generously with marinade. Bake at 375 degrees for 25 minutes, turn and bake additional 35 minutes, basting frequently.
- Season chicken with salt and black pepper.
- Cook remaining marinade in saucepan over medium heat to reduce and thicken slightly. Spoon sauce over chicken to serve. Serves 6 to 8.
- Marinade also works well with small whole turkey or large drumsticks, duck or rolled pork loin roast; be sure to adequately cook pork.

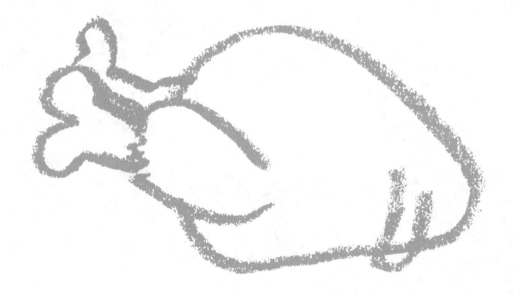

LUCIE ARNAZ

"This chicken would taste best served with a wonderful dish called 'Arnaz Rice' which my father invented and used to serve to all the folks at the Desilu Studio company picnics. But, my Dad tried so hard to keep that recipe a secret, he even forgot to give it to me!"

Sesame Chicken

  3 **eggs, beaten**
1½ **cups milk**
  2 **cups all-purpose flour**
  2 **teaspoons baking powder**
  2 **teaspoons salt**
 ½ **teaspoon black pepper**
  1 **tablespoon paprika**
 ½ **cup chopped almonds**
 ½ **cup sesame seeds**
  6 **small broiler-fryers, cut in halves**
  1 **cup butter or vegetable cooking spray**

- Blend eggs with milk.
- Combine flour, baking powder, salt, black pepper, paprika, almonds and sesame seeds in paper bag.
- Dip chicken pieces in egg liquid, then place in bag and shake to coat thoroughly with dry mixture.
- Melt butter in shallow baking pans or spray with vegetable cooking spray. Place chicken skin side down in single layer in pans.
- Bake at 400 degrees for 20 minutes, turn and bake for additional 20 minutes. Serves 12.

RICHARD CRENNA

"Don't let the simplicity of this recipe fool you. It's delicious."

Barbecued Chicken

¼ **cup lemon juice**
¾ **cup soy sauce**
 4 **chicken breast halves**
 4 **chicken thighs**

- Prepare grill by bringing coals to white ash stage. While coals develop, prepare marinade by blending lemon juice and soy sauce.
- Place chicken bone side down on grill rack and cook for 10 minutes. Baste with marinade, turn, baste and cook for 10 minutes. Baste, turn, baste and cook, with grill hood covered for 15 minutes. Total cooking time should not exceed 35 minutes for large pieces of chicken.
- Serves 4.

PAM DAWBER

"I serve this with chunks of crusty bread and a cucumber and tomato salad. Enjoy!"

Shepherd's Pie

FILLING
4   carrots, cut in bite-sized pieces
½   pound green beans, cut in bite-sized pieces
1   large yellow onion, chopped
2   cloves garlic, chopped
¼   cup olive oil
3   stalks celery with leaves, chopped
2   pounds ground fresh turkey
1   tablespoon poultry seasoning
½   cup dry red wine
1½ cups frozen peas
1   (10¾ ounce) can cream of celery soup, undiluted

- Prepare topping and set aside.
- Steam carrots and green beans until al dente; do not overcook.
- Sauté onion and garlic in oil in large skillet until softened and transparent. Add celery and cook for 5 minutes.
- Crumble turkey and poultry seasoning into vegetable mixture. Cook until meat is browned and some liquid has evaporated.
- Stir in red wine and simmer for 5 minutes.
- Add carrots, green beans and peas to turkey mixture and cook for 3 to 5 minutes.
- Blend 1 can reserved potato-turnip water with soup. Stir into turkey mixture and simmer for 5 to 7 minutes.
- Spoon mixture into 13x9x2-inch baking dish. Spread topping over filling, smoothing with back of spoon and sealing edges. Sprinkle with chives and paprika.
- Bake at 350 degrees for 35 minutes. Broil for 3 to 5 minutes for crispier crust.
- Serves 6 to 8.
- Pie can be assembled and frozen. Allow 45 minutes baking time.

TOPPING
3 or 4 large potatoes, peeled and cubed
1   turnip, peeled and cubed
8   cups water
2 to 3 tablespoons salt
2   tablespoons butter or olive oil
½   cup regular or skim milk or half and half
2   tablespoons chopped chives (optional)
paprika (optional)

- Cook potatoes and turnips in water to which salt has been added for 25 to 30 minutes or until vegetables are very soft. Reserving 1½ cups cooking liquid, drain vegetables.
- Mash or rice vegetables. Add butter and milk or half and half; vegetables should be more moist than regular mashed potatoes so add additional milk or half and half if necessary.

VICE PRESIDENT AND MRS. AL GORE

Spiced Roast Chicken

1 onion, diced
2 tablespoons olive oil
⅔ cup plus 1 teaspoon garam masala, divided
¼ pound button, brown or chestnut mushrooms, chopped
1 cup coarsely grated parsnips
1 cup coarsely grated carrots
¼ cup finely chopped walnuts
2 teaspoons chopped thyme
1 cup fresh white bread crumbs
1 egg, beaten
1 cup chicken broth
salt and black pepper to taste
1 (3½ pound) roasting chicken
olive oil
¼ cup water
1 tablespoon margarine
thyme sprigs for garnish
watercress sprigs for garnish

- Sauté onion in oil in large skillet for 2 minutes or until softened.
- Stir in 1 teaspoon garam masala and cook for 1 minute.
- Add mushrooms, parsnips and carrots. Cook, stirring frequently, for 5 minutes. Remove from heat and stir in walnuts, thyme, bread crumbs, egg, broth, salt and black pepper.
- Spoon stuffing into chicken cavity and truss, using skewers and string. Lightly oil surface of chicken. Place, breast down, in roasting pan and add water to pan.
- Bake at 375 degrees for 45 minutes. Turn chicken over, dot with margarine and bake for additional 45 minutes or until meat thermometer (inserted in thickest part of thigh but not touching bone) registers 185 degrees. Place chicken on platter and keep warm.
- Discard fat from roasting pan. Add remaining ⅔ cup garam masala to cooking liquid, stirring to dislodge browned bits. Bring to a boil and cook for 1 minute to reduce liquid slightly. Check and adjust seasoning.
- Carve, garnish with thyme and watercress and serve with stuffing and flavored roasting liquid. Serves 4.

SAMMY AND TITA CAHN

Chicken Paillards with Herbs

¼ teaspoon minced dried summer savory
1 tablespoon minced fresh or dried thyme
1½ teaspoons minced fresh sage or ½ teaspoon crushed dried sage
1½ teaspoons minced fresh rosemary or ½ teaspoon crushed dried rosemary
¼ teaspoon minced dried marjoram
3 tablespoons minced parsley
1 teaspoon grated lemon peel
pinch of allspice
pinch of cayenne pepper
⅓ cup olive oil
4 chicken breast halves, skin removed and boned
lemon wedges

- A day in advance of serving, prepare chicken for grilling.
- Combine savory, thyme, sage, rosemary, marjoram, parsley, lemon peel, allspice, cayenne pepper and oil in bowl.
- Pound chicken to flatten to ¼-inch thickness. Rub herb mixture into chicken. Place in shallow dish and chill, covered, overnight.
- Season chicken with salt and black pepper.
- Grill on well-oiled rack over glowing coals, cooking for 2 to 3 minutes on each side or until they are firm.
- Serve with lemon wedges. Serves 4.

Jackie Gleason and I would get Sammy in a booth between the two of us at Toots Shor's in New York and wouldn't let him go until he wrote at least two hits, which took about five minutes. And then we still wouldn't let him go. I miss Sammy's humor, his talent, his guidance, and friendship.
— *Frank Sinatra*

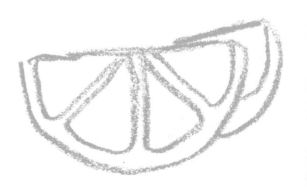

GLEN CAMPBELL

"Delight-ful southern fried chicken is crunchy, messy and better than finger lickin' good!"

Editor's Note: Campbell, if you weren't aware of it, is from Delight, Arkansas.

"Delight"ful Southern Fried Chicken

3 pounds chicken pieces
all-purpose flour
salt and black pepper
vegetable shortening
water

- Generously coat chicken with flour seasoned with salt and black pepper.
- Fry chicken in hot shortening in heavy skillet until golden brown and crunchy on all sides.
- When chicken is done, add small amount of water to skillet, cover and simmer until gravy forms. Serves 3 or 4.

SHIRLEY JONES

Shirley's City Chicken

1 pound top sirloin beef, cut in 1-inch cubes
1 pound center cut boneless pork, cut in 1-inch cubes
1 pound milk veal stewing meat, cut in 1-inch cubes
2 eggs, beaten
cracker meal
¼ cup butter or margarine
herbs to taste: rosemary, dill, thyme or others
salt and black pepper
butter
white wine
6 to 8 cups cooked rice or buttered noodles

- On 8 to 10 wooden skewers, alternate cubes of beef, pork and veal. Dip assembled skewers in egg, then in cracker meal to completely coat meat.
- Brown skewered meats in butter in skillet, turning to brown on all sides. Place in shallow casserole.
- Sprinkle herbs over meat, season with salt and black pepper and dot with butter. Add wine to cover bottom of casserole.
- Bake, covered, at 300 degrees for about 1 hour and 45 minutes, basting several times; remove cover and bake for additional 30 minutes.
- Serve with rice or noodles. Serves 8 to 10.

ROY CLARK

Chicken Potato Bake

6 chicken breast halves, boned
salt and black pepper
1 tablespoon vegetable oil
1 (24 ounce) package frozen hash brown
   potatoes, thawed
1 (10¾ ounce) can cream of chicken, broccoli or
   celery soup, undiluted
1 cup (4 ounces) shredded Cheddar cheese,
   divided
½ cup sour cream
1 cup French fried onions, divided

- Season chicken with salt and black pepper. Briefly fry chicken in oil, turning to brown on both sides.
- Spread potatoes in 13x9x2-inch baking dish. Add soup, ½ cup cheese, sour cream and ½ cup onions, stirring to blend.
- Arrange chicken on potato mixture.
- Bake at 350 degrees for 40 minutes, sprinkle with remaining ½ cup cheese and ½ cup onions and bake for additional 5 minutes.
- Serves 6.

LARRY GATLIN

Chicken Fiesta

1 cup crushed Cheddar cheese crackers
2 tablespoons taco seasoning mix
8 chicken breast halves
4 green onions, chopped
2 tablespoons butter
2 cups whipping cream
1 cup (4 ounces) shredded Monterey Jack
   cheese
1 cup (4 ounces) shredded Cheddar cheese
1 (4 ounce) can green chiles, chopped
½ teaspoon chicken bouillon granules

- Combine cracker crumbs and taco seasoning. Coat chicken in seasoning mixture and place in 13x9x2-inch baking pan.
- Sauté onion in butter until tender.
- Combine onion, cream, Monterey Jack cheese, Cheddar cheese, chiles and bouillon, mixing well. Pour over chicken.
- Bake at 350 degrees for 45 minutes.
- Serves 8.

GARY COLLINS
"This is one of my favorite recipes."

Chinese Walnut Chicken

2 teaspoons cornstarch
2 tablespoons water
2 egg whites
4 chicken breast halves, skin removed, boned
  and cut in 1-inch pieces
¼ cup plus 2 tablespoons soy sauce
2 tablespoons bourbon
1 teaspoon sugar
¼ cup vegetable oil, divided
8 green onions, cut in 2-inch slivers
2 slices ginger root, minced
1 clove garlic, minced
½ cup chopped walnuts
3 cups cooked rice

- Combine cornstarch, water and egg white in large bowl, blending until smooth. Add chicken and toss until well coated.
- In separate bowl, combine soy sauce, bourbon and sugar.
- Stir-fry chicken in 2 tablespoons oil in skillet or wok for 3 to 5 minutes or until cooked. Remove from pan.
- Add remaining 2 tablespoons oil to skillet or wok. Stir-fry onion, ginger and garlic for 1 minute. Stir in soy sauce mixture and cook quickly until sauce is thickened. Add walnuts to sauce.
- Combine sauce and chicken. Serve over rice. Serves 4.

ANDY GARCIA

Mojo Cuban Marinade Criollo

Cuban Marinade

1 cup lime juice
1 cup orange juice
1 head garlic, peeled
freshly ground black pepper to taste
sliced or diced onions (optional)

- Using food processor, blend lime juice, orange juice, garlic, black pepper and onion together.
- Pour marinade over beef, pork, fish or poultry. Let stand overnight.
- Marinade can also be used to baste, grill or sauté or as a dipping sauce for fried green bananas or broiled or sautéed vegetables. Makes 2½ cups.

JILL IRELAND AND CHARLES BRONSON

Chicken Curry

4 onions, chopped
4 apples, chopped
½ cup vegetable oil, divided
1 cup margarine or butter
¼ cup curry powder
¾ cup all-purpose flour
4 cups chicken broth
4 tomatoes, peeled and diced
2 bay leaves
2 cinnamon sticks
6 cloves
⅔ cup mango chutney
1 (16 ounce) can crushed pineapple, drained
1 cup green grapes, cut in halves
2 (2½ pound) broiler-fryers, cut up
all-purpose flour
condiments: flaked coconut, raisins, peanuts,
    fried bananas or yogurt

- Sauté onion and apple in ¼ cup oil in large saucepan until browned.
- In separate saucepan, melt butter. Add curry and cook for 2 minutes. Stir in flour. Gradually add broth, bringing to a boil after each addition.
- Pour sauce into onion and apple mixture. Bring to a simmer.
- Add tomatoes, bay leaves, cinnamon, cloves, chutney, pineapple and grapes to sauce. Simmer for several minutes.
- Lightly coat chicken with flour. In large skillet, fry chicken in remaining ¼ cup oil until lightly browned on all sides.
- Place chicken in 15x10x2-inch baking dish or pan. Spoon sauce over chicken.
- Bake, covered, at 350 degrees for 1½ to 2 hours or until chicken is tender.
- Serve chicken with rice and condiments.
- Serves 6 to 8.

LARRY HAGMAN

Larry's Chili

1 **package Carroll Shelby's Three Alarm Chili mix**
ground turkey
beer

- Follow directions on chili mix package, substituting ground turkey for ground beef and beer for water. Cook as directed.

WHOOPI GOLDBERG

Jewish American Princess Fried Chicken

vegetable oil
lightly salted butter
  1 **cup all-purpose flour**
salt and black pepper to taste
  1 **tablespoon paprika**
1½ **tablespoons Cajun spice mix**
  1 **(2½ to 3 pound) broiler-fryer, cut up**

- Send the chauffeur to your favorite butcher shop for one fresh, cut-up fryer. (Save brown paper bag!)
- Have your cook: Melt oil with butter to about ¼-inch depth in skillet and heat to moderate temperature. Pour flour, salt, black pepper, paprika and Cajun spices into the bag. Rinse chicken parts thoroughly and place into the brown paper bag.
- Tightly close the top of the brown paper bag (watch your nails), shake 10 times, hand back to cook, go dress for dinner.
- While you are dressing — cook will place coated chicken parts into skillet and brown them slowly. When evenly browned, chicken will be placed in an oven-proof baking dish and put into a 350 degree pre-heated oven.
- While cook prepares the rest of the meal — you touch-up your make-up.
- In about a half-hour, voila, dinner for four is served! You must be exhausted.

In my book, all women should be treated like a Princess. Barbara and I are big fans of Whoopi — and this chicken recipe. — Frank Sinatra

DENNIS FARINA

"In 1923, my maternal grandfather, Sabbatino Donati, and a partner opened a small bakery in Chicago. In 1927, this evolved into Donati's Cafe when he moved to a new location with a new partner, my grandmother, Bianca Buonamici Donati. Although my grandparents were from Florence, their restaurant was in a neighborhood known as Little Sicily and it became popular and successful, not only for my grandmother's unique cooking but for my grandfather's homemade beer and wine. His secret was California Zinfandel grapes, quite an exotic ingredient in Chicago at the time, especially during Prohibition! Like so many great cooks, my grandmother never measured anything, so these measurements are mostly approximate. And like so many great family recipes, it didn't have a name, but I hope you enjoy my grandmother's chicken with peppers and peaches and oranges and my grandfather's wine!"

Chicken Bianca

6   chicken breast halves, skin removed and boned
salt to taste
garlic salt to taste
1   clove garlic, minced
1   green bell pepper, cut in strips
1   red bell pepper, cut in strips
1   yellow bell pepper, cut in strips
8   Roma tomatoes, quartered
oregano to taste
1   ripe peach, peeled and diced
white wine
juice of 1 orange
olive oil
½   cup margarine
½   cup (2 ounces) crumbled Gorgonzola cheese
2   tablespoons grated Romano cheese
2   tablespoons grated Parmesan cheese
2   or 3 dashes Worcestershire sauce
4   cups cooked white or brown rice

- Place chicken in mixing bowl. Season with salt and garlic salt. Add minced garlic, bell peppers and tomatoes. Sprinkle with oregano and toss to mix well.
- Spoon peaches on top of chicken mixture, splash with wine and drizzle ½ orange juice over mixture. Let stand for 30 minutes to 1 hour.
- Sauté chicken mixture in small amount of olive oil and splash of wine in large skillet over medium heat for 20 minutes.
- Melt margarine with Gorgonzola, Romano and Parmesan cheeses in saucepan, blending well. Add to chicken mixture.
- Cook over high heat, adding remaining orange juice, Worcestershire sauce and another splash of wine for final 5 minutes of cooking time.
- Serve chicken mixture over buttered rice. Serves 6 to 8.

SQUARE ONE, SAN FRANCISCO, CALIFORNIA
JOYCE GOLDSTEIN, EXECUTIVE CHEF

Petti di Pollo Trifolati

Sautéed Chicken Breasts with Porcini, Prosciutto, Cognac and Cream

⅓ **cup dried Porcini mushrooms**
¾ **cup hot water**
¼ **cup plus 2 tablespoons all-purpose flour**
salt and black pepper to taste
3 **whole chicken breasts, skin removed and boned**
¼ **cup plus 2 tablespoons butter, clarified**
¼ **cup cognac**
2 **cups whipping cream**
¼ **pound sliced prosciutto, cut in 2x¼x⅛-inch strips**
chopped parsley

- Soak mushrooms in hot water. Drain, reserving liquid. Chop mushrooms and set aside.
- Combine flour, salt and black pepper.
- Coat chicken in seasoned flour. Sauté briefly in butter in large skillet for about 3 minutes on each side or until golden. Place on warm platter and cover to keep warm.
- Deglaze skillet with cognac. Add mushroom liquid and cream. Cook over high heat for 5 to 8 minutes to reduce and thicken.
- Add mushrooms and prosciutto to sauce and cook for 1 to 2 minutes. Check seasoning.
- Place chicken in skillet and cook for 1 minute to coat with sauce and reheat.
- Garnish servings with parsley.
- Serves 6.

WIL SHRINER

Cajun Special

"The 'Cajun Special' is very simple. Whenever I burn any dish, I tell everyone it's Cajun food and they never know the difference. Best of luck, Wil."

KATHIE LEE GIFFORD

Polynesian Chicken

4   chicken breast halves, skin removed and
     boned
garlic powder
1   cup apple juice
1   (16 ounce) can low-calorie chunky fruit
½   cup low-sodium soy sauce
1   (10 ounce) jar Chinese sweet and sour sauce
3   to 4 cups cooked rice

- Sprinkle chicken with garlic powder.
- Mix apple juice with juice from chunky fruit,
  reserving fruit. Blend in soy sauce. Pour over
  chicken.
- Bake at 325 degrees for 1 hour. Spread sweet and sour sauce and reserved fruit on chicken
  and bake for additional 30 minutes.
- Serve over rice. Serves 4.

MONTY HALL

Lemon-Basil Chicken Breasts

1   cup fresh bread crumbs
1½   tablespoons minced parsley
1½   teaspoons lemon zest
1   teaspoon dried basil
½   teaspoon salt
½   teaspoon black pepper
3   tablespoons buttermilk
¾   teaspoon lemon juice
6   chicken breast halves, skin removed
lemon slices for garnish
parsley sprigs for garnish

- Combine bread crumbs, parsley, lemon zest, basil, salt and black pepper in plastic bag.
- Blend buttermilk and lemon juice. Brush on both sides of chicken pieces.
- Place chicken in bag of seasonings and shake to coat well. Sprinkle remaining crumbs on
  chicken.
- Arrange chicken on broiler pan prepared with cooking spray.
- Bake at 400 degrees for 35 minutes or until done.
- Garnish with lemon and parsley.
- Serves 6.

ALICE FAYE HARRIS

Chicken in the Bag

1 (2½ to 3 pound) broiler-fryer
baking soda
Canola oil
seasoned salt
black pepper
paprika

- Wash chicken thoroughly with baking soda in water, rinse well and dry. Rub oil on surface and inside of chicken. Sprinkle inside and out with seasoned salt, black pepper and paprika.
- Place chicken, breast side up, in large heavy brown paper bag. Close by folding end twice. Cut 6 slits in top of bag. Place on baking sheet.
- Bake at 400 degrees for 1½ hours, reduce heat to 300 degrees and bake for additional 1 hour.
- Let stand for 15 to 20 minutes before carving.
- Serves 4.

HENRY WINKLER

Hawaiian Chicken

2 (2½ to 3 pound) broiler-
    fryers, cut up
¼ cup butter
2 tablespoons all-purpose
    flour
1 cup orange juice
1 (10¾ ounce) can condensed
    chicken broth, undiluted
1 teaspoon salt
dash of cayenne pepper
dash of cinnamon
dash of garlic salt (optional)
1 (20 ounce) can pineapple
    chunks, undrained
½ cup raisins
½ cup slivered blanched
    almonds
parsley sprigs and orange slices
    for garnish
6 to 8 cups cooked white rice

- Sauté chicken in butter in large heavy skillet, turning to brown on both sides and removing pieces as they brown. Set chicken aside.
- Retain ¼ cup drippings in skillet and discard rest. Blend in flour and cook, stirring often, for 5 minutes. Gradually add orange juice and broth.
- Return chicken to skillet and add salt, cayenne pepper, cinnamon, garlic, pineapple and raisins. Simmer, covered, for 50 to 60 minutes or until chicken is tender.
- Sprinkle chicken and sauce with almonds. Garnish servings with parsley and orange slices. Serve over rice.
- Serves 6 to 8.

**CENTURY PLAZA HOTEL,
LOS ANGELES, CALIFORNIA
CHEF RAIMUND HOFMEISTER**

"This recipe was served to the President of the United States, Mr. Ronald W. Reagan and the First Lady on Dec. 27, 1984, at the new tower suite of the Century Plaza Hotel, for a quiet dinner for two."

Supreme of Capon with Celery and Mushrooms with Tarragon Flavored Lemon Sauce

½   **teaspoon garlic crushed with salt**
1   **tablespoon plus 1 teaspoon minced shallots, divided**
½   **cup finely diced celery**
¼   **cup butter, divided**
¾   **cup diced mushrooms**
white wine
2   **lemons, divided**
2   **tablespoons fresh bread crumbs**
1   **egg yolk**
1   **tablespoon coarsely chopped parsley, tarragon to taste**
salt and black pepper to taste
8   **(8 ounce) capon breast halves, skin removed**
2   **cups chicken broth**
½   **cup California chardonnay**
2   **lemons**
1   **cup cream, reduced**

- Sauté garlic, 1 tablespoon shallots and celery in 1 tablespoon butter for 2 to 3 minutes in skillet.
- Add mushrooms, dash of white wine and juice of ½ lemon. Cook until liquid is evaporated.
- Stir in bread crumbs, egg yolk, parsley and tarragon. Season with salt and black pepper. Set aside to cool.
- Clean wing bones of chicken and chop off tip joint. Split breast from the thick part to create a pocket slit. Spoon stuffing into pocket and fold to enclose. Season with salt and black pepper.
- Brown chicken on both sides and place in buttered 12x8x2-inch baking pan scattered with remaining 1 teaspoon shallots. Add broth and chardonnay.
- Bake, covered with parchment paper, at 375 degrees for 12 to 15 minutes.
- Transfer chicken to serving platter, arranging 4 on the left and 4 on the right.
- Pour cooking liquid through fine strainer into small saucepan. Stir in juice of 1½ lemons and zest of 2 lemons. Bring to a boil and cook for 1 minute. Stir in cream, blend in remaining 3 tablespoons butter and spoon over chicken to thinly coat.
- Serves 8.

DOLORES HOPE
"We like to serve this with a tossed green salad and crusty French bread."

Poulet a L'Espagnole

½ pound lean smoked ham, diced
2 (2 to 2½ pound) chickens, cut up
1 tablespoon lard
1 tablespoon olive oil
salt and black pepper
2 pounds green peas
4 cups veal broth
1¼ cups regular rice
1 large Spanish onion, minced
½ clove garlic, minced
2 green bell peppers, finely chopped
3 tomatoes, peeled, seeded and chopped
dash of cognac
parsley sprigs for garnish

- Sauté ham and chicken pieces in lard and oil in deep heavy skillet, seasoning with salt and black pepper and frying for about 30 minutes or until golden brown on all sides.
- While ham and chicken are cooking, prepare peas and rice. Cook peas in veal broth until tender. Cook rice in 4 cups boiling water.
- Remove chicken and ham from skillet and keep warm.
- Sauté onion and garlic in skillet drippings until tender. Stir in bell pepper, tomatoes, peas with broth, drained rice, ham and chicken. Season with cognac, salt and black pepper.
- Simmer, tightly covered, for 30 minutes. Serve on hot platter and garnish with parsley.
- Serves 8.

JACK WHITAKER

Supremes of Chicken

3 tablespoons butter
4 chicken breast halves, skin removed and boned
seasoned flour
¼ cup quality Madeira wine
1 teaspoon chopped tarragon or ½ teaspoon dried tarragon
½ cup whipping cream
salt and white pepper to taste

- Heat butter until foaming but not colored in large skillet.
- Coat chicken with seasoned flour. Sauté in butter to seal in juices, reduce heat and cook for 5 minutes on each side or until just firm to touch. Place on serving plate and keep warm.
- Add wine and tarragon to skillet, increase heat and bring to bubbling. Stir in cream and cook until thickened, scraping bottom and sides of skillet to loosen bits; sauce will thicken quickly in large skillet.
- Season lightly with salt and black pepper and serve over chicken.
- Serves 4.

BOB HOPE

Bob's Favorite Chicken Hash

2 chicken breast halves, broiled and cut julienne
2 slices bacon, cooked and crumbled
½ small onion, minced
2 tablespoons butter
½ teaspoon lemon juice
salt and black pepper
2 tablespoons sour cream
1 teaspoon dry sherry

- Combine chicken, bacon, onion, butter, lemon juice, salt and black pepper. Sauté until thoroughly heated.
- Just before serving, stir in sour cream and sherry; heat but do not cook. Serves 2.

Bob and I both have streets named after us in Rancho Mirage. I used to tease him that his street was wider and mine was thinner. When he'd tell me his street was prettier, I'd remind Bob that every night around cocktail time his street was dark but mine was always lit up. — *Frank Sinatra*

DIAHANN CARROLL

Marinated Chicken Breast

8 chicken breast halves
lemon pepper to taste
onion powder to taste
dash of salt
1 (8 ounce) bottle low-calorie Italian salad dressing
1 medium-sized white onion, sliced
1 medium-sized green, red or yellow bell pepper, sliced
½ pound mushrooms

- A day in advance of serving, prepare chicken for baking.
- Sprinkle chicken with lemon pepper, onion powder and salt. Lightly rub chicken with salad dressing. Place in baking dish, cover with foil and chill overnight.
- Place onion, bell pepper and mushrooms on chicken.
- Bake at 300 degrees for 45 minutes, add 2 cups water, and bake for additional 45 minutes. Serves 8.

HENRY KISSINGER

Henry Kissinger's Moo Goo Gai Pan

4 chicken breast halves, skin removed and boned
1 teaspoon cornstarch
2 teaspoons dry sherry
¾ teaspoon minced ginger root
1 tablespoon salt, divided
¾ cup walnuts
⅓ cup vegetable oil
1 (15 ounce) can Chinese straw mushrooms, drained
1 cup fresh bamboo shoots
1 cup snow pea pods
3 to 4 cups cooked rice

- Cut thin slices of chicken across grain. Combine chicken, cornstarch, sherry, ginger and 1½ teaspoons salt in bowl and set aside.
- Stir-fry walnuts in oil in wok or large saucepan over medium heat for 3 minutes. Remove walnuts and drain on paper towel.
- Stir-fry mushrooms, bamboo shoots and snow peas with remaining 1½ teaspoons salt for 3 to 5 minutes or until snow peas are crisp tender. Place vegetables in bowl.
- Stir-fry chicken for about 5 minutes or until tender. Add vegetables and mix well. Spoon mixture on warm platter and sprinkle with walnuts.
- Serve over rice. Serves 4.

PHYLLIS DILLER

Tropical Chicken

4 chicken breast halves, skin removed and boned
1 mango or papaya, cut in large strips
¼ cup all-purpose flour
1 tablespoon curry powder
¼ teaspoon white pepper
¼ teaspoon thyme
¼ teaspoon garlic powder
¼ teaspoon seasoned salt
4 eggs, beaten
freshly grated coconut or
   1 (16 ounce) bag

- Pound chicken breasts to flatten. Place mango or papaya strips on each and roll up, tucking edges to enclose fruit. Freeze for a few minutes to make rolls easier to handle.
- Combine flour, curry powder, white pepper, thyme, garlic powder and seasoned salt.
- Coat chicken rolls with seasoning mixture, dip in egg and roll in coconut to completely cover. Place on baking sheet.
- Bake at 350 degrees for 40 minutes. Broil for a few minutes to lightly brown coconut. Serves 4.

PETER MARSHALL

Chicken in Wine Sauce

6 to 8 chicken breast halves, skin removed and
   boned
¼ cup olive oil
¼ cup butter
¼ cup all-purpose flour
2 tablespoons chopped parsley
1 medium-sized onion, chopped
2 (15 ounce) cans chicken consommé
¾ cup tomato juice
½ cup sherry
6 to 8 cups rice or noodles

- Sauté chicken, turning to brown on both sides, in oil and butter in skillet. Remove chicken and set aside.
- Blend flour, parsley and onions into skillet drippings. Stir in consommé, tomato juice and sherry wine. Cook until smooth.
- Place chicken in sauce. Simmer, covered, for 30 minutes.
- Serve over rice or noodles. Serves 6 to 8.

JOHN LODGE
"In our family, this is the favorite. We serve it with new potatoes and fresh mint."

Italian Style Chicken

4 large chicken breast halves,
   skin removed and boned
2 cloves garlic, crushed
2 tablespoons chopped
   tarragon
salt and freshly ground black
   pepper
1 tablespoon butter
3 tablespoons virgin olive oil,
   divided
1 onion, minced
2 shallots, minced
1 (14½ ounce) can tomatoes,
   chopped
2 tablespoons tomato purée
1 tablespoon oregano
½ cup chicken broth
4 slices (5 ounces) Mozzarella
   cheese

- Season chicken with garlic, tarragon, salt and black pepper.
- Sauté chicken in butter and 1 tablespoon oil in skillet for 3 minutes on each side. Place in 12x8x2-inch broiler-proof baking dish.
- Sauté onion and shallots in remaining 2 tablespoons oil for 5 minutes.
- Add tomatoes, purée, oregano and broth to onions and shallots. Season with salt and black pepper. Simmer for 15 minutes. Spoon sauce over chicken.
- Bake, covered with aluminum foil, at 350 degrees for 25 minutes. Remove from oven, place cheese on chicken and broil for 3 to 5 minutes or until cheese is melted.
- Serves 4.

THE OAKS AT OJAI, OJAI, CALIFORNIA
ELEANOR BROWN,
CO-OWNER AND FOOD CONSULTANT

"This is one of my very favorite recipes. My youngest grandchildren enjoy it and my most discriminating gourmet friends have pronounced it sensational. My husband, who is not fond of either chicken or curry, loves this dish. I hope that it turns out well for you."

Cantonese Coconut Curry Chicken

4½ tablespoons low-sodium soy sauce, divided
6 tablespoons dry sherry, divided
3½ teaspoons arrowroot, divided
1½ pounds chicken breast tenders, cut in 1-inch pieces
1 teaspoon peanut oil
4 teaspoons minced ginger root, divided
1 tablespoon minced garlic
1 cup minced onion
dry sherry
1 tablespoon plus 1½ teaspoons curry powder or garam masala
1 tablespoon plus 1½ teaspoons honey
⅔ cup nonfat milk granules
1 teaspoon coconut extract
3 cups cooked brown rice
2 tablespoons slivered almonds or toasted coconut

- Combine 3 tablespoons soy sauce, 3 tablespoons sherry and 1½ teaspoons arrowroot, mixing well.
- Pour marinade over chicken chunks in bowl and let stand for at least 30 minutes.
- Remove chicken from marinade, reserving liquid. Stir-fry chicken in hot oil in wok or heavy skillet until opaque. Remove chicken and set aside.
- Stir-fry 2 teaspoons ginger and garlic for about 1 minute. Add onion and cook until translucent, adding a splash of sherry if needed to prevent sticking or scorching.
- Blend remaining 3 tablespoons sherry, 1½ tablespoons soy sauce, curry powder and honey with reserved marinade. Add to onion mixture and cook, stirring often, until thickened.
- Return chicken to wok or pan and heat thoroughly.
- Combine milk, coconut extract and remaining 2 teaspoons arrowroot. Gradually blend into sauce and simmer until thickened.
- Serve ½ cup chicken and sauce over ⅓ cup rice and top with almonds or coconut.
- Serves 8.

ED McMAHON

Roast Turkey with Ed's Dressing

6 **cups herb seasoned dressing mix**
6 **cups cornbread dressing mix**
1 **cup diced celery**
1 **cup diced onion**
1 **cup chopped pecans**
1 **cup chopped walnuts**
½ **pound mushrooms, diced**
1 **pound country sausage**
1 **to 1½ cups apple sauce**
1 **cup crushed pineapple**
1 **(6 ounce) jar orange marmalade**
brandy
1 **(16 pound) turkey**
olive oil
salt and black pepper

- Except for 2 dressing mixes, amount of each ingredient can be adjusted to taste. Combine dressing mixes, celery, onion, pecans, walnuts, mushrooms and sausage.
- Add applesauce, pineapple and marmalade. Stir in up to 2 cups brandy to moisten for dressing consistency.
- Spoon stuffing into turkey cavity. Place turkey, breast side up, on rack in roasting pan. Brush with oil and season with salt and black pepper. Place aluminum foil tent over turkey.
- Bake at 250 degrees for 6 to 7 hours, basting occasionally during first few hours and frequently during last few hours. Serves 16 to 20.

ZUBIN MEHTA
*"Nancy serves this with her Shahjahani Biryani
(Spiced Saffron Rice)."*
*Editor's Note: Recipe for Spiced Saffron Rice can be
found in Vegetables and Side Dishes.*

Nancy Mehta's Moglai Chicken

- 1 **teaspoon saffron**
- 2 **tablespoons warm milk**
- 8 **chicken breast halves, skin removed and
  boned**
- **seasoned flour**
- ¼ **cup butter**
- 2 **large onions, chopped**
- 6 **large cloves garlic, crushed**
- 1 **(½ inch) piece ginger root, ground**
- 1¼ **teaspoons ground cumin**
- 1¼ **teaspoons cumin seeds**
- 1¼ **teaspoons caraway seeds**
- 1¼ **teaspoons ground turmeric**
- 1 **teaspoon cayenne pepper**
- 1 **green chile, split**
- 1 **large tomato, chopped**
- **hot water**
- 1¼ **teaspoons ground cloves**
- 1¼ **teaspoons ground cardamom**
- ¼ **cup firmly-packed brown sugar**
- 1 **cup sour cream**

- Mix saffron with milk and set aside.
- Coat chicken with seasoned flour. Sauté pieces in butter in heavy skillet over medium heat, turning to brown on both sides. Remove chicken and set aside.
- Sauté onion, garlic and ginger in skillet until onion is transparent. Add cumin powder and seeds, caraway, turmeric, cayenne pepper and chile. Cook, stirring frequently, until chile is browned, spices are mixed and seeds are lightly fried.
- Return chicken to skillet, add tomato and pour in hot water to cover. Simmer, stirring occasionally, for about 25 minutes or until chicken is tender. Place chicken in 13x9x2-inch baking dish.
- Stir cloves, cardamom, brown sugar and saffron into sauce. Blend in sour cream. Pour sauce over chicken.
- Bake at 350 degrees for about 10 minutes or until thoroughly heated. Serves 8.

ROBERT ZEMECKIS

David's Jerk Chicken

CHICKEN
1 onion, minced
2 tablespoons hot pepper sauce
1 sprig thyme, finely chopped
2 scallions, minced
1 (3 to 3½ pound) chicken, cut up

- Prepare jerk seasoning or use prepared product. Combine ½ cup seasoning, onion, hot pepper sauce, thyme and scallions.
- Rub chicken with jerk paste, covering well. Chill for at least 4 hours.
- Grill chicken until cooked. Serves 3 or 4.

JERK RUB
1 onion, minced
½ cup minced scallion
2 teaspoons thyme leaves
2 teaspoons salt
1 teaspoon ground black pepper
1 teaspoon ground Jamaican pimento or allspice
¼ teaspoon nutmeg
½ teaspoon cinnamon
4 to 6 hot peppers, finely ground, or hot pepper sauce

- Mixing by hand or in a food processor, combine onion, scallion, thyme, salt, black pepper, Jamaican pimento or allspice, nutmeg, cinnamon and hot peppers or sauce. Blend to form paste.
- Store in tightly-closed jar in refrigerator for up to 1 month. Makes 1 cup.
- Recipe from "Jerk Barbecue from Jamaica" by Helen Willinsky, reprinted courtesy of The Crossing Press, Freedom, California.

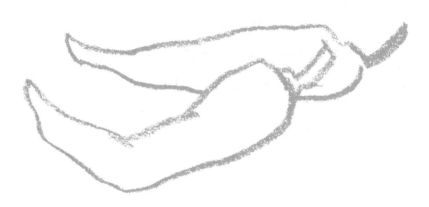

NEHEMIAH PERSOFF

Stuffed Chicken Rolls

- 1 **cup chopped onion**
- ½ **pound chicken giblets, chopped**
- 1 **cup tightly-packed sliced mushrooms**
- 2 **cloves garlic, minced**
- 2 **tablespoons minced mint**
- ¼ **cup vegetable oil**
- ¼ **cup margarine**
- ½ **cup chicken broth**
- 3 **tablespoons sautérne**

pinch of black pepper
- ½ **teaspoon cinnamon**
- ½ **teaspoon cayenne pepper**
- ¼ **teaspoon salt**
- 1 **cup tightly-packed chopped parsley**
- 1 **cup tightly-packed chopped watercress**
- 4 **eggs or 6 egg whites**
- ½ **cup chopped almonds or ½ cup pine nuts, lightly sautéed**
- 12 **chicken breast halves, boned**

vegetable oil, melted butter or margarine or cooking spray
paprika for garnish
mint sprigs for garnish

- Sauté onion, giblets, mushrooms, garlic and mint in oil and margarine in large skillet.
- Add broth, wine and black pepper to giblet mixture. Bring to a boil, reduce heat and simmer for about 30 minutes or until giblets are tender. Remove cover and continue cooking to evaporate most of liquid. Set aside to cool.
- Place chicken breasts, skin side down, on wax paper. Pound to flatten to ¼-inch thickness.
- Mix cinnamon, cayenne pepper and salt together. Sprinkle on chicken.
- Combine parsley, watercress, eggs and almonds or pine nuts in large bowl. Add giblet mixture and mix thoroughly. Check seasoning and adjust if needed.
- Place equal portion of mixture on each chicken breast. Roll up, tuck ends under and secure with string or wooden pick. Blot with paper towel to remove any moisture. Brush with oil, butter, margarine or cooking spray. Place on greased baking sheet.
- Sprinkle rolls with paprika.
- Bake at 375 degrees for 30 minutes. Let stand for 5 minutes, then cut diagonally in 2 or 3 slices.
- Garnish with mint.
- Serves 12.

NEIL AND LEBA SEDAKA

Voodoo Chicken

2   cups white vinegar
2   tablespoons soy sauce
1   large onion, sliced
4   cloves garlic
½   teaspoon black pepper
1   (2½ to 3 pound) broiler-fryer, cut up
¼   cup Dijon mustard
¼   cup plus 2 tablespoons ketchup
2   tablespoons milk
3   to 4 cups cooked white rice

- Combine vinegar, soy sauce, onion, garlic and black pepper. Marinate chicken for several hours in mixture. Drain chicken, reserving marinade.
- Blend mustard with ¼ cup ketchup. Dip each piece chicken in mixture, coating well. Place chicken, skin side down, in 13x9x2-inch baking dish.
- Bake at 350 degrees for 30 minutes. Blend remaining 2 tablespoons ketchup and milk with excess marinade. Pour over chicken and bake for additional 45 minutes.
- Serve over rice. Serves 4.

JOHNNY MATHIS

Chicken Provençal

1   (3½ pound) broiler-fryer, cut in 8 pieces
3   tablespoons olive oil
1½ tablespoons butter
1   cup dry white wine
2   cloves garlic
1   teaspoon salt
white pepper to taste
1   teaspoon sugar
4   large or 6 small tomatoes, peeled, seeded, and chopped
4   anchovy fillets in oil, cut in small pieces
1   tablespoon chopped fresh basil or ½ teaspoon dried basil
16 pitted ripe olives
8   pitted green olives

- Sauté chicken, turning to brown on both sides, in oil and butter in skillet.
- Add wine, bring to a boil, then reduce heat. Stir in garlic, salt, white pepper, sugar and tomatoes. Simmer for 30 minutes.
- Add anchovies, basil, ripe and green olives to sauce. Cook over medium heat for 20 minutes.
- Serves 4.

FRANK SINATRA

Blue Eyes' Italian Chicken, Potato and Onion Dish

2 (2 to 2½ pound) chickens, cut up
salt to taste
olive oil
2 white onions, thinly sliced
8 large potatoes, quartered
black pepper to taste
2 tablespoons oregano
1 cup finely chopped parsley

- Cook chicken in boiling salted water for about 30 minutes. While chicken cooks, pour 1 inch oil into 24x18x2-inch baking pan.
- Remove chicken from water, blot dry with paper towel and place in oil in pan. Separate onion slices and place on chicken. Add potatoes and season with salt and black pepper. Stir in oregano and parsley and mix thoroughly.
- Bake at 350 degrees, stirring every 10 to 15 minutes, for 1 hour or until potatoes and chicken are done. Serves 4.

ELIZABETH TAYLOR

Spicy Chicken

2 teaspoons curry powder
1 teaspoon cumin
½ teaspoon ground ginger
½ teaspoon turmeric
½ clove garlic, crushed
1 onion, chopped
1 teaspoon grated ginger
1 (3 to 4 pound) chicken, cut in 10 pieces and skin removed

- Combine curry powder, cumin, ground ginger, turmeric, garlic, onion and grated ginger.
- Coat chicken with seasoning mixture. Chill for 2 hours or longer.
- Grill chicken over moderately hot coals or broil in oven for about 30 minutes or until done, turning once. Serves 5 or 6.

Barbara and I enjoyed testing Elizabeth's Spicy Chicken — we like heat in our food.
It's a good thing the recipe didn't call for carrots, though, because when that lady asks for carrots it could cost you half a mil! — Frank Sinatra

---

OLIVER STONE

Chicken Parmigiana

2 egg yolks, beaten
salt and black pepper to taste
garlic powder to taste
6 chicken breast halves, skin removed and boned
bread crumbs
vegetable oil
1 cup Parmesan cheese, grated

- Prepare tomato sauce. Blend yolks, salt, black pepper and garlic powder together.
- Dip each chicken piece in egg liquid and roll in bread crumbs. Sauté in oil in large skillet, turning to lightly brown on both sides and cooking just until done.
- Sprinkle cheese on top of each chicken piece and allow to melt. Place chicken on serving platter and spoon tomato sauce on each piece. Serves 6.

SAUCE
1 to 3 cloves garlic, diced
vegetable oil
3 onions, diced
6 tomatoes, peeled and diced
salt and black pepper

- Sauté garlic in small amount of oil in small skillet for 1 minute. Add onion and sauté for 3 minutes.
- Stir in tomatoes and cook for several minutes, stirring to prevent burning. When sauce is thickened, season with salt and black pepper.

ALEX TREBEK

Honey-Pecan Fried Chicken

4 cups buttermilk
8 chicken breast halves
1 cup all-purpose flour
¾ teaspoon salt
¼ teaspoon garlic powder
¼ teaspoon cayenne pepper
1 cup butter
½ cup honey
½ cup coarsely chopped roasted pecans
vegetable oil

- Pour buttermilk into large bowl, add chicken and chill, covered, for 1½ hours. Drain chicken.
- Combine flour, salt, garlic powder and cayenne pepper. Coat chicken in flour, shaking to remove excess. Let stand at room temperature for 20 minutes.
- Melt butter in heavy small saucepan over low heat. Stir in honey and bring to a boil. Add pecans and simmer for 15 minutes.
- Fry chicken in ½ to ¾ inch oil in large heavy skillet, cooking for about 7 minutes on each side or until crisp, golden brown and thoroughly cooked. Drain on paper towel and arrange on platter.
- Pour glaze over chicken. Serve immediately. Serves 4 to 8.
- For lower-fat sauce, use 1 cup chicken broth instead of butter. Dissolve 2 tablespoons cornstarch in ¼ cup broth. Combine remaining ¾ cup broth with honey in saucepan and bring to a boil. Stir cornstarch into mixture and cook until thickened. Add roasted nuts.

CLIFF NORTON

Chicken Cacciatore with Artichokes

1 (6 ounce) jar marinated
   artichoke hearts
2 tablespoons olive oil
1 (3 pound) broiler-fryer, cut
   up
all-purpose flour
1 (14½ ounce) can tomatoes
2 cloves garlic, minced
½ teaspoon garlic powder
1¼ teaspoons salt
½ teaspoon dried oregano
½ teaspoon dried basil
½ cup dry sherry
¼ pound mushrooms, sliced
minced parsley

- Drain artichoke hearts, reserving liquid. Set artichokes aside. Blend artichoke liquid with olive oil in large skillet.
- Coat chicken with flour. Sauté in blended oil in skillet, turning to lightly brown on all sides. Place chicken in 13x9x2-inch baking dish.
- Combine tomatoes, garlic, garlic powder, salt, oregano, basil and sherry. Pour over chicken.
- Bake, uncovered, at 350 degrees for 1 hour. Spoon mushrooms and artichoke hearts on chicken and bake, covered, for additional 10 minutes.
- Garnish with parsley. Serve with pasta, risotto or polenta.
- Serves 4.

IVANA TRUMP

Chicken Paprika

½ cup plus 2 tablespoons all-purpose flour, divided
½ teaspoon salt
½ teaspoon white pepper
2 tablespoons plus 1 teaspoon sweet Hungarian paprika, divided
1 (2½ pound) broiler-fryer, cut up
1½ tablespoons butter
1½ tablespoons vegetable oil
1 cup minced yellow onion
2 cups well-seasoned chicken broth
1 cup sour cream
3 to 4 cups cooked rice, noodles or Czech dumplings

- Combine ½ cup flour, salt, white pepper and 1 teaspoon paprika. Coat chicken with seasoned flour.
- Sauté chicken in butter and oil in heavy skillet, turning to brown on all sides. Remove chicken from skillet.
- Sauté onion in skillet with remaining 2 tablespoons paprika until translucent. Add chicken and broth to onion. Simmer, covered, for about 1 hour.
- Stir remaining 2 tablespoons flour into sour cream. Gradually add sour cream to chicken and sauce. Simmer until thickened and smooth; do not boil or sour cream will separate.
- Serves 4.

**THE GRILLE, SONOMA MISSION INN & SPA,
SONOMA, CALIFORNIA
MARK VANN, EXECUTIVE CHEF**

Stewed Chicken Breast with Pearl Onions, Artichoke Hearts and Creamy Polenta

CHICKEN
- 4 **chicken breast halves**
- 2 **tablespoons olive oil**
- 8 **pearl onions, peeled**
- 1 **cup artichoke hearts, quartered**
- 1 **cup seeded and chopped tomato**
- ¼ **teaspoon sage**
- 2 **teaspoons minced garlic**
- 1 **cup chicken broth**
- ¼ **cup creme fraiche**

salt and black pepper

- Sauté chicken in oil in skillet over high heat, turning to lightly brown on both sides. Remove chicken from skillet.
- Combine onions, artichoke hearts, tomato, sage, garlic, broth and creme fraiche in skillet. Simmer for 20 minutes.
- While vegetables are cooking in sauce, prepare polenta.
- Add chicken to sauce, season with salt and black pepper and simmer for 5 minutes.
- Spoon polenta in individual serving bowls, place chicken breast on polenta and ladle sauce over chicken.
- Serves 4.

CREAMY POLENTA
- 1¼ **cups milk**
- 1 **cup water**
- ½ **cup polenta**
- 2 **tablespoons unsalted butter**
- 2 **tablespoons grated Parmesan cheese**

salt and black pepper to taste

- Combine milk and water in large saucepan. Bring to a boil.
- Whisk polenta into liquid, reduce heat and simmer for 5 minutes, whisking occasionally.
- Whisk butter and cheese into polenta mixture. Season with salt and black pepper. Cover and keep warm.

RAY WALSTON

Chicken Livers Delight

1 **cup all-purpose flour**
1 **teaspoon salt**
½ **teaspoon black pepper**
1 **teaspoon ground ginger**
1 **pound chicken livers**
margarine
1 **large onion, chopped**
2 **cups port wine**
2 **to 3 cups cooked white rice**

- Combine flour, salt, black pepper and ginger in bag. Add livers and shake to coat thoroughly.
- Sauté livers with onion in margarine in large skillet until browned. Add wine and simmer for 20 minutes.
- Serve livers with onion and sauce over rice. Serves 2 or 3.

HENNY YOUNGMAN
"Take my recipe, please!"

Crispy Rice Chicken

1 **(12 ounce) package crispy rice cereal, coarsely crushed**
1 **tablespoon salt**
1 **tablespoon black pepper**
1 **tablespoon paprika**
4 **(2½ to 3 pound) broiler-fryers, cut up**
2 **cups margarine, melted**

- Combine cereal, salt, black pepper and paprika.
- Dip chicken pieces in margarine, then coat with cereal mixture. Place in baking pans.
- Bake at 375 degrees for 1 hour.
- Serves 12 to 15.

JANE WYMAN

Torchy Chicken

- 1 cup thinly sliced onion
- 2 cups chicken stock, divided
- 3 cloves garlic, minced
- 8 chicken breast halves, skin removed and boned
- 2 tablespoons salt
- ¼ cup plus 2 tablespoons curry powder
- 2 teaspoons chili powder
- ½ teaspoon ground ginger
- 6 to 8 cups cooked white or basmati rice

- Sauté onion and garlic in skillet sprayed with vegetable spray; as onion begins to stick, add ½ cup broth and cook until softened.
- Coat chicken with mixture of salt, curry powder, chili powder and ginger. Add chicken to pan and cook, turning once. Stir in remaining herb mixture. Simmer, covered, for 25 to 30 minutes; remove cover and simmer for additional 5 to 15 minutes or until chicken is cooked.
- Serve over rice. Serves 8.
- For thicker sauce, dissolve 1 tablespoon cornstarch in ¼ cup water. Add to sauce, 1 teaspoon at a time, during final cooking time.

DAVID L. AND GLORIA WOLPER

Turkey Pita Pockets

- ½ pound ground raw turkey
- 1 small onion, chopped
- ½ green bell pepper, chopped
- 1 clove garlic, minced
- ⅓ cup tomato sauce
- 1 teaspoon chili powder
- ½ teaspoon ground cumin
- freshly ground black pepper
- 1 cup frozen corn
- 4 whole wheat pita rounds, halved
- 4 cups shredded lettuce
- 1 large tomato, chopped
- 2 green onions with tops, thinly sliced

- Brown turkey, onion, bell pepper and garlic together in non-stick skillet sprayed with cooking spray, stirring to crumble turkey.
- Add tomato sauce, chili powder, cumin, black pepper and corn to turkey mixture. Simmer for about 10 minutes or until corn is tender.
- Warm pita bread. Drain turkey mixture to remove excess liquid. Spoon ⅓ cup mixture into each pita half. Top with ½ cup shredded lettuce, small amount of tomato and green onion.
- Serves 2 to 4.

CAFE DE ARTISTES, NEW YORK, NEW YORK
GEORGE LANG, PROPRIETOR
JENNIFER LANG, PROPRIETOR AND EXECUTIVE CHEF

Chicken Bouillabaisse

5 quarts water
bouquet garni (parsley stems,
    peppercorns, 3 bay leaves,
    fresh fennel leaves and dried
    thyme in cheesecloth bag)
2 tablespoons kosher salt,
    divided
3 (3½ pound) chickens
½ cup extra virgin olive oil
3 medium-sized onions,
    minced
5 fennel bulbs, cut julienne
4 leeks (white portion only, cut
    julienne)
2 medium carrots, thinly sliced
1 stalk celery, thinly sliced
4 large cloves garlic, peeled
    and minced
1 pound ripe tomatoes, peeled,
    seeded and chopped
2 cups white wine
1 sprig thyme
1 sprig rosemary
salt to taste
1 teaspoon freshly-ground
    black pepper
1 teaspoon red pepper flakes
1½ cups Pernod liqueur
¼ cup minced Italian parsley

- Combine water with bouquet garni and 1 tablespoon kosher salt in stock pot. Bring to a boil. Add whole chickens to water. Simmer for 1 hour or until chicken is tender. Set aside to cool in broth.
- Sauté onion, fennel, leeks, carrots, celery and garlic in oil in large heavy saucepan over medium heat, stirring constantly, for 20 minutes or until vegetables are softened but not browned.
- Add tomatoes, 6 cups chicken broth, wine, thyme, rosemary, 1 tablespoon kosher salt, black pepper and red pepper. Simmer, stirring occasionally, for 30 minutes. Check liquid and add additional broth if not soup consistency. Check seasoning and adjust if needed.
- Remove chicken from broth. For each serving, place breast, leg and thigh in soup plate or individual casserole. Ladle portion of soup into bowl, add ¼ cup Pernod and sprinkle with parsley. Serve with garlic toast. Serves 6.

Seafood

Susan, age 8

PETER ALLEN

Baked Fish Peter Allen

"First tasted on the Great Barrier Reef where I have a house."

1 (5 pound) red snapper, cleaned
juice of 3 limes or 1½ lemons
salt
3 cups chopped cashews, almonds, Brazil nuts, hazelnuts or pecans
1 cup (4 ounces) grated mild cheese
1 small clove garlic, crushed
1 small onion, grated
1 cup milk
cayenne pepper to taste
½ teaspoon grated nutmeg
2 bay leaves, finely crushed
¼ cup sherry or Madeira wine
1 cup dry fine bread crumbs
6 tablespoons butter

- Brush exterior and inside of fish with lime juice, sprinkle lightly with salt and ice down for at least 4 hours before cooking.
- Place fish in well-greased baking dish.
- Combine nuts, cheese, garlic and onion. Add milk and mix to form stiff paste. Season with salt and cayenne pepper. Stir in nutmeg, bay leaves and sherry.
- Spread paste on fish, covering well. Sprinkle with bread crumbs and add butter in lumps.
- Bake at 350 to 375 degrees, basting well, until browned and fish flakes easily with fork.
- Serves 6.

FRED DE CORDOVA
"A cool plate is required. Saltines are important."

Sardines á la Fred

1 (4 ounce) can sardines
saltines
1 (12 ounce) bottle of beer, chilled

- Carefully open can of sardines. Pour contents on cold plate. Surround sardines with saltines.
- Open cold bottle of beer. Pour beer in a glass.
- Combine sardines with saltines. Wash down with beer. Repeat procedure as required.
- Serves 1.

CARROLL BAKER

Lobster Oriental

1 small clove garlic, minced
2 tablespoons olive oil
2 pounds uncooked lobster meat, **diced**
2 tablespoons rum
½ cup chicken broth
1 cup snow peas
1 cup bean sprouts
1 cup sliced water chestnuts
2 cups coarsely cut Chinese cabbage
6 cups cooked white rice

- Sauté garlic in large skillet over medium heat until transparent; do not brown.
- Add lobster to garlic and cook, turning pieces.
- Stir rum, broth, snow peas, bean sprouts, water chestnuts and cabbage into lobster mixture. Simmer, uncovered, for 5 minutes.
- Serve over rice. Serves 6.

CHERYL TIEGS
"Thick crusty bread and a good bottle of red wine — 'heaven'. The next day, cold with cold jasmati or basmati white rice — delish."

Fish with Fresh Tomatoes

8 cloves garlic, chopped and pressed
½ cup olive oil
8 large ripe tomatoes, cored, seeded and sliced
1½ to 2 pounds tuna or swordfish
1 (2 ounce) can anchovy fillets, drained and chopped
1 bunch basil, chopped
red pepper flakes to taste

- Sauté garlic in oil until golden brown. Strain through sieve and set aside.
- Layer ½ of tomatoes in casserole large enough to contain fish in single layer. Sprinkle ½ garlic and ½ basil on tomatoes.
- Place fish on tomatoes. Layer anchovies, red pepper and remaining basil on fish.
- Arrange remaining tomatoes on fish with remaining garlic and oil.
- Bake at 400 degrees for 20 to 25 minutes or until fish flakes easily. Serves 5 to 7.

DOUG ARANGO'S, PALM DESERT, CALIFORNIA
CHRIS BENNETT, EXECUTIVE CHEF

Fillet of Sole Milanese

FISH
- 4 (4 ounce) sole fillets
- 2 large eggs
- ½ teaspoon dried oregano
- salt and black pepper
- ½ cup all-purpose flour
- 1 cup unseasoned bread crumbs
- 6 cloves garlic
- ½ cup olive oil
- 1 tablespoon unsalted butter
- chopped parsley

- Prepare lemon butter caper sauce just before cooking fish.
- Wash fish and blot with paper towel.
- Scramble eggs and season with oregano, salt and black pepper.
- Lightly coat fish with flour, dip in egg and coat with bread crumbs.
- Sauté garlic in oil and butter in skillet over high heat until golden brown. Remove garlic.
- Sauté fish in oil and butter for 3 to 5 minutes on each side or until golden brown. Remove from pan and blot excess grease with paper towel.
- Place fish on individual plates. Drizzle lemon butter caper sauce on fish and garnish with parsley. Serves 4.
- Other delicate white fish such as tilapia or John Dory can be substituted for sole.

LEMON BUTTER CAPER SAUCE
- 3 cloves garlic
- 2 tablespoons unsalted butter
- 1 teaspoon capers
- juice of ½ lemon
- salt and black pepper

- Sauté garlic in butter in skillet over medium heat until golden. Remove garlic.
- Turn off heat. Add capers, lemon juice, salt and black pepper to butter.

MRS. ARMAND S. DEUTSCH

Portuguese Fisherman's Stew

- 1 medium-sized onion, thinly sliced
- 1 small clove garlic, pressed
- ½ cup coarsely chopped green bell pepper
- ¼ cup olive oil
- 2 (28 ounce) cans tomatoes, undrained, cut up
- ½ cup minced parsley
- ¼ teaspoon Worcestershire sauce
- 1½ teaspoons salt
- few drops hot pepper sauce
- 2 pounds sea bass, halibut or cod, cut in 2-inch cubes
- ¾ cup dry white wine
- chopped parsley

- Sauté onion, garlic and bell pepper in oil in heavy 4-quart pot over medium-high heat, stirring often, until onion is lightly browned.
- Add tomatoes with juice, parsley, Worcestershire sauce, salt and hot pepper sauce to onion mixture. Bring to a boil, reduce heat and simmer, covered, for 30 minutes, stirring occasionally.
- Sauce is base for stew. It can be stored in refrigerator for up to 5 days or in freezer for up to 4 months.
- About 20 minutes before serving, bring stew base to a boil. Wash fish under cold water before adding to stew. Add fish and wine, cover and simmer for about 15 minutes or until fish is cooked; do not overcook.
- Pour stew into individual soup bowls and sprinkle with parsley. Or serve soup in bread bowls, made by cutting slice from top of sour dough roundette and scooping out interior to form bowl. Fill with stew and cover with top slice. Serves 5 or 6.

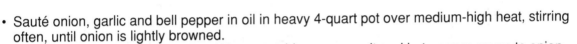

AGUT D'AVIGNON, BARCELONA, SPAIN
MERCEDES R. GIRALT SALINAS, EXECUTIVE CHEF

Sole Nyoca Style

- 6 Petrale sole fillets
- salt to taste
- 1½ cups all-purpose flour
- 2 cups olive oil, divided
- 1 cup coarsely chopped toasted hazelnuts
- 1 cup toasted almonds
- 1 cup pine nuts
- 1 cup raisins
- 2 limes or lemons
- parsley, finely chopped
- 6 small ripe tomatoes, scalded

- Salt fish and coat with flour. Sauté in 1 cup oil in skillet until cooked. Remove from skillet and keep warm.
- Cook hazelnuts, almonds, pine nuts and raisins in remaining 1 cup oil for 2 minutes.
- Place fish on serving platter. Garnish each piece with lime or lemon slice. Sprinkle parsley on lemon and top with tomato. Pour nut and fruit mixture over fish. Serves 6.

PAUL BURKE

"Although this is called barbecued shrimp, it is actually done in the oven. I hope you like spicy food. Be prepared — serve with hot French bread and a cold green salad. Lots of paper napkins as this dish is eaten with your fingers. A bowl of quartered lemons is a must. Serve ice cold beer."

New Orleans Barbecued Shrimp

- 1 **cup butter**
- 1 **tablespoon olive oil**
- 1 **tablespoon minced garlic**
- 2 **teaspoons ground fresh rosemary**
- 2 **teaspoons thyme**
- 1 **teaspoon oregano**
- 2 **teaspoons salt**
- 2 **teaspoons black pepper**
- 2 **teaspoons cayenne pepper**
- ¼ **cup Worcestershire sauce**
- 60 **large shrimp, heads removed but shells intact**
- ¾ **cup beer**
- **chopped parsley**

- Melt butter in skillet. Stir in oil, garlic, rosemary, thyme, oregano, salt, black pepper, cayenne pepper and Worcestershire sauce. Simmer for about 5 minutes.
- Place shrimp in shallow layer in large stainless steel pan or casserole. Pour sauce over shrimp and toss to coat evenly. Marinate in refrigerator for at least 4 hours or overnight.
- Bake at 400 degrees for 10 minutes, stirring once or twice. Add beer and bake for additional 10 minutes, stirring once or twice. Do not overcook shrimp.
- Divide shrimp among soup bowls, pour sauce over shrimp and sprinkle with parsley.
- Serves 4.

KENNY G.

Teriyaki Salmon

- 1 **fresh thick salmon fillet, boned**
- 1 **tablespoon olive oil**
- **teriyaki sauce**
- **organic honey**

- Cut salmon lengthwise in 2-inch strips.
- Sear salmon on both sides in oil in skillet over high heat until lightly browned. Add teriyaki sauce, turn salmon, drizzle with honey; repeat addition of teriyaki sauce and honey, turning until salmon is very dark brown and thoroughly cooked.
- Serves 1.

WRIGHT'S, THE ARIZONA BILTMORE RESORT & VILLAS, PHOENIX, ARIZONA
BRIAN TESS, EXECUTIVE CHEF

Parmesan Scallopini of Sea Bass

12 Jerusalem artichokes (sunchokes), peeled and cut in ¼-inch cubes
 8 cloves garlic, sliced
olive oil
 1 cup dry white wine
 1 cup chicken broth
 ¼ cup butter
salt and black pepper to taste
 3 medium parsnips, peeled and cut julienne
 2 cups vegetable oil
 4 eggs
 2 cups (8 ounces) grated Parmesan cheese
 1 pound striped sea bass fillets
 ¾ cup all-purpose flour
 ¼ cup olive oil
 4 sprigs Italian parsley

- Sauté artichokes and garlic in small amount of olive oil in saucepan over medium heat for a few minutes.
- Add white wine and cook to reduce liquid by ½. Stir in broth, reduce heat and simmer to reduce liquid by ½ and artichokes are tender.
- Fold butter into sauce and season with salt and black pepper. Remove from heat and set aside.
- Fry parsnip strips in vegetable oil at 325 degrees until golden brown. Remove with slotted spoon and place on paper towel to absorb grease.
- Whisk eggs, add cheese and blend thoroughly.
- Thinly slice fish fillets across grain. Season with salt and black pepper. Coat with flour, dip in egg and cheese mixture and sauté in olive oil in non-stick sauté pan over medium high heat, turning to brown on both sides.
- Spoon about 2 tablespoons artichoke sauce in center of individual dinner plates. Place 2 slices fish on mixture, arrange a few parsnip strips on fish and garnish with parsley.
- Serves 4.

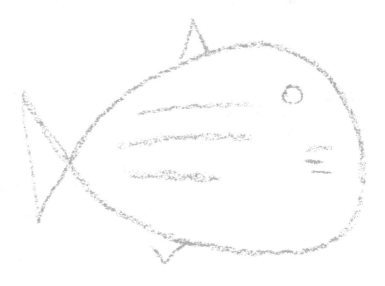

BORDER GRILL, SANTA MONICA, CALIFORNIA
SUSAN FENIGER AND MARY SUE MILLIKEN, OWNERS AND EXECUTIVE CHEFS
"Whenever possible, we would make our own yogurt to have at home (of course, owning a couple of restaurants makes that much easier since we just bring it home) but this dish works best with homemade yogurt."

Grilled Salmon with Tziki and Marinated Peppers

FISH
4 (7 ounce) fresh salmon fillets
1 tablespoon olive oil
salt and black pepper

- Prepare Tziki and Marinated Peppers.
- Heat grill as hot as possible or preheat broiler.
- Lightly brush salmon with oil and season with salt and pepper. Grill for about 3 minutes on each side. Heat source must be very hot to quickly cook fish and retain moisture; slow cooking will dry fish.
- To serve, spoon ¼ of tziki in center of each individual plate. Top with salmon fillet and garnish with marinated bell peppers.
- Fish can be served cold with the same sauce the following day. Serves 4.

TZIKI
2 cups yogurt
2 pickling cucumbers
1 teaspoon kosher or regular salt
1½ tablespoons freshly puréed garlic
salt and black pepper to taste

- In towel or cheesecloth, drain yogurt for 1 to 2 hours. Discard liquid.
- Trim bitter ends from cucumber, peel and coarsely grate. Add kosher salt to cucumber, place in colander and drain for 1 hour or longer.
- Combine cucumber, yogurt, garlic, salt and black pepper.
- Tziki can be prepared a day in advance and stored in refrigerator. Use as dip or beneath grilled or broiled fish.

MARINATED PEPPERS
2 red bell peppers
3 tablespoons olive oil
1 tablespoon red wine vinegar
2 tablespoons chopped oregano
salt and black pepper to taste

- Roast peppers by charring on all sides under a preheated broiler or directly over a gas flame. Make sure the peppers are darkened to maximize flavor of smokiness. Place in plastic bag, close tightly and set aside to steam for about 10 minutes. Under cold running water, carefully peel and split peppers open and remove seeds and excess pulp.
- Cut bell pepper in julienne strips. Add oil, vinegar, oregano, salt and black pepper. Check seasonings and adjust if necessary. Marinate for 1 hour.
- Peppers can be marinated for 2 or 3 days before serving.

JULIO IGLESIAS

"When I was a child, this was our family dinner on Sundays. My father always told me that if I ate all I was served I would become a very good singer...who knows. Maybe this recipe will produce more singers."

Paella Valenciana

18 clams or mussels
 1 (2 to 2½ pound) broiler-fryer, cut in 8 pieces
 1 thick slice ham or prosciutto, diced
 1 cup olive oil
 1 large red bell pepper, diced
 1 large clove garlic, minced
 1 large squid, cut in rings
 3 or 4 medium tomatoes, peeled and diced
 1 teaspoon paprika
 4 to 6 large shrimp in shells
 1 (14 ounce) package paella or arborio rice
water or fish and chicken broth
 ¼ cup cooked peas
 1 red snapper fillet, cut in small pieces
salt and black pepper
 3 saffron threads, pulverized
 1 lemon, quartered

- Cook clams or mussels in small amount of water until shells open. Discard ½ of shell and retain ½ with meat. Strain and reserve broth.
- Sauté chicken and ham in oil in Dutch oven until golden.
- Add bell pepper, garlic and squid. Cook over low heat, stirring and adding more oil if necessary. Stir in tomatoes, paprika and shrimp and cook until done.
- Combine clam or mussel broth with enough water or fish and chicken stock to equal twice the volume of rice. Add liquid, rice, peas, clams or mussels and red snapper to chicken mixture. Bring to a boil, cook for 2 to 3 minutes and reduce heat.
- Season with salt, black pepper and saffron.
- Continue cooking but do not stir. As liquid evaporates, reduce heat until paella appears almost dry. Let stand for a few minutes before serving.
- Serve from pan in which paella is cooked. Garnish with lemon. Serves 4.

PRESIDENT AND MRS. GERALD FORD
"This recipe is based on one found in the Arnaud's Creole Cookbook. With that basis and some adding, subtracting and experimentation, we finally came up with 'Betty's Blue Bayou'."

Betty's Blue Bayou

2 tablespoons chopped shallots
2 tablespoons butter
2 pounds medium-large shrimp, peeled and deveined
6 tablespoons white wine
salt and freshly ground black pepper
dash of cayenne pepper
1 tablespoon grated Swiss cheese
1 tablespoon grated Parmesan cheese
4 cups cooked white rice

- Prepare Bechamel sauce and use portion of it to prepare Mornay sauce.
- Sauté shallots in butter in large skillet over high heat until translucent.
- Add shrimp to shallots and cook for about 3 minutes or until pink.
- Stir in wine and cook for 2 minutes. Season with salt, black pepper and cayenne pepper.
- Add 2½ cups Mornay sauce and Swiss cheese. Bring to a boil and cook for 1 minute.
- Pour shrimp and sauce into 13x9x2-inch broiler-proof baking dish. Sprinkle with Parmesan cheese. Broil until golden brown.
- Serve with rice.
- Serves 4.

BECHAMEL SAUCE
4 cups milk
1½ cups sliced white onion
1 bouquet garni
4 cloves
3 bay leaves
pinch of white pepper
½ cup roux

- Combine milk, onion, bouquet garni, cloves, bay leaves and white pepper in saucepan. Bring to a boil.
- Whisk roux into simmering liquid. Simmer for 10 to 15 minutes, check seasoning and strain.

MORNAY SAUCE
4 cups Bechamel sauce
1½ cups (6 ounces) grated Swiss cheese
½ cup (2 ounces) crumbled Danish blue cheese
¼ teaspoon nutmeg

- Pour Bechamel sauce in saucepan. Stir in Swiss cheese, blue cheese and nutmeg. Heat over low heat, stirring occasionally, until cheese is melted and blended.

SPAGO, HOLLYWOOD, CALIFORNIA
WOLFGANG PUCK,
OWNER AND EXECUTIVE CHEF
Wolfgang Puck is credited with reviving California culinary heritage. Blending fresh California ingredients and classical French training, his innovation in cooking has been enjoyed and praised by world leaders, Hollywood stars and fellow chefs alike.

Alaskan Salmon with Ginger and Black Pepper

FISH
3 tablespoons chopped ginger
3 tablespoons chopped black pepper
4 (6 ounce) Alaskan King salmon fillets
salt to taste
olive oil

- Prepare sauce and celery purée.
- Combine ginger and black pepper. Season salmon with salt and coat with ginger-black pepper mixture. Sprinkle with oil.
- Grill or sauté salmon to medium doneness.
- Divide sauce among 4 warmed dinner plates. Spoon equal portions of celery purée on sauce and top with salmon.
- Serves 4.

SAUCE
¼ cup plus 2 tablespoons unsalted butter, divided
1 shallot, chopped
1 clove garlic, minced
1 tomato, peeled, seeded and chopped
2 cups Cabernet Sauvignon wine
2 tablespoons Balsamic vinegar
1 cup chicken broth
salt and black pepper to taste

- Heat 2 tablespoons butter in sauté pan until foaming. Sauté shallot, garlic and tomato for several minutes or until shallot is translucent.
- Pour wine and vinegar into pan and cook over medium heat to reduce liquid by ½. Add broth and cook to reduce again by ½.
- Stir in remaining butter to desired consistency. Season with salt and black pepper. Keep sauce warm.

CELERY PURÉE
1 medium baking potato, peeled and cut in 1-inch cubes
1 celery root, peeled and cut in 1-inch cubes
½ cup whipping cream
2 tablespoons butter
salt and black pepper to taste

- Cook potato and celery root in boiling salted water for 15 to 20 minutes or until softened. Drain water and return vegetables to pan. Add cream and simmer over medium heat for about 15 minutes and thickened, stirring occasionally.
- Remove from heat. Add butter, salt and black pepper.
- Process in food mill or for several seconds in food processor. Purée should be creamy but not sticky.

QUINCY DELIGHT JONES

Quincy's Papaya Delight

    4 large ripe papayas
    2 cloves garlic, crushed
    3 tablespoons butter
    3 stalks celery, diced
    1 medium-sized onion, diced
    1 medium apple, diced
    1 cup vegetable, fish or chicken broth
    ½ teaspoon salt
    1 tablespoon curry powder
    1 tablespoon ground red chilies
    1 pound chunk crab meat
    6 to 8 cups cooked white rice
chutney
mint sprigs for garnish

- Cut papayas in halves. Scoop pulp from center and reserve. Set shells aside.
- Sauté garlic in butter in large saucepan until brown. Discard garlic and retain butter in pan.
- Sauté celery, onion, apple and papaya in butter until softened. Gradually add broth, stirring constantly. Season with salt, curry and chili and mix well. Simmer for 20 minutes.
- Gradually add cream to mixture. Fold in crab meat and simmer for 5 minutes.
- Arrange shells in well-oiled baking pan. Spoon mixture into shells.
- Bake, covered with aluminum foil, at 350 degrees for 30 minutes.
- Serve on bed of rice with chutney on side. Garnish with mint sprigs. Serves 8.

JACK LEMMON

Broiled Shrimp

    2 cloves garlic, crushed
    ¼ cup peanut oil
    ¼ cup soy sauce
    ¼ cup seafood cocktail sauce
    1 tablespoon lemon juice
    3 tablespoons chopped dill
pinch of freshly ground black pepper
    2 pounds fresh medium shrimp, peeled and
       deveined

- Combine garlic, oil, soy sauce, cocktail sauce, lemon juice, dill and black pepper, mixing well. Marinate shrimp in sauce for 2 hours.
- Remove shrimp from marinade and place on broiler pan. Broil for 2 minutes on each side.
- Place shrimp on platter and spoon portion of remaining marinade over shrimp. Serve as appetizer or main dish. Serves 4.

JIMMY'S, BEVERLY HILLS, CALIFORNIA
JIMMY MURPHY, OWNER AND EXECUTIVE CHEF

Peppered Salmon on Bed of Spinach-Cabernet Sauvignon Sauce

4 bunches spinach, steamed
2 cups Cabernet wine, divided
2 shallots, diced
1 cup brown veal stock or low-sodium chicken broth
2 teaspoons cornstarch
salt and black pepper to taste
8 (7 ounce) fresh salmon steaks, skin removed and boned
3 tablespoons coarsely ground black pepper
salt
½ cup olive oil
½ cup butter

- Steam spinach until tender, drain well and set aside.
- Combine 1½ cups wine and shallots in saucepan. Bring to a boil.
- Add stock or broth and cook to reduce by ½.
- Dissolve cornstarch in remaining ½ cup wine, gradually add to boiling sauce and cook until thickened. Season to taste and strain sauce.
- Sprinkle salmon with black pepper and salt lightly.
- Sauté salmon in oil until golden brown on each side. Place in baking pan.
- Bake at 400 degrees for about 5 minutes or until tender but not dry.
- While salmon is baking, sauté spinach in butter.
- Place spinach on plate, arrange salmon on spinach and pour sauce over salmon. Serve very hot. Serves 8.

ALAN KING

Crab Meat Alan King

2 **pounds fresh lump crab meat**
juice of 1 lemon, strained
½ **bunch watercress leaves, chopped**
¼ **cup prepared horseradish, drained**
¼ **cup prepared chili sauce**
½ **cup mayonnaise**
salt and freshly ground black pepper to taste

- Examine crab meat and discard slivers of cartilage. Sprinkle with lemon juice.
- Add watercress and horseradish to crab meat.
- Blend chili sauce with mayonnaise and add to crab meat. Season with salt and black pepper. Mix gently with fork to avoid breaking crab meat.
- If preparing 1 to 2 hours in advance of serving, store crab meat mixture in refrigerator.
- Prepare Mornay sauce.
- Pour crab meat mixture into heavy saucepan and heat, stirring constantly, for a few minutes until crab meat is very warm but not hot. Mixture can be warmed in microwave oven.
- Divide crab meat among 10 to 12 small lightly-buttered ramekins or in large buttered clam shells. Top each with 2 tablespoons Mornay sauce. Place ramekins or shells in large baking pan.
- Bake on top oven rack at 375 degrees for 15 to 20 minutes or until sauce is bubbling and top is golden brown. Serve immediately. Serves 10 to 12.

MORNAY SAUCE
¼ **cup butter**
3 **tablespoons all-purpose flour**
2 **cups half and half, scalded and hot**
2 **egg yolks, well beaten**
2 **tablespoons grated Gruyere cheese**
2 **tablespoons Parmesan cheese**
salt to taste
cayenne pepper to taste
butter

- Melt butter in saucepan. Blend in flour and cook for a few minutes. Add half and half and bring to a boil. Remove from heat and rapidly whisk in egg yolks.
- Stir Gruyere cheese and Parmesan cheese into sauce. Season with salt and cayenne pepper. Heat over low heat, stirring occasionally, until cheese is melted and blended.
- If preparing 1 to 2 hours in advance of using, spread small amount of butter on top of sauce to prevent film.

**LA COSTA RESORT AND SPA,
CARLSBAD, CALIFORNIA
JOSEPH LAGEDER**

Baked Salmon with Saffron Couscous

1 **pound salmon fillet, cut in half lengthwise**
olive oil
¼ **cup white wine**
2 **cups chicken broth**
¼ **teaspoon saffron**
1½ **cups couscous**
½ **cup finely diced carrots**
½ **cup chopped dry sun-dried tomatoes**
salt and black pepper to taste
2 **tablespoons chives**
2 **tablespoons chopped parsley**
4 **(½ ounce) slices smoked turkey**
1 **cup water**

- Sauté salmon in oil in saucepan for 1 minute.
- Add wine and simmer to reduce liquid by ½.
- Stir in broth and saffron. Simmer for 5 minutes. Add couscous, carrots and tomatoes. Season with salt and black pepper, mixing well, and set aside to cool. Blend in ½ chives and parsley mix.
- Place sheet of plastic wrap on work surface and sprinkle with remaining chives and parsley. Arrange turkey slices on herbs, add 1 slice salmon, spread with couscous mixture, top with second slice salmon and wrap tightly.
- Place salmon stack in 9x9x2-inch baking dish and add water.
- Bake at 300 degrees for 15 to 20 minutes.
- Slice salmon before serving. Serves 4.

JOANNE POITIER

Chilean Sea Bass in Lemon Sauce

1 **pound Chilean sea bass, cut in 4 pieces**
¼ **cup chopped parsley**
1 **teaspoon salt**
1 **teaspoon black pepper**
3 **tablespoons butter or margarine**
¼ **cup Chardonnay wine**
¼ **cup chicken broth**
2 **tablespoons lemon juice**
superfine flour for thickening

- Season fish with parsley, salt and black pepper. Sauté in butter in sauté pan over high heat, browning on both sides.
- Add wine, broth and lemon juice to fish. Reduce heat to medium, bring to a boil and cook for 2 minutes.
- Place fish on platter.
- Whisk superfine flour into pan juices and cook to desired consistency. Strain sauce through sieve over fish. Serves 4.

**UMBERTO'S,
VANCOUVER, BRITISH COLUMBIA, CANADA
UMBERTO MENGHI, OWNER AND CHEF**

Risota Alla Aragosta

Risotto with Lobster Tails

2 cups Arborio rice
2 shallots, minced
2 tablespoons olive oil
1 cup dry white wine
4 cups fish stock
2 medium-sized fresh lobster tails
3 tablespoons finely chopped cilantro
salt and white pepper

- Prepare fish stock.
- Wash rice in cold water, drain and set aside.
- Sauté shallots in oil in skillet for 1 minute or until translucent.
- Combine shallots, rice and wine in saucepan, stirring with wooden spoon for 1 to 2 minutes. Begin to cook rice over medium heat. Begin ladling fish stock into rice mixture, stirring gently and adding next portion when previous is nearly absorbed, always keeping rice moist and stirring gently. Cook rice for 15 to 18 minutes or until rice is tender and creamy but firm.
- While rice is cooking, peel and devein lobster tails and cut meat into ½-inch thick medallions. About 4 minutes before rice is cooked, add lobster and cilantro to mixture.
- Season with salt and white pepper. Serve immediately.
- Serves 4 to 6.

FISH STOCK

½ pound fish bones (no skin)
1 cup white wine
3 cups cold water
1 medium-sized onion, coarsely chopped
1 laurel leaf
1 bouquet garni

- Rinse fish bones under cold running water for 10 minutes. Crack bones and place in large saucepan.
- Pour water and wine into pan with bones. Bring to a boil, skimming foam from surface of liquid.
- Add onion, laurel leaf and bouquet garni. Simmer for 25 minutes. Strain through linen-lined sieve.
- Store stock in sealed plastic container in refrigerator for up to 10 days or freeze for up to 3 months.
- Makes 4 cups.

JOE GARAGIOLA

Risotta Alla Marinara

Italian Rice with Seafood

7 cups fish stock
½ pound mussels
1 cup diced onion
¼ cup olive oil
½ cup diced carrot
½ cup diced celery
1 (16 ounce) package Arborio rice
1 cup dry white wine
salt and black pepper to taste
2 bay leaves
½ teaspoon ground fennel
pinch of saffron
¼ pound mixed seafood: prawns, scallops,
    squid rings, cooked crab and oysters
1 tablespoon butter
1 tablespoon chopped chives
1½ teaspoons chopped parsley
2 tablespoons grated Parmesan cheese
dash of Marsala wine

- Bring stock to a boil and keep at low boil while preparing dish.
- Cook mussels in small amount of water to open shells. Discard shells and set meat aside.
- Sauté onion in oil until translucent. Add carrots and celery and cook until softened.
- Stir rice into vegetables and sauté for 1 minute. Add wine and cook until liquid is evaporated. Season with salt and black pepper.
- Begin ladling fish stock into rice mixture, stirring continuously and adding next portion when previous is nearly absorbed. Rice should be cooked until al dente or crunchy and moist but not soupy.
- Add bay leaves, fennel and saffron. When rice is ¾ cooked, begin adding seafood. Prawns and scallops should be cooked just to opaqueness and mussels, oysters and crab require only warming.
- Season with salt and black pepper, remove bay leaves. Add butter, chives, parsley, cheese and wine.
- Serves 6.

LARRY MANETTI

Tuna Cutlets in Parsley and Bread Crumbs

6   **(6 ounce) tuna steaks**
½   **cup white wine vinegar**
¾   **cup all-purpose flour**
1   **egg, beaten**
¾   **cup dry bread crumbs**
1   **tablespoon chopped parsley**
¾   **cup extra virgin olive oil**
salt
1   **lemon, cut in wedges**

- Rinse tuna and blot dry with paper towel.
- Place vinegar, flour and egg in separate shallow bowls. Combine bread crumbs and parsley and place in shallow bowl.
- Dip tuna steaks, 1 at a time, in vinegar and drain, dredge in flour, dip in egg and dredge in bread crumb mixture, coating both sides.
- Brown cutlets in oil in heavy iron skillet for a few minutes on each side. Sprinkle with salt and drain on paper towel.
- Serve immediately with lemon wedges. Serves 6.
- Swordfish steaks can be substituted for tuna.

A few days after Frank and I returned from Hawaii where Blue Eyes did a "Magnum P.I.," Larry and his wife, Nancy, gave us one of their parrots, Rocky. We adore Rocky and over the years his vocabulary has greatly expanded. He now shows off by singing a few bars of "My Way." And Rocky loves a party. He often climbs off his perch and waddles across the living room floor to the den and onto the back of a couch to join Frank and me and guests when we gather for cocktails before dinner — a welcome uninvited guest! — Barbara Sinatra

---

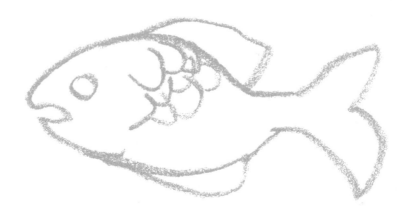

BROOKS ROBINSON
"The secret of this recipe is using only jumbo lump crab meat without a trace of shell."

Maryland Crab Cakes

1 teaspoon seafood seasoning
¼ teaspoon salt
1 tablespoon mayonnaise
1 tablespoon Worcestershire sauce
1 tablespoon chopped parsley
1 tablespoon baking powder
1 egg, beaten
2 slices white bread, chopped
1 pound jumbo lump crab meat
vegetable oil
lemon wedges for garnish
parsley sprigs for garnish

- Combine seafood seasoning, salt, mayonnaise, Worcestershire sauce, parsley, baking powder, egg and bread, mixing well.
- Gently fold crab meat into mixture, keeping large lumps intact.
- Shape mixture into 4 large cakes or several small cakes.
- Sauté cakes in oil in skillet over medium-high heat, cooking quickly and turning until golden on both sides.
- Garnish with lemon and parsley.
- Serves 4 as entree or 8 for starter course.

ROGER WHITTAKER

Trout in Almonds

1 trout, cleaned
all-purpose flour
2 tablespoons butter
¼ cup blanched almonds
¼ cup chopped parsley
salt and black pepper to taste

- Coat trout with flour.
- Fry trout in butter in skillet for about 6 minutes on each side, adding almonds and parsley for final 2 minutes of cooking. Serve immediately.
- Serves 1.

PAUL NEWMAN

Italian Baked Scrod

2 pounds scrod fillets
salt and black pepper to taste
2 onions, sliced
1 (14½ ounce) can stewed tomatoes, chopped
¼ cup sliced black olives
¼ cup sliced green olives
2 tablespoons chopped basil or 1 tablespoon dried basil
2 tablespoons chopped parsley or 1 tablespoon dried parsley
1 clove garlic, crushed
½ to ⅔ cup clam juice

- Wash scrod and blot with paper towel. Arrange in single layer in 13x9x2-inch baking dish. Season with salt and black pepper.
- Cover scrod with onion, tomatoes, ripe and green olives, basil, parsley and garlic. Moisten with clam juice.
- Bake at 375 degrees for 20 minutes or just until fish flakes easily. Drain most of liquid before serving.
- Serves 4.

Paul Newman has blue eyes; Frank has blue eyes.
Paul is a great actor and Frank is a great actor.
Paul is very handsome and so is Frank
Paul won an Oscar; Frank won an Oscar.
Frank's picture is on albums, and Paul's is on salad dressing, pasta, and popcorn.
Joanne and I are just lucky, I guess. — *Barbara Sinatra*

WAYNE NEWTON

Shrimp á la Nichols

    2 cups all-purpose flour
    1 teaspoon salt
    ½ teaspoon black pepper
   12 jumbo shrimp, peeled and deveined
    4 eggs, well beaten
    ½ cup virgin olive oil
    ½ cup finely chopped bacon
    2 tablespoons minced garlic
    ¼ cup minced shallots
    ¼ cup minced leeks
    ½ cup peeled, seeded and diced tomatoes
    ¼ cup dry white wine
    ¼ cup clam broth or juice
    1 (16 ounce) package linguine
fresh basil leaves for garnish

- Prepare garlic butter and set aside.
- Combine flour, salt and black pepper. Coat shrimp in seasoned flour, dip in egg, drain excess and coat again with flour.
- Sauté shrimp in hot oil in skillet over medium high heat, browning well on both sides. Drain on paper towel and set aside.
- While preparing remainder of sauce, cook linguine according to package directions.
- Sauté bacon in large skillet over medium-high heat until crisp. Discard excess grease from skillet.
- Add garlic to bacon and cook over medium heat for 1 minute.
- Stir shallots, leeks and tomatoes into garlic-bacon mixture and cook over high heat, stirring frequently.
- Add wine, clam juice and about ½ garlic butter to vegetable mixture. Cook for 2 to 3 minutes, stirring to blend. Season with salt and black pepper.
- Reheat shrimp in pan in oven at 400 degrees for 2 to 3 minutes.
- Drain linguine well. Add remaining garlic butter and toss to coat thoroughly. Place pasta on serving platter, top with shrimp and pour sauce over shrimp and pasta. Garnish with basil. Serve immediately. Serves 3 or 4.

GARLIC BUTTER
    1 cup butter, softened
    1 clove garlic, lightly sautéed and chopped
chopped parsley
dash of Dijon mustard
dash of Worcestershire sauce
salt and black pepper to taste

- Combine butter, garlic, parsley, mustard, Worcestershire sauce, salt and black pepper. Beat until smooth and fluffy.

MONTRACHET, NEW YORK, NEW YORK
DEBRA PONZEK, EXECUTIVE CHEF
"My food is modern French. It's not typically classic but it is based in French technique. I favor bold seasonings and enjoy using lots of herbs in my dishes."

Black Sea Bass with Grilled Vegetables, Provençal Vinaigrette

FISH AND VEGETABLES
3 tomatoes, peeled, seeded and quartered
olive oil
pinch of curry powder
pinch of ground cumin
2 fillets of 2½ pound sea bass, cut in halves
2 baby fennel bulbs, split and cored
2 pieces leek (white only)
salt and black pepper
1 zucchini, cut in ⅛-inch slices
1 yellow squash, cut in ⅛-inch slices

- A day in advance of using, prepare Provençal vinaigrette.
- Place tomatoes on baking sheet. Sprinkle with 2 tablespoons oil, curry and cumin.
- Bake at 300 degrees for about 40 minutes or until tender. Set tomatoes aside.
- Coat fennel and leek lightly with oil. Season with salt and black pepper. Grill briefly to mark, then place in baking pan.
- Bake at 300 degrees for about 15 minutes or until softened.
- Lightly brush zucchini and squash with oil. Season and mark on the grill.
- Season bass with salt and black pepper. Sauté in oil for about 2 minutes on each side or until light golden brown; bass should be rare to medium rare.
- Arrange grilled vegetables and roasted tomatoes on serving plate. Place bass on vegetables and drizzle with vinaigrette. Serves 2.

PROVENÇAL VINAIGRETTE
10 shallots, chopped
10 cloves garlic, chopped
1 cup olive oil, divided
2 large tomatoes, chopped
4 anchovy fillets
1 bunch basil
½ cup red wine vinegar
salt and black pepper to taste

- Sauté shallots and garlic in 2 to 3 tablespoons oil until translucent. Add tomatoes, anchovies, basil and remaining oil. Simmer for 30 minutes.
- Stir vinegar into sauce. Cool, cover and let stand overnight.
- Strain through fine chinois and season with salt and black pepper.

arbara & Frank nd friends and riends and friends...

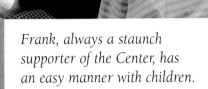

Frank, always a staunch supporter of the Center, has an easy manner with children.

Talented Jaime McEnnan donates his work to Barbara Sinatra for a fund-raising art auction.

A cheerful atmosphere, bright designs, a sense of love and privacy, plus Barbara's natural warmth, create a trusting background. Interiors at the Children's Center are the work of famed designer Hal Broderick and art curator Calvin Vander Woude.

Despite their busy schedules, the couple devotes valuable time to the Center. Barbara oversees planning and meets often with staff and volunteers.

This lucky pup, Wiggles, enjoys a snuggle with his "pop."

The smiling chef at right is Sinatra himself, barbecuing for friends at home.

During a concert tour of South America, Barbara and Frank surprised a young fan with a bicycle.

Ground-breaking ceremony for the Barbara Sinatra Children's Center, December 12, 1985, which was also Frank's 70th birthday. The Sinatras are featured with John Sinn, Eisenhower Medical Center president and Rancho Mirage official Bob Craig.

Frank Sinatra, President Gerald Ford, and Gregory Peck get together at a gala benefiting American Friends of The Hebrew University.

Angela Lansbury joins the "Sinatra: & Years My Way" benefit party in 1995

Frank Sinatra, Diana Ross, Luciano Pavarotti and opera great Frederica von Stade, a quartet of world-class talent, appear at a Memorial Sloane-Kettering Cancer Center gala.

Laurance Rockefeller, Luciano Pavarotti, and Frank Sinatra appear at a benefit for Memorial Sloane-Kettering Cancer Center, New York City.

Frank makes a point with friends Jolene and George Schlatter. Schlatter is an award-winning television producer of "Laugh-In" and many other hits.

al Ed McMahon, announcer straight-man for Johnny son on the long-running e Tonight Show," is a Beverly s friend and neighbor of Sinatras.

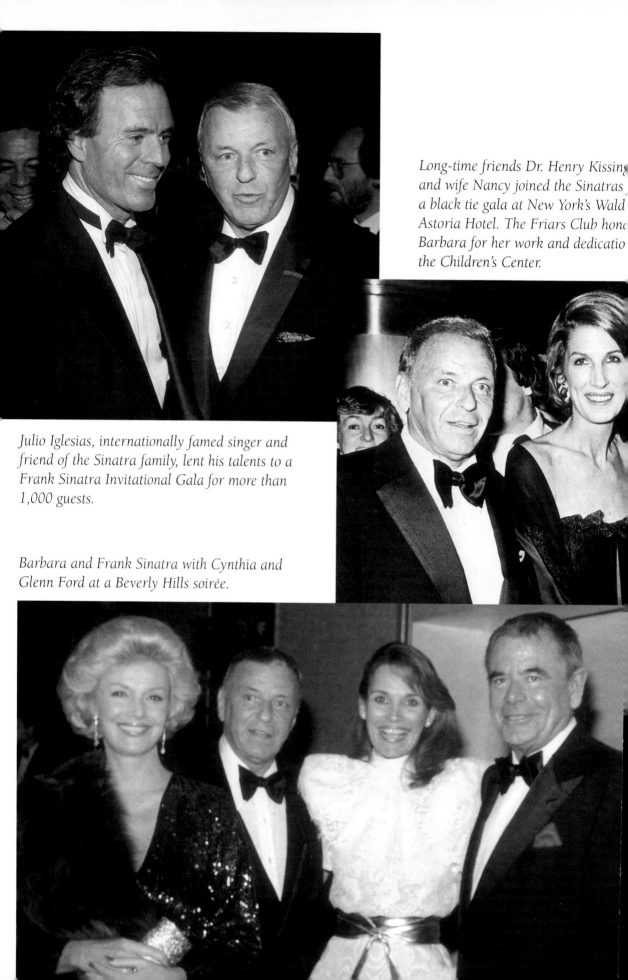

Long-time friends Dr. Henry Kissing
and wife Nancy joined the Sinatras
a black tie gala at New York's Wald
Astoria Hotel. The Friars Club hon
Barbara for her work and dedicatio
the Children's Center.

Julio Iglesias, internationally famed singer and
friend of the Sinatra family, lent his talents to a
Frank Sinatra Invitational Gala for more than
1,000 guests.

Barbara and Frank Sinatra with Cynthia and
Glenn Ford at a Beverly Hills soirée.

Though these two brilliant screen talents never made a film together, Ginger Rogers and Frank Sinatra were great friends.

A life-long model train collector, Frank holds a rare treasure from his collection.

omedian Don Rickles
d Barbra Streisand
lebrate with Frank at
American Friends of
he Hebrew University
ent at Chasen's restau-
nt in Beverly Hills.

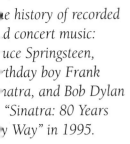

...e history of recorded
...d concert music:
...uce Springsteen,
...rthday boy Frank
...natra, and Bob Dylan
... "Sinatra: 80 Years
...y Way" in 1995.

...otables representing the best and
...ightest in the entertainment
...mmunity, including top artists,
...lt 'n Pepa, joined Ol' Blue Eyes
...r his 80th birthday celebration
... Los Angeles' Shrine Auditorium.

...rank and Barbara receive acco-
...des and applause at "Sinatra:
...0 Years My Way," the birthday
...arty that aired around the world.
...roceeds benefited the Barbara
...natra Children's Center and
...IDS Project Los Angeles.

Barbara and Frank are joined by Sidney and Joanna Poitier at a Barbara Sinatra Children's Center fund-raising event.

Frank reunited Dean Martin and Jerry Lewis on one of Lewis' annual Muscular Dystrophy telethons.

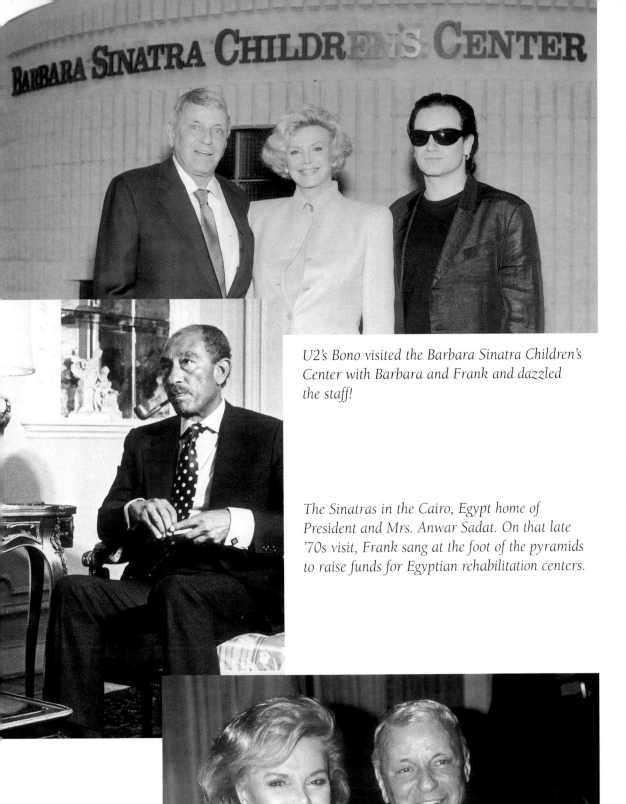

BARBARA SINATRA CHILDREN'S CENTER

U2's Bono visited the Barbara Sinatra Children's Center with Barbara and Frank and dazzled the staff!

The Sinatras in the Cairo, Egypt home of President and Mrs. Anwar Sadat. On that late '70s visit, Frank sang at the foot of the pyramids to raise funds for Egyptian rehabilitation centers.

Sinatras at an 80th day party hosted in New City by Capitol Records. k's tie design is based on f his original paintings.

Barbara and Frank have generated millions of dollars for the Children's Center through the annual Frank Sinatra Celebrity Golf Tournament.

The Sinatras and long-time friend and Children's Center supporter Gregory Peck on a Hebrew University Caravan in Israel.

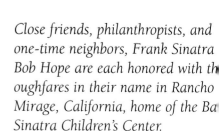

Close friends, philanthropists, and one-time neighbors, Frank Sinatra Bob Hope are each honored with th oughfares in their name in Rancho Mirage, California, home of the Ba Sinatra Children's Center.

Barbara and Frank with radio-TV personality Larry King and U.S. Senator Paula Hawkins, guests at a Barbara Sinatra Children's Center educational forum on child abuse.

y Bennett and Frank
tra are superb performers
great friends. In 1994,
nett headlined the Sinatra
brity Golf Gala.

k Sinatra describes Perry
o as the "sweetest, kindest,
talented of singers, and a
erful friend."

A hug from the heart. Frank referred to Sammy Davis, Jr. as "my real brother."

Johnny Carson helps celebrate Frank's 65th birthday at a western-theme party.

Frank, guest-hosting on "The Tonight Show," shares a laugh with George Burns.

Frank Gifford, Susan and Don Meredith, Esther and Walter Schoenfeld at the Skins Polo Game benefitir the Children's Center.

An afternoon fund-raiser. Randy Russell of the Eldorado Polo Club, California, with Affiliate members Nelda Linsk, Virginia Zamboni, and Barbara Sinatra.

Adlin deCardi and Barbara Sinatra at a holiday party held each December for the Center's clients.

Meats

Greg, age 8

RICHARD CRENNA

Flank Steak Barbecue

¼ **cup soy sauce**
3 **tablespoons honey**
2 **tablespoons vinegar**
1½ **teaspoons garlic powder**
1½ **teaspoons ginger**
¾ **cup olive oil**
1 **green onion, minced**
1 **(1½ pound) flank steak**

- Combine soy sauce, honey and vinegar. Blend in garlic powder and ginger. Add oil and green onion.
- Pour sauce over steak in small pan. Marinate for at least 4 hours or overnight, turning occasionally.
- Drain marinade. Grill steak over glowing coals for about 5 minutes on each side for medium rare or to preferred doneness; do not overcook. Or use oven broiler, broiling about 2 minutes on each side for medium rare.
- Let stand a few minutes before cutting diagonally in thin slices. Serves 4.

NEIL DIAMOND
Recipe is from his mother, Rose.

Gedempte Fleish

Beef Pot Roast

1 **packet onion soup mix**
1 **cup water**
4 **pounds chuck roast, fat trimmed, cut in bite-sized pieces**
1 **teaspoon salt or to taste**
½ **teaspoon black pepper or to taste**
1 **teaspoon minced garlic or to taste**
6 **potatoes, quartered**
1 **green bell pepper, seeded and quartered**
6 **carrots, quartered**
2 **stalks celery, quartered**
ketchup

- Blend soup mix with water in large skillet. Add beef to liquid and season with salt, black pepper and garlic. Simmer, covered, for 1 hour.
- Arrange potatoes, bell pepper, carrots and celery on meat. Lightly sprinkle ketchup on vegetables and meat. Simmer, covered, for 1 to 1½ hours. Serves 10.

EDWARD ASNER

Mediterranean Stew

1	pound chuck steak, cut in 1½-inch cubes
1	pound sweet Italian sausage links
1½	cups burgundy
2	cups water
1	(6 ounce) can tomato paste
¾	teaspoon black pepper
2	teaspoons paprika
3	cloves garlic, minced
1	pound cubed cooked ham
3	medium-sized onions, coarsely chopped
1	red bell pepper, coarsely chopped
¼	cup chopped parsley
2	(16 ounce) cans garbanzo beans, drained
1	teaspoon grated lemon peel
1	head cabbage, cut in 6-8 wedges

- Prepare stew a day in advance of serving.
- Sauté beef cubes and sausage in large skillet until browned. Drain excess fat, slice sausage and place meat in Dutch oven.
- Add wine, water, tomato paste, black pepper, paprika and garlic to meat. Bring to a boil, reduce heat, cover and simmer for 1½ to 2 hours or until steak is tender.
- Stir ham, onion, bell pepper, parsley, beans and lemon into meat and sauce. Cook, covered, for about 20 minutes. Add cabbage and cook for about 15 to 20 minutes or until cabbage is crisp-tender.
- Chill overnight to develop flavors.
- Skim fat from surface and let stand until room temperature. Reheat on stove top for 15 to 20 minutes or in microwave oven at high (100%) setting for 4 to 5 minutes or until hot.
- Serves 6 to 8.

BILL BLASS

Bill Blass Meat Loaf

1 cup chopped celery
1 cup chopped onion
¼ cup butter
2 pounds chopped sirloin
½ pound veal
½ pound pork
1 egg
1 tablespoon Worcestershire sauce
½ cup chopped parsley
⅓ cup sour cream
1½ cups soft bread crumbs
salt and black pepper to taste
pinch of thyme
pinch of marjoram
1 (8 ounce) bottle chili sauce

- Sauté celery and onion in butter until tender. Grind sirloin, veal and pork together. Beat egg and Worcestershire sauce together.
- Combine sautéed vegetables, meat, egg liquid, parsley, sour cream, bread crumbs, salt, black pepper, thyme and marjoram, mixing well.
- Shape mixture into loaf and place in 9x5x3-inch loaf pan or in baking dish. Spread chili sauce on loaf.
- Bake at 350 degrees for 1 hour. Serves 6.

EL TOULA RESTAURANT, ITALY
ARTURO FILIPPINI, OWNER

Medallion Veal of Princess Art

4 (6 to 7 ounce) veal
  medallions
salt and black pepper to taste
3½ tablespoons butter
12 stalks asparagus, tip
  portions, cooked
grated Parmesan cheese

- Lightly pound veal to flatten and shape. Season with salt and black pepper.
- Sauté veal in butter in skillet, turning frequently to cook but avoid coloring. Drain, remove from skillet and keep warm.
- Place asparagus in skillet and warm. Place 3 stalks on each medallion and sprinkle with small amount of cheese. Serves 4.

PAT BOONE

"It was because of this chili I met Clark Gable. At a big Hollywood premiere, I got separated from my wife, Shirley, in the crowd. When I caught up, she was talking to Kay and Clark Gable! Kay was saying, 'I saw your recipe in a magazine. I fixed it for Clark and now he wants it once a week.' Then my wife said ever-so-casually, 'Honey, this is Kay and Clark Gable...'."

Grammy's Chili Mac

1 **(8 ounce) package spaghetti**
2 **medium-sized onions, chopped**
2 **tablespoons vegetable oil**
2 **pounds lean ground beef**
2 **(14½ ounce) cans solid pack tomatoes, undrained**
2 **(8 ounce) cans tomato sauce**
1 **(6 ounce) can tomato paste**
2 **(16 ounce) cans red kidney beans, partially undrained**
chili pepper to taste
chopped green onion, low-fat sour cream or shredded Cheddar cheese for garnish

- Prepare pasta according to package directions. Drain well before using.
- Sauté onion in oil until softened. Add ground beef and cook, stirring to crumble, until browned. Drain excess fat.
- Combine tomatoes, tomato sauce, paste and beans in large pot. Stir in onion and beef mixture and cooked pasta. Season with chili pepper. Simmer for 1 hour.
- Sprinkle individual servings with green onion, dollop of sour cream or cheese.
- Serves 6 to 8.

TOVA AND ERNIE BORGNINE

Pevronatta á la Borgnine

    4 cloves garlic
olive oil
    1 large onion, chopped
   10 green bell peppers, diced
    1 pound sweet Italian sausage, casing
       removed
    1 to 1½ pounds ground sirloin
chopped parsley or parsley flakes to taste
    ½ pound mushrooms, sliced
    1 (16 ounce) jar Italian-seasoned tomato sauce
    1 cup red wine
    1 (16 ounce) package pasta

- Sauté garlic in oil in skillet. Add onion and cook until lightly browned. Stir in bell pepper and cook, turning frequently, until softened.
- In separate skillet, sauté sausage and beef, stirring to crumble, until cooked and no longer red in center. Combine meat mixture with sautéed vegetables.
- Add parsley, mushrooms and tomato sauce to meat mixture. Stir in red wine. Simmer for 20 minutes.
- While sauce is cooking, prepare pasta according to package directions. Drain well. Serve sauce over pasta. Serves 4 to 6.
- Chicken wings or drummettes can be substituted for sausage and beef.

I'm a cook who sings; Ernie is a cook who gets as many requests in the kitchen as I do on stage. I can't wait to eat a medley of his hits. — Frank Sinatra

---

MIKE CONNORS

Belgian Beef Stew

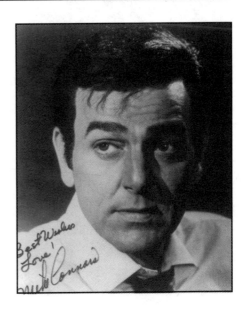

¼ cup unsifted all-purpose flour
1½ teaspoons salt
½ teaspoon black pepper
2 pounds beef chuck, cut in 1-inch cubes
2 pounds onions, sliced
1 clove garlic, crushed
1 cup vegetable oil, divided
1 (12 ounce) can light beer
1 tablespoon soy sauce
1 tablespoon Worcestershire sauce
1 tablespoon steak sauce
2 bay leaves
¼ teaspoon thyme (optional)

- Combine flour, salt and black pepper. Coat beef with seasoned flour and set aside.
- Sauté onion and garlic in ½ cup oil in Dutch oven for 8 to 10 minutes. Remove onion and garlic.
- Pour remaining ½ cup oil in pan. Add beef and brown on all sides.
- Add onion and garlic, beer, soy sauce, steak sauce, Worcestershire sauce, bay leaves and thyme to meat. Bring to a boil, reduce heat and simmer, covered, for 2 hours or until meat is done. Or cook stew by baking at 350 degrees until meat is done. Serves 4 or 5.

MARVIN HAMLISCH
"This is my Mother's recipe — it's my favorite meal."

Chuck Roast

5 large onions, divided
6 cloves garlic
vegetable salt seasoning to taste
black pepper to taste
1 (4 pound or larger) chuck roast
1 (16 ounce) bottle ketchup
red wine
chicken broth

- Chop 3 onions with garlic. Season with vegetable salt and black pepper.
- Make large slit, stuff roast with seasoning, place in small roasting pan and let stand for 3 hours.
- Bake at 325 degrees for 3 hours. Cool, then slice.
- Chop remaining 2 onions and combine with ketchup in saucepan. Simmer for 45 minutes, adding red wine and chicken broth to thin for sauce consistency as needed.
- Place beef slices in sauce and simmer for 20 minutes. Serves 6 to 8.

DOM DE LUISE

"For as long as I can remember, my mother has never worn makeup. Also, she simply combs her hair straight back in a bun. Can you believe that when I was a child, I thought that bun was filled with meatballs? Good old Mom."

Dom's Mom's Meatballs

    2 pounds ground chuck
    ½ pound ground pork
    2 cups Italian-flavored bread crumbs
    4 eggs
    1 cup milk
    1 cup chopped parsley
    ½ cup grated Romano cheese
    1 tablespoon olive oil
    2 cloves garlic, minced
    1 onion, minced
    ½ cup pine nuts (optional)
olive oil
spaghetti sauce

- Combine beef, pork, bread crumbs, eggs, milk, parsley, cheese, oil, garlic, onion and pine nuts, mixing thoroughly. Let stand for 30 minutes.
- Shape mixture into medium-sized meatballs. Sauté in oil, turning to lightly brown on all sides, or place on foil-lined baking sheet and bake at 350 degrees for 30 minutes.
- Carefully add meatballs to spaghetti sauce and simmer for 1 hour.
- Meatballs freeze well. Quadruple recipe, bake meatballs in large baking pan, cool, place 20 each in plastic bags and freeze. Thaw before adding to sauce. Serves 10.

PHIL HARRIS

"These hamburgers are much like the White Castle hamburgers, still served in the South and Midwest."

Phil Harris' New Orleans Hamburgers

    1 pound ground round
    2 large onions, minced
salt and black pepper to taste
    4 hamburger buns

- Sauté onions in skillet prepared with vegetable cooking spray until translucent.
- Shape beef into 4 patties and place on onions. Patties should never touch bottom of pan.
- Steam, covered, until hamburgers are done. Place bun tops on hamburgers, cover again for 1 to 2 minutes, remove hamburger with onions and place on bun bottom.
- Serves 4.

GLENN FORD

"This is a traditional pie served at Christmas by my family in Quebec, Canada, where I was brought up. It is named after the pottery casserole it was originally baked in, the 'tourte'. It is not only a Christmas specialty but also great when served hot on a cold winter day."

Tourtiere

2	pounds lean ground pork
1	pound ground beef
1½	cups water or 1 cup chicken broth plus ½ cup water
3	large potatoes, peeled
1	onion, ground
1½	teaspoons salt
¼	teaspoon black pepper
½	teaspoon cinnamon
2	unbaked 9-inch pastry shells

- Simmer pork and beef with water in large skillet for 45 minutes.
- While meat is cooking, cook potatoes in boiling salted water, drain and mash.
- Add onion, salt, black pepper and cinnamon to meat. Stir in potatoes and let stand until cool.
- Spread meat mixture in 1 pastry shell and cover with second shell, crimping edges to seal. Cut slits in top to vent steam.
- Bake at 400 degrees for 30 minutes. Serves 8.

HENRY KISSINGER

Veal Stew

1	onion, chopped
2	cloves garlic, minced
1	tablespoon olive oil
2	pounds veal stew meat, fat trimmed
all-purpose flour	
salt and black pepper	
1	(14½ ounce) can chicken broth
1	carrot, sliced
1½	teaspoons all-purpose flour
1	teaspoon cayenne pepper
12	pearl onions, parboiled
12	small potatoes
12	small carrots
12	peppercorns, crushed
parsley sprigs	

- Sauté onion and garlic in oil in Dutch oven. Lightly coat veal with flour, add to onion and garlic and sauté until lightly browned on all sides.
- Season veal with salt and black pepper. Add broth and carrots.
- Blend 1½ teaspoons flour with cayenne pepper. Brown seasoned flour in dry skillet, stirring to avoid browning. Add to veal mixture.
- Simmer for about 45 minutes. Add onions, potatoes, carrots and peppercorns and simmer until vegetables are tender and veal is done.
- Garnish with parsley. Serves 4 to 6.

BUDDY HACKETT

Buddy Hackett's Chinese Chili

- 2 pounds ground chuck
- 1 large onion, diced
- 1½ teaspoons salt, divided
- 1 tablespoon chili powder
- 2 tablespoons ground red chili peppers

pinch of oregano

- ½ teaspoon granulated garlic

all-purpose flour

- 1 (14½ ounce) can beef consommé
- 3 cups diagonally sliced celery
- 1 cup sliced onion
- ¼ cup vegetable oil
- 1 cup sliced water chestnuts
- 1 cup sliced bamboo shoots
- 1 cup bean sprouts

- Sauté beef, onion, 1 teaspoon salt, chili powder, ground chili, oregano and garlic, stirring to crumble beef, until well done.
- Stir enough flour into meat mixture to absorb fat. Simmer for 20 minutes.
- Add consommé to meat mixture and simmer, covered, for 2 hours, stirring frequently.
- Stir-fry celery and onion in oil in large skillet or wok until crisp-tender.
- Add water chestnuts, bamboo shoots, bean sprouts and remaining ½ teaspoon salt. Cook for 5 minutes.
- Drain excess liquid from vegetables. Add meat mixture and mix thoroughly. Serves 6 to 8.

SUZANNE SOMERS

Medallions of Lamb with Cumin

- 12 to 15 shallots, chopped
- 2 tablespoons butter
- 2 tablespoons olive oil
- 4 cloves garlic, chopped
- 6 fresh or canned tomatoes, chopped
- 1 bunch basil, chopped

salt and black pepper to taste

- 2 racks of lamb (boned and fat trimmed)
- ¼ cup ground cumin

olive oil

- 4 to 6 basil leaves for garnish

- Sauté shallots in butter and oil until golden. Stir in garlic, tomatoes, basil, salt and pepper. Sauté for 5 minutes to evaporate most of liquid. If tomatoes are very acidic, add a pinch or two of sugar to balance.
- Cut lamb in 1-inch medallions. Coat well in cumin.
- Sauté lamb in oil for 1 minute on each side; meat will be pink.
- Spoon portion of tomato sauce in center of each serving plate, top with 2 medallions and garnish with basil.
- Serves 4 to 6.

JACK HALEY, JR.

Boston Shepherd's Pie

2 pounds ground sirloin
1 medium-sized onion, chopped
½ cup butter, divided
¼ cup Worcestershire sauce, divided
½ cup sherry, divided (optional)
1 cup beef broth
¼ cup all-purpose flour
6 medium potatoes
1 cup peas
1 cup chopped carrots
1 cup chopped green beans
salt and black pepper

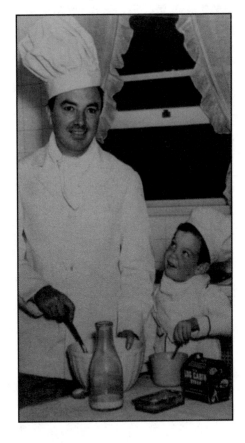

- Cook potatoes in boiling salted water until tender. Drain well and mash.
- While potatoes are cooking, sauté beef, onion and 2 tablespoons Worcestershire sauce in ¼ cup butter in skillet, stirring to crumble, until browned. Remove beef mixture from skillet, stir in ¼ cup sherry and set aside.
- Skim fat from pan drippings. Add broth, butter, flour, remaining 2 tablespoons Worcestershire sauce and sherry. Cook over very low heat, stirring often, until thickened. Set aside.
- While gravy is cooking, parboil or steam vegetables. Drain well and season with salt and black pepper.
- Arrange vegetables into 2-quart casserole. Layer beef mixture on vegetables, spread gravy on beef and cover completely with potatoes, swirling to form peaks. Sprinkle generously with paprika.
- Bake at 375 degrees for 45 minutes or until potatoes are well browned. Serves 6.

KIM HUNTER

"It's really better to make the dish early and reheat, allowing the flavors time to blend. To reheat, put the stew pot over a pan of boiling water and take care not to mush up the macaroni by overstirring."

Mexican Stew

1 large Spanish onion, minced
1 large clove garlic, minced
1 medium-sized green bell pepper, finely chopped
1½ tablespoons butter
1½ tablespoons vegetable oil
1½ pounds lean ground beef
1 (28 ounce) can Italian plum tomatoes in purée, crushed
salt and freshly ground black pepper to taste
1 teaspoon chili powder
½ teaspoon basil
½ teaspoon oregano
1 (8 ounce) package elbow macaroni
freshly grated Parmesan cheese
1 tablespoon chopped fresh parsley

- Sauté onion, garlic and bell pepper in butter and oil in large skillet for about 15 minutes or until onion is golden brown.
- Add beef to onion mixture and cook over medium heat, stirring to crumble, until lightly browned.
- Stir tomatoes, salt, black pepper, chili powder, basil, oregano and parsley to beef mixture and mix well. Simmer, covered, for 30 minutes. Check seasoning.
- While meat mixture is cooking, prepare macaroni according to package directions. Drain well and return to pot.
- Pour meat mixture into macaroni and stir gently with wooden spoon to blend.
- Serve with grated Parmesan cheese. Serves 4.

MITCHELL LAURANCE AND EWA MATAYA

Swedish Meatballs

⅓ **cup bread crumbs**
¾ **cup milk**
1 **pound ground beef**
1 **teaspoon salt**
¼ **teaspoon white or black pepper**
1 **to 2 tablespoons minced onion**
1 **egg (optional)**
1½ **tablespoons butter or margarine**
water
1½ **teaspoons soy sauce**
2 **tablespoons all-purpose flour**
whipping cream

- Combine bread crumbs and milk. Let stand for at least 10 minutes.
- Mix beef with salt, white or black pepper and onion. Add bread with liquid and egg and mix thoroughly.
- Shape or roll meat into small to medium balls, rinsing hands occasionally to avoid sticking.
- Sauté meatballs, several at a time, in butter or margarine in skillet, shaking pan to turn to brown on all sides. Reduce heat and fry, uncovered, for 3 to 5 minutes. Remove meatballs and set aside. Rinse skillet with ¼ to ½ cup water after frying each group of meatballs and reserve water.
- When all meatballs are browned, return 1¼ cups water to skillet. Blend flour with ¼ cup water and add to other liquid with soy sauce. Cook for 3 to 5 minutes, stirring constantly.
- Add small amount of cream to liquid.
- Serve meatballs separately or in sauce. Serves 4 to 6.

JOHNNY MANN

Sharon Hickey's Award Winning Meat Loaf

1½ pounds ground chuck
⅔ cup evaporated milk
1 egg
½ cup chopped green bell pepper
½ cup finely crushed saltine cracker crumbs
¼ cup grated onion
1½ teaspoons salt
¼ teaspoon black pepper
1 teaspoon dry mustard
3 bacon slices, cut in halves

- Combine beef, milk, egg, bell pepper, cracker crumbs, onion, salt, black pepper and mustard, mixing until smooth.
- Shape mixture into oblong loaf and place in baking pan. Arrange bacon on top of loaf.
- Bake at 350 degrees for 1 hour. Let stand for 10 minutes before slicing. Serves 6.

HUGH O'BRIAN

Hugh O'Brian's Wyatt Earp Stew

1 (16 ounce) can corn, undrained
2 (15 ounce) cans beef stew
2 (10¾ ounce) cans cream of mushroom soup, diluted
2 (10¾ ounce) cans chicken noodle soup, diluted
2 (10½ ounce) cans consommé
1 (6 ounce) can black olives, drained and sliced
6 large carrots, cut in 1-inch chunks
2 onions, coarsely chopped
3 tomatoes, chopped
3 large potatoes, peeled and cut in chunks
water
1 cup whiskey

- Combine corn, stew, mushroom soup, chicken noodle soup, consommé, olives, carrots, onions, tomatoes and potatoes in stock pot.
- Bring to a boil, reduce heat and simmer, covered, until carrots and potatoes are tender.
- Stir whiskey into stew after it is cooked.
- Serves 6 to 8.
- For variation, eliminate potatoes and serve stew over rice or noodles.

ANTHONY NEWLEY

Shepherd's Pie

  4 **large potatoes, peeled and cubed**
  1 **cup milk, heated**
  2 **tablespoons butter, melted**
  ¼ **cup whipping cream**
pinch of black pepper
pinch of nutmeg
  1 **large onion, minced**
  2 **tablespoons olive oil**
  1 **pound ground beef**
salt and black pepper to taste
  ¼ **teaspoon oregano**
  ¼ **teaspoon rosemary**
  ¼ **teaspoon thyme**
water
  2 **beef bouillon cubes (optional)**
  1 **tablespoon cornstarch (optional)**

- Cook potatoes in boiling salted water until tender.
- While potatoes are cooking, sauté onion in oil until softened. Add beef, salt, black pepper, oregano, rosemary and thyme, mixing well.
- Place meat mixture in saucepan. Add water to cover and bouillon cubes. Cook until beef is tender, stirring to avoid sticking. To thicken, dissolve cornstarch in 2 tablespoons water and add during cooking time. Spoon meat mixture into broiler-proof casserole.
- Drain potatoes well. Mash until smooth. Add milk, butter, cream, black pepper and nutmeg, beating thoroughly.
- Spread potatoes on meat. Broil until browned; avoid burning. Serves 4 to 6.

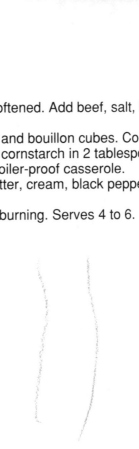

ARNOLD PALMER

Hawaiian Meatballs with Sweet and Sour Sauce

MEATBALLS
1½ **pounds ground beef**
⅔ **cup cracker crumbs**
½ **cup chopped onion**
⅔ **cup evaporated milk**
1 **teaspoon seasoned salt**
⅓ **cup flour**
3 **tablespoons shortening**

- Prepare sweet and sour sauce.
- While sauce is cooking, combine beef, cracker crumbs, onion, milk and seasoned salt, mixing lightly but thoroughly.
- Shape mixture into 30 balls. Roll in flour and sauté in shortening in skillet, turning to brown on all sides. Drain excess fat.
- Pour sauce over meatballs. Simmer, covered, for 15 minutes. Serves 6.

SWEET AND SOUR SAUCE
1 **(13½ ounce) can pineapple chunks**
water
2 **tablespoons cornstarch**
½ **cup vinegar**
½ **cup firmly-packed brown sugar**
2 **tablespoons soy sauce**
2 **tablespoons lemon juice**
1 **cup coarsely chopped green bell pepper**
1 **tablespoon chopped pimento**

- Drain pineapple, reserving chunks and pouring syrup into measuring cup. Add water to make 1 cup liquid.
- Blend pineapple liquid and cornstarch in saucepan until smooth. Stir in vinegar, brown sugar, soy sauce and lemon juice. Cook until thickened and clear.
- Add pineapple, bell pepper and pimento to sauce. Simmer, covered, for 15 minutes.

BURT REYNOLDS

Burt's Beef Stew

3 slices bacon, diced
¼ cup all-purpose flour
¼ teaspoon black pepper
2 pounds lean chuck, cut in chunks
1 large onion, chopped
2 cloves garlic, minced
1 (28 ounce) can tomato sauce
1 cup beef broth
1 cup dry red wine
1 bay leaf (optional)
pinch of thyme
4 carrots, coarsely chopped
2 stalks celery, coarsely chopped
4 large potatoes, peeled and quartered
10 to 12 mushrooms, sliced

- Fry bacon in large pot or Dutch oven until lightly browned.
- Combine flour and black pepper. Thoroughly coat beef with seasoned flour.
- Brown beef in bacon drippings, turning often. Add onion and garlic to beef. Cook until lightly browned. Skim and discard excess fat.
- Stir tomato sauce, broth, wine, bay leaf and thyme into beef mixture. Simmer, covered, for about 1½ hours.
- Add carrots, celery, potatoes and mushrooms to beef mixture. Simmer, covered, for about 30 minutes or until vegetables are tender. Serves 6.

DINAH SHORE

"This is a Ukranian specialty. It's cold a lot of the time there. Perhaps that is one of the reasons they have large families and even in a medium-sized family they have large appetites. However, for smaller families and eaters, freeze half of the patties before coating. Wrap separately in aluminum foil or freezer paper with directions on top for coating, cooking and serving."

Russian Meat Cakes

½ **cup minced onion**
2 **tablespoons butter**
⅔ **cup regular oats**
⅔ **cup milk**
1 **pound twice-ground beef**
1 **pound twice-ground pork**
2 **eggs, lightly beaten**
2 **teaspoons salt**
½ **teaspoon black pepper**
1 **teaspoon basil**
1 **teaspoon thyme**
3⅓ **tablespoons chilled butter**
2 **cups sour cream**
1 **cup fresh bread crumbs**
⅓ **to ½ cup clarified butter**
snipped dill for garnish

- Sauté onions in butter until softened.
- Soak oats in milk for 5 minutes.
- Combine beef and pork. Blend in eggs, oats with liquid, onions, salt, black pepper, basil and thyme, mixing well.
- Divide mixture in 10 portions and flatten each to ½-inch thick patty. Press 1 teaspoon butter in center of each, wrap meat around butter to enclose and flatten to ½-inch thickness.
- Thinly coat each patty with about 1 teaspoon sour cream and roll in bread crumbs.
- Sauté patties in clarified butter in large skillet for about 4 minutes on each side or until golden brown. Top each with 2 tablespoons sour cream and cook, covered, for 5 minutes.
- Garnish patties with dill and place on warmed serving platter. Potatoes are good accompaniment. Serves 8 to 10.

I met Dinah many years before I was introduced to Frank. Dinah was a fabulous cook and had sensational parties. She told a great story, played a mean game of tennis, and was an avid gin rummy player – and a great friend. — Barbara Sinatra

SINATRA'S KITCHEN

Barbara Ann's Meatballs

  2 (8 ounce) containers seasoned bread crumbs
  1 cup (4 ounces) grated Parmesan cheese
  2 large onions, chopped
  1 cup chopped parsley
  1 tablespoon salt
1½ teaspoons black pepper
red pepper to taste
  6 pounds ground sirloin
1½ pounds ground pork or veal
  8 eggs
milk
vegetable oil
 10 to 12 cups marinara sauce
  1 (48 ounce) package pasta

- Combine bread crumbs, cheese, onion, parsley, salt, black pepper and red pepper.
- Add dry ingredients to beef and pork or veal and eggs, mixing well. Gradually add milk until consistency is soft but firm enough to form balls.
- Shape meat mixture into balls. Sauté in oil until lightly browned.
- Drop meatballs into marinara sauce and simmer for about 30 minutes. While meatballs are cooking, prepare pasta according to package directions.
- Serve meatballs and sauce over pasta. Serves 16 to 18.

HARRIS AND IRENA KATLEMAN

Russian Leg of Lamb

- 1 (5 to 6 pound) leg of lamb, fell and excess fat removed
- 2 tablespoons lemon juice
- 1 to 2 tablespoons olive oil
- ½ teaspoon salt
- ½ teaspoon freshly ground black pepper
- 2 cloves garlic, sliced
- 6 to 8 sprigs fresh rosemary

- Blot lamb with paper towel to dry. Rub with lemon juice, then olive oil, and season with salt and black pepper.
- Using knife tip, cut slits in lamb and insert garlic slices and rosemary sprigs.
- Place lamb on oiled rack in roasting pan. Insert meat thermometer in thickest part of leg, avoiding bone.
- Bake at 350 degrees for 1½ to 1¾ hours or until thermometer registers 130 to 135 degrees for pink, medium rare lamb. Remove and let stand for 10 minutes.
- Discard garlic and rosemary. Cut lamb into slices. Serves 10 to 12.

THE HONORABLE TOM HARKIN

Stuffed Iowa Chops

- ½ cup corn
- ½ cup bread crumbs
- salt and black pepper to taste
- 2½ teaspoons parsley flakes
- pinch of sage
- 1½ teaspoons minced onion
- ½ cup diced apple
- 1 tablespoon milk
- 2 thick pork chops
- ¼ cup honey
- ¼ cup mustard
- ¼ teaspoon rosemary leaves
- ½ teaspoon salt
- pinch of black pepper

- Combine corn, bread crumbs, salt, black pepper, parsley, sage, onion, apple and milk, mixing well.
- Cut slit in side of each chop. Spoon stuffing into slit. Brown chops on each side and place in small baking pan.
- Blend honey, mustard, rosemary, ½ teaspoon salt and pinch of black pepper.
- Basting chops often with sauce, bake at 350 degrees for about 1 hour. Serves 2.

SHIRLEY MACLAINE

Gourmet Lamb Stew

- 1 (5 to 6 pound) leg of lamb, fell and bone removed and excess fat trimmed
- 1 tablespoon lard or vegetable shortening
- 2 tablespoons all-purpose flour
- 1 clove garlic, minced
- 3 cups water
- 2 tablespoons tomato paste
- ¼ teaspoon bouquet garni
- 1 teaspoon salt
- ⅛ teaspoon freshly ground black pepper
- 10 sugar cubes
- 1 tablespoon water
- 1 teaspoon beef extract
- 1 small yellow onion, chopped
- 8 to 10 pearl onions, peeled
- 2 small yellow turnips, coarsely diced
- 2 small carrots, chopped
- 3 tablespoons sweet butter
- 1 teaspoon sugar
- 1 tablespoon chopped parsley

- Cut lamb in 1½-inch cubes. Sauté lamb in lard or shortening in large skillet, turning until golden on all sides.
- Sprinkle flour over meat and cook, stirring constantly, for a few minutes.
- Add garlic and cook over very low heat until garlic gives off aroma.
- Pour up to 3 cups water into skillet, just covering meat. Blend in tomato paste, bouquet garni, salt and black pepper. Simmer, covered, for 15 minutes.
- While meat is cooking, combine sugar cubes and 1 tablespoon water in small saucepan. Cook over low heat until sugar caramelizes. Add with meat extract to meat and mix well. Simmer, covered, for 45 minutes, stirring occasionally.
- Cook onion, pearl onions, turnips and carrots in butter in large skillet, sprinkling with 1 teaspoon sugar. Simmer until golden, stirring occasionally.
- Add vegetables to meat and simmer, covered, for 50 minutes or until vegetables and meat are fork-tender, stirring often.
- Remove vegetables and meat to heated platter. Skim fat from surface before pouring sauce over meat. Garnish with chopped parsley. Serves 6 to 8.

BETSY BLOOMINGDALE

"Pork is a great favorite today because it is so lean. I admire this simple but delicious recipe and the hostess who introduced me to it."

Sautéed Medallions of Pork

8 (3 ounce) slices boneless pork loin, fat trimmed
salt and freshly ground black pepper to taste
2 teaspoons ground cumin
1 teaspoon paprika
2 tablespoons olive oil
½ cup minced onion
1 teaspoon minced garlic
¼ cup port
1 tablespoon red wine vinegar
¼ cup water or chicken broth
2 tablespoons butter
2 tablespoons coarsely chopped coriander

- Season pork slices with salt, black pepper, cumin and paprika.
- Sauté pork in single layer in oil in non-stick skillet over medium high heat for about 5 minutes or until browned, turn and sauté for about 5 minutes. Reduce heat and cook for about 2 minutes, turning slices occasionally. Transfer pork to serving dish.
- Discard most of fat from skillet. Sauté onion and garlic until onion is softened and lightly browned.
- Add port, vinegar and water to onion and garlic. Stir to dislodge browned bits from skillet and cook until ingredients reduce to about ⅓ cup. Blend in butter.
- Spoon sauce over pork and sprinkle with coriander. Serve immediately. Serves 4.

**CUISTOT RESTAURANT,
PALM DESERT, CALIFORNIA
BERNARD DERVIEUX,
OWNER AND EXECUTIVE CHEF**

Veal Chop with Wild Mushrooms

CHOPS
 4 **veal chops**
salt and black pepper to taste
 ½ **cup butter, divided**
 1 **shallot, chopped**
 ½ **pound shitake mushrooms**
 ½ **cup dry white wine**

- A day in advance, prepare veal stock.
- Season chops with salt and black pepper. Sauté chops in 1 tablespoon butter in large skillet until lightly browned on both sides. Place in single layer in baking dish.
- Bake at 450 degrees for 8 minutes.
- While chops are baking, prepare sauce in same pan in which chops were browned. Sauté shallots and mushrooms. Add wine and cook to reduce liquid by ⅔. Stir in 2 cups veal stock and cook to reduce by ½. Add remaining butter and season with salt and black pepper.
- Place veal chops on 4 dinner plates. Pour sauce over chops and garnish with sautéed vegetables. Serves 4.

VEAL STOCK
 5 **pounds veal bones**
 2 **carrots, sliced**
 2 **onions, sliced**
 2 **cups chopped celery**
 ¼ **cup butter**
 8 **quarts water**
 2 **tablespoons black peppercorns**
 1 **sprig thyme**
 3 **bay leaves**
 5 **Roma tomatoes**

- Place bones in baking pan. Bake at 450 degrees for about 1 hour or until browned.
- Sauté carrots, onion and celery in butter in large skillet until softened.
- Combine bones, sautéed vegetables, water, peppercorns, thyme, bay leaves and tomatoes in stock pot. Simmer for 10 to 12 hours, adding water to replace loss by evaporation. Skim and discard fat. Pour stock through medium strainer, discard bones and vegetables and reserve stock.

HUBERT DE GIVENCHY

Pork Tenderloin Basted with Chinese Sauce

½ **cup soy sauce**
½ **cup ketchup**
¼ **cup honey**
3 **cloves garlic, minced**
pork tenderloin
1 **teaspoon dry mustard**
sesame seeds to taste

- Combine soy sauce, ketchup, honey and garlic.
- Brush sauce on pork before and occasionally during roasting period.
- Bake pork at 325 degrees until meat thermometer registers 170 degrees. Let stand for 20 minutes before carving.
- Add mustard and sesame seeds to remaining sauce and serve with sliced pork.
- Serves 8 to 10.

ARTE JOHNSON

Ouiseau de Veau

6 **large slices leg veal**
1 **cup chopped parsley**
½ **cup chopped ham**
¼ **cup raisins**
¼ **cup (1 ounce) grated Parmesan or Romano cheese**
salt and black pepper
½ **cup pine nuts**
3 **tablespoons olive oil**
½ **cup Marsala wine**
4 **to 6 cups cooked kasha (buckwheat groats) or buttered rice**

- Pound veal slices until thin and set aside.
- Combine parsley, ham, raisins and cheese. Season with salt and black pepper and add pine nuts.
- Divide filling among veal slices, roll up and secure with string or wooden skewers.
- Slowly sauté veal rolls in single layer in oil in large skillet, turning to brown on all sides. Add wine and simmer, covered, for about 25 minutes.
- Serve on kasha or rice. Serves 6.

RUTH BUZZI

"I happen to love beans. If time permits, I cook lentils with onions and brown rice every other week for a healthy snack, or to add to my homemade soup that needs more body. But as a youngster, my favorite sandwich was one my Mom made with B&B baked beans on buttered bread. Joy! Joy!"

Salsicce Fagioli in Unido

Sausage and Beans in Tomato Sauce

1½ **cups dried white kidney beans or other white beans**
cold water
2 **cloves garlic, chopped**
1 **tablespoon olive oil**
1 **(28 ounce) can Italian style tomatoes, crushed**
salt and black pepper to taste
1½ **pounds sweet Italian sausage**
2 **tablespoons chopped parsley**

- Place beans in bowl and add cold water to generously cover. Soak overnight.
- Sauté garlic in oil in saucepan until softened. Press tomatoes through sieve to remove seeds and add pulp to garlic. Simmer for 15 to 20 minutes. Season with salt and black pepper.
- Drain beans, rinse under cold running water, drain and place in saucepan. Add salted water to cover.
- Bring beans and water to a boil, reduce heat and simmer, covered, for 40 to 50 minutes or until tender but firm.
- While beans are cooking, wash sausages and puncture casing with fork tines. Place in large skillet with 1 to 2 cups water.
- Bring water with sausages to a boil and cook over medium heat for 10 to 15 minutes, turning sausages. Water should evaporate by end of cooking time.
- Pour 2 cups tomato sauce into skillet, season with salt and black pepper and add cooked beans. Simmer, uncovered, for 5 minutes. Stir in parsley and cook for 5 minutes.
- Serves 4 to 6.

KIRK DOUGLAS

Veal Oscar

  1 **(3½ pound) veal tenderloin, cut in serving pieces**
 ¼ **cup plus 3 tablespoons all-purpose flour, divided**
 ¾ **teaspoon salt**
 ¾ **teaspoon black pepper**
 ¾ **pound or more fresh shelled crab legs**
  2 **eggs, beaten**
 ½ **cup bread crumbs**
 ½ **cup butter, divided**
  1 **cup Sautérne wine**
 12 **large mushrooms**
  2 **tablespoons minced shallots**
  2 **cups Hollandaise sauce**

• Pound veal pieces to flatten. Combine ¼ cup flour, salt and black pepper. Lightly coat veal with seasoned flour and set aside.
• Dredge crab legs in remaining 3 tablespoons flour, dip in eggs, roll in bread crumbs and set aside.
• Brown veal in ¼ cup butter in large skillet on both sides until golden brown. Place on hot platter. Heat wine, pour over veal and keep warm.
• In clean skillet, fry crab legs in remaining ¼ cup butter for 5 to 6 minutes or until browned. Sauté mushrooms and shallots until softened.
• Spoon Hollandaise sauce over veal, add crab meat and top with mushrooms and shallots.
• Serves 6 to 8.

LENA HORNE

Veal Chops Flamenco

6 veal loin chops
all-purpose flour
 ¼ cup vegetable oil
 1 (10½ ounce) can beef consommé
 1 tablespoon Worcestershire sauce
 2 tablespoons grated lemon peel
 ½ cup black olives, pitted
 ½ cup chopped green bell pepper
 ½ cup chopped pimento
 2 tablespoons capers
orange slices for garnish
 4 to 6 cups hot cooked rice

- Coat chops with flour, shaking to remove excess. Brown chops in single layer in oil in large skillet. Drain excess oil.
- Add consommé, Worcestershire sauce, lemon peel. olives, bell pepper, pimento and capers.
- Simmer, covered, for 40 to 45 minutes or until tender, turning chops occasionally.
- Garnish servings with oranges and serve over rice. Serves 6.

**DOROS RESTAURANT,
SAN FRANCISCO, CALIFORNIA
PAOLO BERMANI, EXECUTIVE CHEF**

Veal Scallopini á la Doros

 18 thin slices veal loin
salt and black pepper
all-purpose flour
 1½ cups plus 3 tablespoons
   butter, divided
 1½ tablespoons minced shallots
 ⅓ cup dry Sautérne wine
 ¾ cup brown sauce
 1½ pounds mushrooms, sliced
 18 slices eggplant

- Pound veal slices to thin cutlets, season with salt and black pepper and lightly coat with flour.
- Melt 1½ cups butter in large skillet and heat to bubbling. Brown veal in butter on both sides.
- Remove excess butter from skillet. Add shallots and wine and simmer for 3 minutes. Stir in brown sauce.
- In separate skillets, sauté mushrooms and eggplant until softened.
- Place mushrooms on serving platter. Arrange alternate slices of veal and eggplant on mushrooms.
- Stir remaining 3 tablespoons butter into veal skillet juices. Pour sauce over veal and eggplant. Serve immediately. Serves 6.

PRESIDENT AND MRS. RONALD REAGAN

Piccata of Veal

12 **thin slices veal, trimmed**
salt and white pepper
½ **cup all-purpose flour**
2 **eggs, beaten**
1 **tablespoon chopped parsley**
½ **cup vegetable oil**
¼ **cup (1 ounce) grated Romano cheese**
   (optional)

- Season veal on both sides with salt and white pepper. Lightly dip veal pieces in flour to coat on both sides.
- Blend egg and parsley. Dip veal in egg, turning to moisten on both sides. Sauté in oil in large non-stick skillet or iron skillet until golden brown on both sides. Place on serving platter and top with cheese, if desired. Serves 6.

LOUIS JOURDAN

Veal Stew á la Marseillaise

2 **pounds veal, cut in 12 to 16 pieces**
½ **cup corn oil, divided**
2 **medium-sized onions, chopped**
1 **clove garlic, crushed**
salt and black pepper to taste
12 **slices Polish kielbasa sausage**
1 **(10½ ounce) can consommé**
½ **can water**
12 **medium mushrooms, cut in halves**
finely chopped parsley
8 **medium potatoes, cooked, tossed with parsley, or 3 cups pasta, rice or polenta**

- Sauté veal in 6 tablespoons oil in cast iron pot, stirring with wooden spoon, until browned on all sides. Add onion and fry until veal and onion are darkly browned. Add garlic and season with salt and black pepper. Reduce heat but do not cover.
- In separate pan, fry sausage in 1 tablespoon oil, until browned on all sides. Remove excess oil and add sausage to veal mixture. Cook over medium heat until meat is darkly browned.
- Pour consommé and water into stew.
- Bake, covered, at 350 degrees for 1¼ hours.
- Just before serving, sauté mushrooms in 1 tablespoon oil in skillet over high heat for 3 to 4 minutes until browned. Remove stew from oven, place over low heat on stove top, stir in mushrooms and cook for 1 minute; mushrooms should remain firm.
- Sprinkle stew with parsley. Stew should be dark brown with liquid consistency of gravy.
- Serve with potatoes, pasta, rice or polenta. Serves 4.

**THE HONORABLE AND MRS.
JOHN D. ROCKEFELLER IV**

Scallopini of Veal Avocado

12 small veal scallops
 2 tablespoons all-purpose flour
fresh lemon juice
 ¼ cup butter, divided
drop of vegetable oil
salt and black pepper to taste
 1 large ripe firm avocado
 ¼ cup sherry, Madeira or Marsala wine
 ½ cup beef broth
chopped chives or parsley for garnish

- Pound veal scallops until thin. Lightly rub each piece with flour.
- Cut avocado in half lengthwise, peel and remove seed. Cut halves lengthwise in thin slices and moisten with lemon juice to prevent discoloration.
- Sauté veal in 3 tablespoons butter plus drop of oil in heavy skillet over medium heat until golden brown. Season with salt and black pepper. Place on platter and keep warm.
- Pour wine, broth and remaining 1 tablespoon butter in same skillet. Carefully place avocado in skillet and cook for 5 minutes over low heat.
- Collect juices from scallop platter, add to liquid in skillet and shake gently to mix with avocado and sauce.
- Place avocado slices on scallops, pour sauce on avocado and garnish with chives or parsley. Serves 6 to 8.

**DRIMCONG HOUSE, GALWAY, IRELAND
GERRY GALVIN, PROPRIETER AND EXECUTIVE CHEF**

Grilled Loin of Lamb in a Salad

 2 cups sunflower oil
 ½ to ⅔ cup combination of
    chopped rosemary, mint,
    lemon balm, chives and
    parsley
 2 cloves garlic, crushed
salt and black pepper
 4 boned loins of lamb, fat
    trimmed
salads of seasonal greens
salad dressing of choice

- Blend oil, herb mixture, garlic, salt and black pepper.
- Cut each loin in 5 small steaks. Marinate lamb in herbed oil for 30 minutes.
- Prepare 4 individual salads from seasonal greens and fresh vegetables of choice.
- Grill lamb for 1 minute on each side for rear meat.
- Arrange steak pieces on each salad and drizzle with small amount of lamb gravy.
- Serves 4.

ENZO STUARTI

Arista di Maile Alla Toscana
Roast Pork

1 **(5 pound) rib or loin roast of pork**
3 **cloves garlic, cut in halves**
8 **sprigs rosemary or 1 tablespoon dried rosemary**
virgin olive oil
salt and freshly ground black pepper
1 **cup dry white wine**
1 **cup beef or veal broth**

- Cut small slits in pork roast. Insert garlic pieces and rosemary sprigs in slits. Rub roast with oil and season generously with salt and black pepper. If using dried rosemary, rub rosemary on roast.
- Place roast, fat side up, in shallow roasting pan.
- Bake at 450 degrees for 30 minutes, reduce heat to 325 degrees and bake for 30 minutes to the pound or until juices run clear, with no trace of pink when pierced with fork.
- After first hour of baking, add wine to pan liquid and baste at 15 to 20 minute intervals. Steam from liquid will render much of fat in pork.
- Place pork on hot serving platter and keep warm.
- Reduce liquid in pan by cooking over high heat, boiling away liquid and leaving only fat; avoid burning drippings in pan. Pour off fat, add broth and deglaze over medium high heat by scraping sides and bottom of pan with wooden spoon and cooking to reduce liquid by ¼.
- Cut pork into slices on platter and spoon sauce over slices. Serves 6.

Vegetables & Side Dishes

James, age 7

RESTAURANT LE LOUIS XV, HOTEL DE PARIS, MONTE CARLO, MONACO
ALAIN DUCASSE

Provençal Garden Vegetables with Truffle

16 baby carrots, trimmed
16 very small turnips, trimmed
2 very small fennel, trimmed
8 radishes, trimmed
¼ cup plus 2 tablespoons butter
olive oil
rich chicken stock
white beef stock
8 small artichokes
light lemon stock
8 stalks asparagus
boiling water
8 scallions, trimmed
1 pound small green peas
1 pound fresh fava beans
½ pound tiny French green beans
1 ounce truffle, chopped
salt and white pepper to taste
butter
aged vinegar
coarse sea salt

- In 4 separate sauté pans, gently cook carrots, turnips, fennel and radish in butter and olive oil over medium heat. Add blend of chicken stock and beef stock to each pan and cook to reduce liquid to glossy glaze as vegetables finish cooking. Cool quickly and set aside.
- Cut artichokes in bite-sized wedges and cook in very light lemon stock.
- Using tips only, cook asparagus in boiling salted water and plunge in ice water. Cook peas, fava beans and green beans in same manner.
- Divide all vegetables between 2 large sauté pans. Add beef stock, oil and truffle. Season with salt and white pepper. Add small amount of butter and drizzle of vinegar.
- Place vegetables in 4 soup bowls. Spoon pan liquid over vegetables and sprinkle each lightly with sea salt. Serves 4.

STEVE GARVEY
"Once a week, I step up to the plate with my wife Candace and we cook together. Here is my favorite All-Star recipe that is sure to be a hit with any man."

All-Star Corn and Rice Sauté

2 tablespoons unsalted butter
2 tablespoons olive oil
1 tablespoon minced garlic
6 medium ears fresh white sweet corn or 3 cups canned corn, drained, or 3 cups frozen corn, thawed
2 cups cooked wild rice
3 tablespoons minced sundried tomatoes in olive oil, well drained
⅓ cup minced basil
salt and black pepper to taste
fresh basil sprigs for garnish

- Melt butter with oil in skillet over medium-high heat. Add garlic and sauté for 30 seconds.
- Add corn, rice and tomatoes to garlic. Sauté for 4 to 8 minutes or until corn is cooked.
- Season with minced basil, salt and black pepper.
- Garnish with basil sprigs. Serve warm or cold. Serves 4 to 6.

PHIL HARRIS

Phil's Favorite Mushrooms

¼ cup plus 2 tablespoons butter
2 or 3 cloves garlic, chopped
1 pound mushrooms
¼ cup Marsala wine
¼ cup oyster sauce

- Sauté garlic in butter in skillet until softened but not browned. Add mushrooms (whole for side dish or sliced for sauce) and sauté for about 4 minutes.
- Stir wine and oyster sauce into mushroom mixture. Simmer until bubbly.
- Serve with steak.
- Serves 6.

EYDIE GORME AND STEVE LAWRENCE
Recipe by Eydie Gorme from her cookbook "Easy Gorme," based on her mother's recipe for "Fasoulia."

String Beans and Olive Oil

1 pound fresh or frozen string beans
2 tablespoons olive oil
salt and black pepper to taste
lemon juice
lemon wedges (optional)
cooked potatoes, cut in chunks
extra virgin olive oil
grated Romano or Parmesan cheese

- Boil or steam beans for 6 minutes. Drain well and scatter on baking sheet to dry.
- Place beans, olive oil, salt, black pepper and small amount of lemon juice in large skillet. Heat quickly and shake while cooking.
- Pour beans into warmed serving bowl and garnish with lemon wedges.
- For variation, allow beans to cool. Toss with potatoes, small amount of oil and lemon juice. Sprinkle with Romano or Parmesan cheese.
- Serves 4.

LINDA McCARTNEY

Beefless Stroganoff

¾ pound mushrooms, sliced
1 large onion, chopped
1 teaspoon paprika
¼ cup butter or margarine
⅓ cup all-purpose flour
6 vegetable burgers, cubed
¾ cup white wine
vegetable stock or water
¼ cup plus 2 tablespoons sour cream
½ teaspoon mild prepared mustard

- Sauté onion and mushrooms with paprika in butter or margarine in skillet for 10 minutes.
- Stir flour and burger cubes into mushroom mixture and sauté for 2 minutes, mixing well.
- Add wine and simmer for 10 to 15 minutes, stirring frequently and adding stock or water if mixture appears dry.
- Blend in sour cream and mustard. Heat thoroughly but do not boil or simmer. Serve immediately. Serves 6.

JOE PESCI

Stuffed Peppers Italian Style

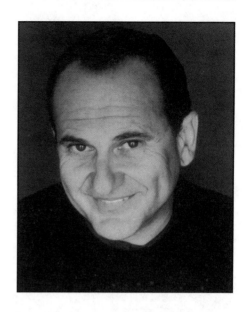

1　loaf Italian bread, crust removed
water
1　large clove garlic, minced, or garlic powder to
　　taste
1　(2¼ ounce) can ripe olives, cut in halves
½　cup (2 ounces) grated Parmesan cheese
salt to taste
parsley flakes to taste
½　cup olive oil
3　large pickled red bell peppers or 3 fresh red
　　bell peppers plus ½ cup red wine vinegar

- Moisten bread and crumble in mixing bowl. Add garlic, olives, cheese, salt, parsley and oil, mixing well.
- Cut bell peppers in strips and add to bread mixture. Spread in roasting pan. Pour liquid (from jar if pickled or vinegar if fresh peppers) over mixture and combine.
- Bake, covered with foil, at 400 degrees for 30 minutes, remove foil and bake for additional 30 minutes. Serves 8 to 10.

SIDNEY POITIER

Sautéed Broccoli

4　cloves garlic
⅓　cup olive oil
¼　cup chicken broth
1　bunch broccoli, cut in bite-sized pieces
salt and black pepper to taste

- Sauté garlic in oil in wok or deep pan over medium heat until golden brown. Remove garlic.
- Pour broth into pan, bring to a boil, add broccoli and lightly season with salt, tossing to coat.
- Simmer, covered, for 3 to 4 minutes or until crisp-tender. Serves 4 to 6.

SUGAR RAY AND MILLIE ROBINSON

Sugar's Spicy Squash

3 **pounds medium-sized banana squash**
water
1 **(8 ounce) can crushed pineapple, undrained**
½ **cup butter or margarine**
½ **cup honey**
½ **cup sugar**
pinch of salt
½ **cup lemon juice**
1 **teaspoon lemon extract**
1 **tablespoon nutmeg**
1 **tablespoon allspice**
1 **teaspoon cinnamon**

- Cook squash in water until tender. Drain well, peel and slice.
- Arrange layer of squash in 12x8x2-inch baking dish sprayed with vegetable cooking spray.
- Blend pineapple, butter or margarine, honey, sugar, salt, lemon juice and extract, nutmeg, allspice and cinnamon. Spread ½ of mixture on squash. Repeat layers.
- Bake, covered with aluminum foil, at 325 degrees for 30 minutes, remove foil and bake for additional 15 minutes or until sauce is thickened and squash is browned. Serves 6.

FRANK SINATRA

Veggie Beans

1 **pound pinto beans**
1 **carrot, finely chopped**
1 **onion, chopped**
1 **or 2 tomatoes, chopped**
assorted chopped chili peppers
1 **teaspoon ground cumin**
1 **tablespoon chili powder**
salt and black pepper to taste
water
4 **to 6 cups cooked shell pasta**
salsa to taste

- Combine beans, carrot, onion, tomatoes, chili peppers, cumin, chili powder, salt and black pepper in large saucepan.
- Add water to cover vegetables by 1 inch.
- Simmer for 3 to 4 hours, adding water as necessary.
- Mix vegetables with pasta. Stir in salsa.
- Serves 4 to 6.

FRANK SINATRA

Eggplant Parmigiana

EGGPLANT
¼ cup all-purpose flour
½ teaspoon salt
1 medium eggplant, peeled and cut crosswise
  in ½-inch slices
1 egg, beaten
¼ cup vegetable oil
⅓ cup (1½ ounces) grated Parmesan cheese
1 (6 ounce) package Mozzarella cheese

- Prepare tomato sauce and set aside.
- Combine flour and salt. Dip eggplant in egg, then in
  seasoned flour.
- Sauté eggplant slices in hot oil in large skillet for 3
  minutes on each side, adding more oil if necessary.
  Drain slices well on paper towel.
- Place ½ of eggplant in single layer in 10x6x2-inch baking dish, cutting slices to fit. Sprinkle
  with ½ of Parmesan cheese, ½ sauce and ½ Mozzarella cheese. Cut remaining Mozzarella
  into triangles. Repeat layers.
- Bake, uncovered, at 400 degrees for 15 to 20 minutes or until hot. Serves 6.

TOMATO SAUCE
½ cup chopped onion
¼ cup chopped celery
1 small clove garlic, minced
2 tablespoons vegetable oil
1 (14½ ounce) can tomatoes, cut up
⅓ cup tomato paste
½ teaspoon salt
¼ teaspoon black pepper
1 teaspoon parsley flakes
½ teaspoon dried oregano, crushed
1 bay leaf

- Sauté onion, celery and garlic in oil in large skillet until tender.
- Add tomatoes, tomato paste, salt, black pepper, parsley, oregano and bay leaf.
- Simmer, uncovered, for about 15 minutes or until desired consistency, stirring occasionally.
- Remove bay leaf.

ROBERT STACK
"Easy, fast. Friends will be thrilled and it tastes as if you spent hours in the kitchen. Serve with chicken, fish and meat dishes."

Curried Creamed Spinach

1 **(10 ounce) package frozen chopped spinach**
1 **cup white sauce**
1 **teaspoon Worcestershire sauce**
¼ **teaspoon curry powder**
juice of ½ lemon

- Prepare spinach according to package directions. Drain well.
- Combine spinach, white sauce, Worcestershire sauce, curry powder and lemon juice in saucepan.
- Simmer until thoroughly heated. Serves 3.

DWIGHT HICKS

Dwight's Thanksgiving Yams

⅓ **cup pecans or walnuts**
2 **Macintosh or Red Delicious apples, peeled and sliced**
⅓ **cup firmly-packed brown sugar**
½ **teaspoon cinnamon**
1 **(27 ounce) can yams, drained and mashed**
¼ **cup margarine or butter**
2 **cups miniature marshmallows**

- Toss pecans or walnuts, apples, brown sugar and cinnamon together, coating apples well.
- Alternate layers of yams and apple mixture in 12x8x2-inch baking dish. Dot with butter.
- Bake at 350 degrees for 35 minutes or until apples are soft. Sprinkle marshmallows on yams and broil until lightly browned.
- Serves 6 to 8.

RED BUTTONS
"If you don't feel like cooking, spend a buck and go out to eat."

Puerto Rican Potato Pancakes

6 medium potatoes
2 medium-sized onions
1 cup matzo meal
3 eggs
½ cup chopped ripe olives
½ cup chopped pimento
vegetable oil
applesauce (optional)
sour cream (optional)

- Using food processor, grate potatoes and onions together. Add matzo meal and eggs and pulse to blend.
- Pour mixture into bowl. Stir in olives and pimentos.
- Shape into pancakes and fry in oil in skillet, turning to lightly brown on both sides.
- Serve with applesauce and/or sour cream. Serves 6.

PERRY COMO

Brown Rice Casserole

1 cup uncooked brown rice
3 cups chicken broth
1 cup diced cooked chicken
1 onion, minced
2 carrots, shredded
¼ teaspoon salt
⅛ teaspoon black pepper
¼ teaspoon parsley flakes
¼ teaspoon dried oregano

- Combine rice, broth, chicken, onion, carrots, salt, black pepper, parsley and oregano in 2-quart casserole, mixing well.
- Bake, tightly covered with lid or aluminum foil, at 350 degrees for 1 hour. Serves 4.

OPRAH WINFREY

Oprah's Potatoes

2½ pounds red potatoes, cut in halves
2½ pounds Idaho potatoes, cut in halves
water
  ½ cup Butter Buds
  1 cup chicken broth
  2 cups skim milk
1½ tablespoons black pepper
  ⅛ teaspoon cayenne powder (optional)
  ¼ cup creamy puréed horseradish

- Place potatoes in large saucepan and add water to cover. Bring to a boil, reduce heat and simmer, covered, until potatoes are very tender. Drain well.
- Add Butter Buds to potatoes and begin to mash. Stir in broth, skim milk, black pepper, cayenne pepper and horseradish. Mash until creamy but slightly lumpy. Serves 12.

ADRIENNE BARBEAU

Thanksgiving Yams

7 pounds yams
¾ cup butter, divided
1 teaspoon salt
½ teaspoon black pepper
⅓ cup honey
½ teaspoon nutmeg
3 Pippin or Granny Smith Apples, thinly sliced
cinnamon to taste

- Cook yams in boiling water for about 45 minutes or until softened. Drain, cool, peel and mash with ¼ cup melted butter, salt and black pepper.
- Melt ¼ cup butter with honey and nutmeg. Pour into 13x9x2-inch baking dish.
- Layer apples, then yams on honey mixture. Sprinkle with cinnamon and dot with remaining ¼ cup butter.
- Bake at 350 degrees for 45 minutes or until bubbly. Serves 6 to 8.

GENE KELLY

"One of the great treats of the world, preferably to be eaten accompanied by a pitcher of good beer or ale. Eat late at night."

Potato Sandwich

 2 slices white bread
butter, softened
 ⅔ to 1 cup leftover mashed potatoes
salt to taste
 ⅓ cup leftover baked beans

- Butter 1 side of each bread slice.
- Spread potatoes ½-inch thick on 1 slice, lightly salt, add layer of beans and top with second bread slice. Serves 1.

I used to tease Gene about working me so hard. But that Irish task master made this skinny Italian kid who walked off the streets of Hoboken actually dance. Any recipe from Gene Kelly has a place of honor on my table. — Frank Sinatra

---

HAL LINDEN

Rice Casserole

 4 cups chicken broth
 2 cups uncooked long-grain rice
 ⅓ cup butter
 ¾ cup finely chopped celery
 ¾ cup finely chopped parsley
 ¾ cup finely chopped carrots
 ½ cup minced green onion
 1 cup pine nuts or shredded blanched almonds
    or both

- Pour broth into saucepan and bring to a boil. Heat 2-quart casserole in oven at 375 degrees.
- Sauté rice in butter in large skillet over high heat, stirring until well coated and cooking for about 5 minutes or until lightly browned. Remove from heat.
- Spread rice in heated casserole and add boiling broth.
- Bake, covered, at 375 degrees for 30 minutes, add celery, parsley, carrots, onions and nuts or almonds, mixing well with fork, and bake for additional 30 minutes. Serves 6 to 8.

DICK MARTIN

Martin's Junk Fried Rice

  1 **cup uncooked white rice**
peanut oil
  2 **cloves garlic, sliced, divided**
  1 **teaspoon crushed dried chili peppers, divided**
1½ **cups diced lean barbecued pork, cooked ham, chicken or shrimp**
  1 **cup green onion in ½-inch pieces**
  1 **red bell pepper, diced**
  1 **cup diced green bell pepper**
  1 **(8 ounce) can water chestnuts, drained and chopped**
  1 **(2 ounce) jar pimentos, drained and finely chopped**
  1 **cup sliced small mushrooms**
  ¼ **cup light soy sauce**
  1 **tablespoon sake or sherry**
  ½ **teaspoon sugar**
  1 **egg, beaten**

- Two days in advance, prepare rice according to package directions. Cool and store in refrigerator.
- Pour 2 tablespoons oil in preheated wok, swirling to coat sides.
- Stir fry ½ of garlic and ½ teaspoon chili peppers in oil over medium-high heat until garlic is well-browned. Discard garlic.
- Add pork and stir-fry for 1 minute. Drain on paper towel.
- Pour 2 to 3 tablespoons oil into wok. Cook remaining garlic and chili peppers until garlic is well browned. Discard garlic.
- Stir-fry green onion, red bell pepper, green bell pepper, water chestnuts, pimento and mushrooms for 2 to 3 minutes. Drain on paper towel.
- Pour 1½ tablespoons oil into wok, swirling to coat sides. Add rice and toss to coat with oil. Spread evenly around sides of wok and cook for about 2 minutes.
- Add vegetables and pork to rice and mix well.
- Blend soy sauce, sake or sherry and sugar. Add to rice mixture and toss to mix thoroughly.
- Scrape rice away from center of wok, leaving small well. Pour egg into well and cook, stirring with chopstick, for about 30 seconds or just until egg begins to set. Serve hot. Serves 6.

NANCY (MRS. ZUBIN) MEHTA

Spiced Saffron Rice

- 2 chicken breast halves, skin removed, boned and cut in ½-inch cubes
- 1½ cups butter, divided
- 4 medium-sized onions, minced
- 1 tablespoon minced ginger
- 2 cloves garlic, minced
- 16 whole cloves
- 4 (4 inch) cinnamon sticks
- 2 teaspoons turmeric
- 2 teaspoons cumin seeds
- 1½ teaspoons ground nutmeg
- 1½ teaspoons ground mace
- ¾ teaspoon cardamom seeds
- ¾ teaspoon cayenne pepper
- 2 cups uncooked converted rice
- 4 cups chicken broth
- 2 teaspoons salt
- 1 teaspoon sugar
- 1½ teaspoons saffron threads
- 2 medium-sized onions, cut lengthwise in thin strips
- ¾ cup dark raisins
- ¼ cup golden raisins
- water
- ½ cup unsalted raw cashews
- ½ cup slivered almonds
- ½ cup shelled pistachios
- silver leaf for garnish (optional)

- Sauté chicken in 2 tablespoons butter in 6-quart pan over medium heat until golden. Remove and set aside.
- Melt ½ cup butter in pan, add minced onion and cook until softened. Stir in ginger and garlic. Sauté for 1 or 2 minutes.
- Stir cloves, cinnamon sticks, turmeric, cumin, nutmeg, mace, cardamom seeds, cayenne pepper and ½ cup butter into ginger and garlic mixture. When butter is melted, add rice and cook over medium heat until golden, stirring frequently.
- Add broth, salt, sugar and saffron. Return chicken to pan.
- Bring to a boil and simmer, covered, for 45 to 50 minutes or until liquid is absorbed.
- Sauté onion strips in ¼ cup butter in skillet until well browned. Drain on paper towel.
- Plump raisins in water, then drain. Sauté cashews and almonds in 2 tablespoons butter.
- Arrange rice on platter. In order listed, layer dark raisins, light raisins, cashews, pistachios, almonds, onions and silver leaf.
- Serves 8.

ROBERT AND MARION MERRILL
"The Potato Latkes recipe is one passed on to me from my mother. It is a family generational pass-down."

Potato Latkes

3 **large onions, cut in chunks**
2 **eggs**
4 **or 5 medium to large baking potatoes, unpeeled and cut in chunks**
1 **teaspoon baking powder**
salt to taste
3 **to 5 tablespoons matzo meal**
vegetable oil
sour cream
applesauce

- Combine onion and eggs in blender. Blend until onion is liquefied.
- Using food processor, coarsely chop potatoes. Pour into bowl.
- Pour egg mixture over potatoes and mix. Add baking powder, salt and matzo meal, mixing thoroughly. If mixture appears too moist, add matzo meal for proper consistency.
- Drop pancake mixture by tablespoonful into ¼-inch depth hot oil in skillet over medium heat, turning to brown on both sides. Place pancakes on several layers of paper towel to absorb excess oil.
- Serve hot with sour cream or applesauce.
- Latkes can be kept warm in oven until ready to serve. To freeze, place on baking sheet, freeze and transfer to plastic bag. To use, remove from freezer, place on baking sheet and heat at 450 degrees for about 10 minutes. Serves 4 to 6.

If I thought Bob's recipe for Potato Latkes would make me sing like him, I'd move to Idaho!
— Frank Sinatra

SUPER DAVE OSBORNE

Super Dave's Homemade Mashed Potatoes

2 **pounds potatoes (about 6 medium), peeled**
⅓ **to ½ cup milk**
¼ **cup margarine or butter, softened**
½ **teaspoon salt**
dash of black pepper

- First, wash the potatoes. Remove eyes and peel if desired... I'm talking about the potatoes. Boil in 1 inch of salt water (30-35 minutes for whole potatoes, 20-25 for potato pieces). Drain potatoes.
- Mash until no lumps remain. Beat in desired amount of milk. Add in other ingredients.
- Climb to top of 40 foot tower and dive head first into bowl. Paddle vigorously until potatoes are light and fluffy. Makes 4 to 6 servings; or, if the wind is blowing, a very big mess.

STEFANIE POWERS

Pierogie

PASTRY
7½ **cups all-purpose flour**
  4 **eggs**
  2 **cups sour cream**
salt to taste
warm water

- Prepare cheese filling and kraut filling.
- Combine flour, eggs, sour cream and salt. Add warm water and mix to dough consistency.
- Knead in bowl, cover with towel and let stand for 10 minutes.
- Knead until smooth. Cut off piece of dough, place on lightly-floured surface, roll out, cut in squares, spoon filling in center, fold dough over filling and pinch to seal.
- Drop stuffed pierogies into boiled salted water in large pan and cook until they float to surface.
- Serves 10 to 12.
- Dough can be frozen.

CHEESE FILLING
  2 **large potatoes, cooked and mashed**
  ½ **cup margarine**
salt and black pepper to taste
  2 **(16 ounce) containers pot cheese or hoop cheese**
  3 **eggs**

- Combine potatoes, margarine, salt, black pepper, cheese and eggs, mixing well.

KRAUT FILLING
  1 **(16 ounce) can sauerkraut, rinsed and drained**
water
  1 **onion, diced**
  ½ **cup margarine**
salt and black pepper

- Cook sauerkraut in small amount of water for 20 minutes. Rinse and press to remove excess moisture.
- Sauté onion in margarine until softened. Add to sauerkraut and season with salt and black pepper, mixing well.

PETER BROWN
"You may want to have copies of this recipe handy; you will be asked for it."

Zucchini de Pedro

  2 **pounds small firm zucchini (no more than 6 ounces each), stems trimmed**
extra virgin olive oil
  5 **large cloves garlic, sliced**
 ½ **cup chopped basil**
 ¼ **cup Balsamic vinegar**
salt and freshly ground black pepper

- Cut zucchini lengthwise in ⅛-inch thick slices.
- Generously brush 2 baking sheets with olive oil. Place zucchini in single layer on sheets and brush tops with oil.
- Bake at 500 degrees for 7 minutes, turn slices, brush tops with oil and bake for additional 8 minutes.
- In serving dish, layer ⅓ of zucchini, drizzle generously with oil, add ⅓ garlic, ⅓ basil and ⅓ vinegar and season with salt and black pepper; repeat layers twice.
- Chill, covered, overnight.
- Let warm to room temperature before serving with small slices of sourdough bread or crackers. Serves 10 to 12.

PAUL BURKE
"In New Orleans, this dish would serve six people; however, to the normal appetite this will serve 12."

Creole Roasted Peppers

  6 **large red bell peppers with**
      green stem
  8 **medium tomatoes**
boiling water
cold water
  5 **cloves garlic**
 24 **anchovy fillets, drained**
freshly cracked black pepper
oregano
fresh basil
extra virgin olive oil

- Cut peppers, top to bottom, so each half has portion of stem. Remove seeds and white membrane. Place, cut side up, on oiled baking sheet.
- Blanch tomatoes in boiling water and plunge in cold water. Peel, discard core and cut in quarters. Place 3 wedges in each pepper half.
- Peel and thinly slice garlic. Place 4 or 5 slices in each pepper half.
- Snip or cut 2 anchovies and scatter over each pepper half.
- Sprinkle with black pepper, oregano and basil. Drizzle with oil.
- Bake on upper oven rack at 350 degrees for 50 to 60 minutes; edges of pepper should be toasted.
- Place in serving dish and pour any pan liquid over peppers.
- Serves 6 to 12. Serve with hot French bread.

Desserts

Donald, age 6

LLOYD BRIDGES

"These cookies are a family affair, a project for little and big kids to get their hands into, literally. Beau, Jeff, Lucinda and our eight grandchildren take turns around the kitchen table and go to it. If anyone is out of town or on location at Christmas time, no matter how far away, we pack up a tin of these to send the family holiday spirit to them."

Cardamom Christmas Cookies

2½ **cups all-purpose flour**
1 **teaspoon baking powder**
¼ **teaspoon powdered cardamom**
1 **cup butter or margarine**
2 **cups sugar**
1 **egg**
½ **cup coarsely chopped almonds**

- Sift flour. Add baking powder and cardamom and sift again.
- Melt butter or margarine in saucepan and boil until browned. Let stand until cool and skim.
- Blend sugar and egg into butter, mixing well. Gradually add dry ingredients, blending well after each addition. Stir in almonds and mix by hand.
- Shape dough into large walnut-sized balls, break each ball in halves and place broken side down on ungreased baking sheet.
- Bake at 350 degrees for 15 minutes or until lightly browned. Immediately transfer to wire cooling rack. Store cooled cookies in tightly-covered container. Makes 6 dozen.

JAMIE FARR

Peanut Butter Snack Bars

¼ **cup butter or margarine**
½ **cup plus 2 tablespoons peanut butter, divided**
¼ **cup honey**
⅓ **cup firmly-packed brown sugar**
3 **cups natural granola cereal**
½ **cup semi-sweet chocolate chips**

- Combine butter or margarine, 2 tablespoons peanut butter, honey and brown sugar in saucepan. Heat over low heat, stirring occasionally, until sugar is melted and mixture is smooth.
- Pour mixture over cereal and stir to thoroughly coat. Spread in foil-lined 9x9x2-inch baking pan, pressing evenly. Set aside to cool.
- Combine chocolate chips and remaining ½ cup peanut butter in top of double boiler over hot but not boiling water. Stir until chocolate is melted and mixture is smooth. Spread over cereal layer.
- Chill until firm. Cut into bars. Makes 2 dozen.

LONI ANDERSON

Fudge Meltaways

¾ **cup butter, divided**
2½ **(1 ounce) squares unsweetened chocolate**
¼ **cup sugar**
2 **teaspoons vanilla, divided**
1 **egg, beaten**
2 **cups graham cracker crumbs**
1 **cup flaked coconut**
½ **cup chopped nuts**
1 **tablespoon milk**
2 **cups powdered sugar**

- Melt ½ cup butter and 1 square chocolate in saucepan over low heat.
- Blend sugar, 1 teaspoon vanilla, egg, crumbs, coconut and nuts into butter mixture and mix well.
- Press mixture in 8x8x2-inch baking pan. Chill until firm.
- Combine remaining ¼ cup butter, milk, powdered sugar and remaining 1 teaspoon vanilla, mixing thoroughly. Spread on chilled chocolate coconut layer and chill until firm.
- Melt remaining 1½ squares chocolate and spread over chilled filling. Chill until partially firm, cut into squares and chill until completely firm.
- Makes 5 dozen.

PAUL BOCUSE RESTAURANT, COLLONGES, FRANCE
PAUL BOCUSE, PROPRIETOR AND EXECUTIVE CHEF

Caramel Custard

3 **cups whipping cream**
1 **cup milk**
⅔ **cup sugar**
7 **egg yolks**
vanilla to taste
brown sugar

- Combine cream, milk, sugar, egg yolks and vanilla, blending well. Pour into ramekins or ovenproof individual casseroles.
- Bake at 250 degrees for 45 minutes. Chill thoroughly.
- Sprinkle sugar on cold custard. Broil for a few minutes to caramelize.
- Serve cold or lukewarm.
- Serves 6.

**THE MANSION ON TURTLE CREEK,
DALLAS, TEXAS
DEAN FEARING, EXECUTIVE CHEF**

Mansion on Turtle Creek Cheesecake

- 1 tablespoon unsalted butter, softened
- 2 cups graham cracker crumbs
- 2 cups sugar, divided
- ½ cup unsalted butter, melted
- 4½ (8 ounce) packages cream cheese, softened
- 5 eggs, at room temperature
- 1 teaspoon vanilla extract
- 1 cup whipping cream
- 1 tablespoon powdered sugar
- shaved chocolate

- Coat bottom and sides of 10-inch springform pan with softened butter.
- Combine crumbs, ½ cup sugar and melted butter, mixing with fork until well blended. Evenly press crumb mixture on bottom and to 1-inch depth on sides of springform pan.
- Beat cream cheese until smooth. Add remaining 1½ cups sugar and beat until smooth.
- Add eggs, 1 at a time, beating after each addition and scraping sides of bowl, until very smooth and well blended. Add vanilla.
- Pour batter into prepared pan.
- Bake at 325 degrees for 1¼ hours or until center is consistency of congealed gelatin. Cool on wire rack away from drafts.
- Remove springform and chill until ready to serve.
- Whip cream with powdered sugar. Pipe cream in rosettes on top of cheesecake and garnish with chocolate.
- Serves 12.

DOM DE LUISE

Dom's Doodlewoppers

- 3 cups all-purpose flour
- 1 teaspoon baking soda
- 2 teaspoons cream of tartar
- ½ cup butter or margarine, softened
- ½ cup vegetable shortening
- 1¼ cups sugar, divided
- 1 teaspoon ground ginger
- 4 eggs
- 1 teaspoon vanilla
- 2 teaspoons cinnamon
- 2 cups pecan halves

- Combine flour, baking soda and cream of tartar.
- Add butter or margarine, shortening, 1 cup sugar, ginger, eggs and vanilla, mixing to form dough.
- Using 1 tablespoon dough, shape into balls. Roll in mixture of remaining ¼ cup sugar and cinnamon. Place on ungreased baking sheet. Gently press pecan half in center of each.
- Bake at 350 degrees for 10 to 12 minutes.
- Makes 4 dozen.

SID CAESAR

Healthy "Mush"

1 **cup dry cereal: shredded wheat, puffed brown rice or red wheat**
1 **cup strawberries or canned fruit in light syrup**
¼ **cup dried apricots or other dried fruit**
¼ **cup chopped walnuts**
¼ **cup raisins**
¼ **teaspoon finely chopped ginger**
2 **bananas**
1 **cup skim milk**

- Combine cereal, strawberries or fruit, apricots or other dried fruit, walnuts, raisins, ginger and bananas in blender. Blend until thoroughly mixed, adding milk to desired consistency.
- Serves 2.

CAROL CHANNING

"Hello Dolly" Bars

½ **cup butter**
1 **cup graham cracker crumbs**
1 **cup flaked coconut**
1 **cup semi-sweet chocolate chips**
1 **cup chopped nuts**
1 **(15 ounce) can sweetened condensed milk**

- Melt butter in 9x9x2-inch baking pan.
- In order listed, layer: crumbs, coconut, chocolate chips and nuts on butter.
- Pour milk over layered ingredients.
- Bake at 350 degrees for 30 minutes.
- Cool in pan. Cut into 16 squares.

THE HONORABLE DAN BURTON

Chocolate Meltaway

CRUST
  1 **cup all-purpose flour**
  ¼ **cup powdered sugar**
  ½ **cup margarine, melted**
  ½ **to ¾ cup chopped nuts**

- Combine flour, sugar and margarine, mixing well.
- Press mixture in 9-inch round baking pan. Sprinkle with nuts.
- Bake at 350 degrees for 15 minutes.

FILLING
  4 **(1 ounce) squares bitter chocolate**
  1 **cup margarine, melted**
  2 **cups firmly-packed powdered sugar**
  4 **eggs**
  1 **teaspoon vanilla**
frozen whipped topping
chocolate curls for garnish

- Melt chocolate in top of double boiler. Remove from heat.
- Blend in margarine and powdered sugar.
- Add eggs 1 at a time, beating well after each addition. Stir in vanilla.
- Spoon filling on baked crust. Let stand until cool.
- Spread whipped topping on filling and add chocolate curls for garnish.
- Serves 6 to 8.

**BRENNAN'S RESTAURANT,
NEW ORLEANS, LOUISIANA
MICHAEL ROUSSEL, EXECUTIVE CHEF**
*"Don't be afraid to attempt the dish in your own
kitchen. It really is simple to prepare. Just remember
to wait until the rum gets hot so you will get a good
flame when it is ignited. The dish can be prepared
over a regular stove burner and then brought to the
dinner table to be flamed."*

Brennan's Bananas Foster

¼ **cup butter**
1 **cup firmly-packed brown sugar**
½ **teaspoon cinnamon**
¼ **cup banana liqueur**
4 **bananas, cut lengthwise in halves, then
   crosswise in halves**
¼ **cup rum**
4 **scoops vanilla ice cream**

• Melt butter in flambé pan or attractive skillet over an alcohol burner.
• Stir sugar, cinnamon and liqueur into butter until blended. Heat for a few minutes, then place
  bananas in sauce and sauté until soft and slightly browned.
• Add rum and heat well. Tip pan to ignite sauce from flame of burner.
• Lift bananas from pan and place 4 pieces on each scoop of ice cream. Spoon hot sauce from
  pan over bananas.
• Serves 4.

JACKIE COLLINS

Orange Chocolate Cheesecake

CRUST
  2 **cups crushed chocolate wafer cookies**
  ½ **cup butter, melted**

- Combine cookie crumbs and butter, mixing to paste consistency. Spread mixture in 8x8x2-inch baking dish.
- Bake at 450 degrees for 5 minutes. Let stand until cool.

FILLING
  1 **(8 ounce) carton whipped cream cheese, softened**
  ½ **cup butter, softened**
  ¾ **cup sugar**
  2 **teaspoons orange extract**
  ½ **cup finely grated orange peel**
  2 **eggs, beaten**
  ½ **cup whipping cream**

- Combine cream cheese, butter and sugar, beating until smooth. Blend in orange extract, peel, eggs and whipping cream, mixing thoroughly.
- Pour batter over cooled crust.
- Bake at 350 degrees for 20 minutes. Let stand until cool.
- Prepare topping. Pour over cake.
- Bake at 350 degrees for 5 minutes. Serve cold. Serves 6 to 8.

TOPPING
  1 **cup sour cream**
  ¼ **cup sugar**
  1 **teaspoon orange extract**

- Combine sour cream, sugar and orange extract, blending until smooth.

CATHY LEE CROSBY

Apple Cobbler Cathy Lee

    5 pounds small red Delicious apples, peeled
   10 cups water, divided
    1 cup golden raisins
    1 teaspoon cinnamon
    1 teaspoon ground cloves
    1 teaspoon nutmeg
    2 cups honey
    1 cup freshly grated coconut
    1 tablespoon cornstarch
    ½ cup cold water
pastry for double-crust 9-inch pie

- Core and cut each apple in 6 pieces. Combine apples and 8 cups water in large saucepan. Cook for 15 to 20 minutes. Drain water from apples.
- Add raisins, cinnamon, cloves, nutmeg, honey and coconut to apples. Dissolve cornstarch in ½ cup cold water and add with remaining 2 cups water to apple mixture.
- Cook, stirring constantly, over medium heat for 10 minutes.
- Roll pastry dough to fit bottom of 18x12x2-inch baking pan, reserving excess dough. Place in pan and prick with fork tines.
- Pour apple mixture into pan. Cut excess dough into strips and arrange in lattice design on top of filling.
- Bake at 350 degrees for 1 hour or until browned. Serves 30 to 35.

ROLAND YOUNG
SINATRA PERSONAL CHEF
"Be sure to put a foil liner on the bottom of the oven because the pie will most likely drip."

Fresh Blueberry Pie

    3 pints fresh blueberries,
       rinsed and blotted dry
   1⅔ cups sugar
    ⅓ cup all-purpose flour
    2 tablespoons cornstarch
    ½ teaspoon almond extract
pastry for double crust 9-inch pie
    1 egg mixed with
       2 tablespoons water
sugar

- Pour blueberries into mixing bowl and mash about ⅓ of the berries to form juice.
- Add sugar, flour, cornstarch and almond extract to berries, mixing well.
- Spread filling in bottom pastry shell and top with remaining pastry. Roll and crimp edges, brush top with egg wash and sprinkle with sugar.
- Bake at 400 degrees for 45 minutes to 1 hour. Serves 6 to 8.

TIM CULBERTSON
"Here's a wonderful low-calorie pie. Hope you'll enjoy it!"

Apple Strawberry Pie

¾ **cup uncooked regular oats**
½ **cup all-purpose flour**
1 **teaspoon sugar**
¼ **teaspoon salt**
3 **tablespoons skim milk**
3 **tablespoons vegetable oil**
1 **cup strawberries**
¾ **cup cold water**
⅓ **cup frozen apple juice concentrate**
3 **tablespoons cornstarch**
1 **tablespoon lemon juice**
red food coloring (optional)
5 **cups strawberry halves**

- Grind oats in blender for about 1 minute. Mix oats with flour, sugar and salt.
- Combine milk and oil. Add to dry ingredients and stir until moistened. Form dough into a ball.
- Flatten ball, place on wax paper on moist work surface and top with wax paper square. Roll to form 12-inch circle. Peel away top wax paper, place dough side down in 9-inch pie plate and discard wax paper. Prick bottom and sides of pastry with fork tines and flute edge.
- Bake at 450 degrees for 10 to 12 minutes or until golden. Cool on wire rack.
- Mash 1 cup strawberries in saucepan and add 1 cup water. Bring to a boil, reduce heat and simmer, uncovered, for 2 minutes. Strain through a sieve and discard pulp.
- In same saucepan, combine apple juice concentrate, cornstarch and strained berry liquid. Cook, stirring often, until thickened and bubbly, then cook for 2 additional minutes. Remove from heat and stir in lemon juice. Cool for 5 minutes.
- Add several drops food coloring to sauce. Gently fold in strawberry halves and pour into baked crust.
- Chill, covered, for at least 5 hours. Serves 8.

I know we're supposed to eat slowly and chew carefully. But, when I was a kid growing up in Hoboken, you had to eat fast before someone grabbed the plate. — Frank Sinatra

---

BARBARA DAVIS

White Chocolate Cheesecake

1¼ **pounds creme filled chocolate sandwich cookies**
½ **cup margarine**
4 **(8 ounce) packages cream cheese, softened**
¾ **cup sugar**
8 **eggs**
1 **cup whipping cream**
4 **(6 ounce) packages white chocolate chips**
2 **teaspoons vanilla**

- Grind cookies in food processor to form fine crumbs. Add margarine, mixing by hand, until well blended. Press mixture on bottom and sides of 10-inch springform pan.
- Beat cream cheese and sugar together until smooth. Blend in vanilla.
- Add eggs 1 at a time, beating well after each addition.
- Pour cream into saucepan over low heat, bring to a boil, turn off heat and add chocolate, whisking until smooth.
- Gradually add chocolate mixture to cream cheese batter, blending thoroughly. Pour into prepared crust.
- Wrap aluminum foil around pan. Place in pan of hot water.
- Bake at 350 degrees for about 1½ hours. Serves 12 to 16.

CLAUDETTE COLBERT

Eggs á la Neige

2 **cups milk**
8 **eggs, separated**
1½ **cups sugar, divided**
1 **teaspoon vanilla**
½ **teaspoon cream of tartar**
toasted almonds for garnish

- Combine milk, egg yolks and ½ cup sugar in top of double boiler. Cook until mixture coats spoon, stir in vanilla and remove from heat.
- Cook ½ cup sugar in saucepan until caramelized. Spread in bottom of non-stick 10-inch fluted tube pan.
- Beat egg whites with remaining ½ cup sugar. Add cream of tartar and beat until peaks form. Spoon mixture into tube pan. Place tube pan in larger pan with hot water.
- Bake at 350 degrees for 30-45 minutes. Remove tube pan from hot water and let cool for 30 minutes.
- Pour custard into glass serving bowl. Invert egg mold on custard and garnish with almonds.
- Serves 8.

RICK DEES

Dees-Licious Peach Cobbler

4 **cups peeled and sliced peaches**
1 **cup sugar**
1 **cup firmly-packed brown sugar**
¼ **cup butter**
1 **tablespoon vanilla extract**
1 **teaspoon cinnamon**
½ **teaspoon nutmeg**
3 **tablespoons all-purpose flour**
2 **tablespoons fresh lemon juice**
vanilla ice cream

- Combine peaches, sugar, brown sugar, butter, vanilla, cinnamon, nutmeg, flour and lemon juice.
- Spoon fruit mixture into two 13x9x2-inch baking dishes. Place pieces of pastry on filling, pressing into fruit.
- Bake at 400 degrees for 50 to 55 minutes. Cool slightly and serve with vanilla ice cream.
- Serves 32.

DEES' FOOLPROOF PIE CRUST

4 **cups all-purpose flour**
1 **tablespoon sugar**
1 **teaspoon salt**
1 **cup vegetable shortening**
¾ **cup butter**
1 **egg**
½ **cup cold water**
1 **tablespoon white vinegar**
1 **teaspoon almond extract**

- Sift flour, sugar and salt together.
- Cut shortening and butter into dry ingredients until consistency of meal.
- In separate bowl, mix egg, water, vinegar and almond extract. Add to dry ingredients and mix thoroughly.
- Form dough into a ball. Chill for 15 minutes. Roll dough to form two 9-inch pastry crusts or pull apart into medium pieces for peach cobbler.
- Makes 2 pastry shells.

FARRAH FAWCETT

"My mother made this pie for me for as long as I can remember. I actually had a piece for breakfast almost every morning from the sixth to the twelfth grade. Obviously I wasn't very health conscious then but I started my day in the happiest mood."

Pauline's Pecan Pie

1   **cup white corn syrup**
3   **eggs, lightly beaten**
⅛   **teaspoon salt**
1   **teaspoon vanilla**
1   **cup sugar**
2   **tablespoons margarine, melted**
½   **cup chopped pecans**
½   **cup pecan halves**
1   **unbaked 9-inch pastry shell**

- Combine syrup, eggs, salt, vanilla, sugar and margarine. Stir pecans into batter. Pour into pastry shell.
- Bake at 400 degrees for 15 minutes, reduce oven temperature to 350 degrees and bake for additional 30 to 35 minutes or until filling edges are firm and center is slightly soft.
- Serves 8.

DORAL SATURNIA
INTERNATIONAL SPA RESORT, MIAMI, FLORIDA
RECIPE CREATED BY CHEF RONALD HOOK
WITH ALIX LANDMAN, R.D.

Mango Raspberry Creme Brulée

10 **egg whites**
 1 **cup peeled and puréed mango**
 ¼ **cup sugar, divided**
 1 **teaspoon cornstarch**
 ⅛ **teaspoon salt**
 1 **cup skim evaporated milk**
 2 **tablespoons half and half**
 ⅓ **pound whole fresh raspberries**
sugar
mint sprigs for garnish

- Combine egg whites, mango, ¼ cup sugar, cornstarch, salt, evaporated milk and half and half, whisking until well mixed.
- Divide creme among 10 ovenproof individual bowls. Place equal portion of raspberries in each bowl.
- Set bowls in shallow baking pan and add hot water to ½ the depth of bowls.
- Bake at 300 degrees for 40 minutes or until firm. Remove from water bath and chill for several hours.
- Sprinkle 1 teaspoon sugar over brulée in each bowl. Broil until sugar darkens and caramelizes; do not burn. Top with mint sprig.
- Serves 10.

ELIZABETH BERKLEY

Carrot Cake

CAKE
1¼ cups vegetable oil
2 cups sugar
3 eggs
2 cups all-purpose flour
2 teaspoons baking soda
1 teaspoon salt
1 teaspoon cinnamon
2 teaspoons vanilla
1 cup shredded coconut
2 cups shredded carrots
1 (8 ounce) can crushed pineapple, undrained
1½ cups chopped pecans or walnuts

- Beat oil, sugar and eggs together until smooth.
- Combine flour, baking soda, salt and cinnamon. Add with vanilla, coconut, carrots, pineapple and pecans or walnuts to egg mixture, mixing thoroughly. Pour batter into ungreased 13x9x2-inch baking pan.
- Bake at 350 degrees for 1 hour. Cool before frosting and cutting into squares. Serves 16.

FROSTING
2 (3 ounce) packages cream cheese, softened
½ cup butter, softened
1¾ to 2 cups powdered sugar

- Beat cream cheese and butter together until smooth. Add powdered sugar and beat until smooth.

ERNIE'S, SAN FRANCISCO, CALIFORNIA
VICTOR AND ROLAND GOTTI, PROPRIETORS

Tiramisu

4 eggs, separated
¼ cup plus 3 tablespoons sugar
1 (8 ounce) package marscapone cheese
½ cup half and half
¼ cup rum
2 (12 count) packages ladyfingers
¾ cup espresso coffee
¼ cup coffee liqueur
¼ cup unsweetened cocoa

- Beat egg yolks and sugar together. Add cheese and blend until smooth creamy consistency. Blend in half and half.
- Beat 2 egg whites until stiff. Add whites and rum to cheese mixture, blending until consistency of whipped cream.
- Arrange ladyfingers in shallow serving dish. Pour coffee, liqueur and creme mixture over ladyfingers. Chill for about 10 minutes.
- Sprinkle with cocoa. Serves 4.

BARBARA GRANT

Apple Almond Crisp

8 cups peeled and sliced tart apples
1½ cups blanched slivered almonds, toasted, divided
1 cup raisins
¼ cup plus 2 tablespoons all-purpose flour, divided
1 cup raw sugar
1 cup uncooked regular oats
1 teaspoon cinnamon
1 teaspoon nutmeg
½ cup butter
ice cream or whipped cream

- Toss apples with ½ cup almonds, raisins and 2 tablespoons flour. Spread mixture in greased 8x8x2-inch baking pan.
- Combine sugar, remaining ¼ cup flour, oats, cinnamon and nutmeg. Cut in butter until crumbly. Stir in remaining almonds and sprinkle over apples.
- Bake at 375 degrees for 30 to 35 minutes or until apples are tender and topping is browned.
- Serve warm with ice cream or whipped cream.
- Serves 6 to 8.

BUDDY GRECO

"I do not use an electric mixer. I beat by hand."

Buddy's Italian Cheesecake

2 **tablespoons butter, softened**
2 **cups graham cracker crumbs**
1 **(48 ounce) can or 3 (16 ounce) cartons Ricotta cheese**
2 **cups sugar, divided**
8 **eggs, separated**
½ **cup sifted all-purpose flour**
grated peel of 1 lemon
1 **teaspoon vanilla**
½ **cup chopped citron and candied cherries**

- Coat bottom and sides of 12-inch springform pan with softened butter and sprinkle with cracker crumbs. If large pan unavailable, prepare two 9-inch springform pans.
- Beat cheese until smooth, gradually adding 1½ cups sugar and egg yolks, beating well after each addition.
- Add flour, lemon peel and vanilla.
- Beat egg whites with remaining ½ cup sugar. Blend into cheese mixture and add citron and cherries.
- Pour batter into prepared pan.
- Bake at 425 degrees for 10 minutes, reduce oven temperature to 350 degrees, bake for 1 hour, turn oven off and leave in oven, with door closed, for 3 hours or longer. Chill for 6 hours before serving. Serves 16 to 20.

**ANTOINE'S RESTAURANT,
NEW ORLEANS, LOUISIANA
BERNARD R. GUSTE, PROPRIETOR**

*"Traditionally at Antoine's, the lights are dimmed as
the waiter prepares this drink so that all can enjoy the
senses. Blue flame rising from the cognac, the
fragrance of special spices, the aroma of French
roast coffee and finally, the wonderfully different and
marvelous taste of Cafe Brulot Diabolique. This great
drink was made popular here at Antoine's during
Prohibition when my great-grandfather, Jules
Alciatore, would disguise the cognac for his guests
with our coffee and drink it all from coffee cups."*

Cafe Brulot Diabolique

    8 whole cloves
    1 (1 inch) stick cinnamon
peel of 1 lemon
    6 cubes sugar
    4 jiggers cognac
    4 demi-tasse cups strong black coffee

- Combine cloves, cinnamon, lemon peel, sugar and cognac in a brulot bowl.
- Heat coffee and keep hot.
- Light cognac in bowl and let burn for 1 to 2 minutes, stirring constantly. Gradually add the hot coffee, stirring to blend flavors; flame will extinguish.
- Serve immediately.
- Serves 4.

KATHARINE HEPBURN

Lace Cookies

    ¼ cup butter, softened
    1 egg
    ½ teaspoon vanilla
    ⅓ cup raw sugar
    ⅔ cup firmly-packed light brown sugar
  1⅓ tablespoons all-purpose flour
    1 cup finely chopped walnuts

- Beat butter, egg and vanilla together until smooth.
- Add raw sugar, brown sugar and flour to egg mixture, mix thoroughly. Stir in walnuts.
- Drop dough by teaspoonfuls on greased baking sheet.
- Bake at 350 degrees for 7 to 8 minutes. Cool on baking sheet. Makes 2½ dozen.

BERNICE KORSHAK

Macadamia Nut Bars

CRUST
½ **cup butter, softened**
¼ **cup sugar**
1 **cup all-purpose flour**

- Cream butter and sugar together until smooth.
- Add flour and mix to dry, crumbly consistency.
- Press mixture into 9x9x2-inch baking pan.
- Bake at 350 degrees for 20 minutes.

FILLING
2 **eggs, lightly beaten**
1½ **cups firmly-packed brown sugar**
1 **teaspoon vanilla**
½ **cup flaked coconut**
1 **cup chopped macadamia nuts**
2 **tablespoons all-purpose flour**
½ **teaspoon baking powder**

- Combine eggs, brown sugar, vanilla, coconut, nuts, flour and baking powder, mixing to blend.
- Pour filling over baked crust.
- Bake at 350 degrees for 20 minutes. Serves 9.

ANNE JEFFREYS

Jeffreys' Chess Pie

PIE
¼ **cup butter, softened**
½ **cup sugar**
1 **cup firmly-packed brown sugar**
⅛ **teaspoon salt**
2 **eggs**
1 **teaspoon vanilla**
2 **tablespoons all-purpose flour**
½ **cup whipping cream**
1 **cup chopped pecans**
1 **unbaked 9-inch pastry shell**
pastry leaves for garnish
pecan halves for garnish

- Prepare apricot glaze.
- Cream butter with sugar and salt until smooth and light. Add eggs, 1 at a time, beating after each addition.
- Stir in vanilla, flour, cream and pecans.
- Brush pastry shell with 2 teaspoons apricot glaze. Pour filling into shell.
- Bake at 375 degrees for 40 to 50 minutes or until knife tip inserted between center and edge of filling comes out clean; do not overbake.
- Serve slightly warm or cold. Garnish with tiny baked pastry leaves and pecan halves.
- Serves 8.

APRICOT GLAZE
1 **(11 ounce) jar apricot preserves**
¼ **cup apricot brandy or orange liqueur**

- Combine preserves and brandy or liqueur in blender or food processor. Blend or pulse until puréed.
- Store glaze in glass jar in refrigerator.

HOWARD KEEL

Sticky Toffee Pudding

PUDDING
¾ (8 ounce) package pitted dates, chopped
1 cup water
1 teaspoon baking soda
¼ cup butter, softened
¾ cup sugar
2 eggs
1 cup plus 2 tablespoons all-purpose flour
½ teaspoon vanilla

- Combine dates and water in saucepan, bring to a boil and remove from heat. Stir in baking soda and set aside.
- Cream butter and sugar together until smooth. Add eggs, 1 at a time, beating well after each addition.
- Fold flour into creamed mixture. Add dates with liquid and vanilla.
- Pour batter into greased 7x7x2-inch baking pan.
- Bake at 350 degrees for 30 to 40 minutes.
- While pudding is baking, prepare sauce.
- Pour some of sauce over baked pudding, then return to oven for about 7 minutes. Pudding should absorb sauce and turn to golden brown.
- Cut into squares and serve with extra sauce. Serves 6 to 8.

SAUCE
1 cup firmly-packed brown sugar
¼ cup plus 2 tablespoons whipping cream
½ cup butter
½ teaspoon vanilla

- Combine sugar, cream, butter and vanilla in saucepan. Bring to a boil, reduce heat and simmer for 3 minutes.

ROLAND YOUNG
SINATRA PERSONAL CHEF
"Be sure to put a foil liner on the bottom of oven because it will most likely drip."

Roland's Deep Dish Apple Crumble Pie

PIE
```
  1  unbaked deep-dish pastry shell
1¼  cups water
  ½  cup sugar
  ⅓  cup firmly-packed brown sugar
  ½  teaspoon cinnamon
  ½  teaspoon nutmeg
  ¼  cup Grand Marnier liqueur
  5  medium Granny Smith apples, peeled and sliced
  ½  cup currants
2½  tablespoons cornstarch
```
cold water

- Bake pastry shell at temperature on package directions until pastry is firm but not browned.
- While shell is baking, prepare topping and set aside.
- Combine water, sugar, brown sugar, cinnamon, nutmeg and liqueur in saucepan. Bring to a boil and simmer for 2 minutes.
- Add apples to syrup and cook for 4 minutes. Stir in currants and cook for 2 minutes
- Blend cornstarch with ⅓ cup cold water, add to apple mixture and cook until thickened.
- Pour filling into partially-baked crust and top with crumb mixture.
- Bake at 350 degrees for about 45 minutes. Serves 8.

TOPPING
```
1¾  cups all-purpose flour
  ½  cup sugar
  ½  cup firmly-packed brown sugar
  ½  teaspoon cinnamon
  ½  teaspoon nutmeg
  ½  teaspoon vanilla
  ½  cup butter
```

- Combine flour, sugar, brown sugar, cinnamon, nutmeg and vanilla.
- Using pastry blender, cut butter into dry ingredients.

MICHELE LEE

Michele Lee's Double Chocolate Surprise Muffins

CHOCOLATE FILLING
¾ cup whipping cream
6 (1 ounce) squares semi-sweet chocolate, finely chopped
3 tablespoons raspberry preserves

- Pour cream into medium saucepan. Bring to a gentle boil over medium-high heat. Remove from heat and add chocolate, stirring until very smooth.
- Place chocolate cream in bowl. Stir raspberries into cream, mixing thoroughly.
- Chill for about 30 minutes or until pudding consistency.

MUFFINS
3 cups all-purpose flour
½ cup unsweetened cocoa powder
1 tablespoon plus 1 teaspoon baking powder
1 teaspoon baking soda
1½ teaspoons salt
2¼ cups sour cream
¾ cup unsalted butter, melted and cooled
¾ cup sugar
2 eggs (at room temperature), lightly beaten

- Sift flour, cocoa, baking powder, baking soda and salt together.
- Using hand-held electric mixer at medium speed, mix sour cream, butter, sugar and eggs together until blended.
- Make a well in center of dry ingredients, add liquid mixture and stir just until moistened.
- Spoon batter into lightly-buttered muffin pans, filling each cup ⅓ full. Place 1 teaspoon filling on each and top with remaining batter, filling each cup ¾ full.
- Position a rack in center of oven. Preheat to 350 degrees.
- Bake for 15 minutes or until wooden pick inserted near center of batter portion of muffin comes out clean.
- Cool muffins in cups for 5 minutes, place on wire rack to complete cooling and store in airtight container.
- Makes 2 dozen.

JANET LEIGH

Jack Daniel's Cake

1 (18½ ounce) package yellow cake mix
1 (4 ounce) package vanilla instant pudding mix
5 eggs
¾ cup butter or margarine, softened
½ cup sweetened condensed milk
½ cup Jack Daniel's
1 (6 ounce) package butterscotch chips
1 cup coarsely chopped pecans

- Combine cake mix and pudding mix.
- Add eggs, butter or margarine, milk and Jack Daniel's to dry ingredients, mixing thoroughly.
- Stir in butterscotch chips and pecans.
- Spread batter in 13x9x2inch baking pan.
- Bake at 350 degrees for 45 minutes to 1 hour, checking doneness after 45 minutes.
- Serves 16 to 20.

ANNE MURRAY

Mom's Cherry Cake

2 cups maraschino cherries, drained and dried
4 cups all-purpose flour, divided
1½ cups butter, softened
2 cups sugar
4 eggs
1 teaspoon vanilla
1 teaspoon almond extract
1 teaspoon lemon extract
2 teaspoons baking powder
1 teaspoon salt
1 cup milk

- Toss cherries with 1 cup flour and set aside.
- Cream butter and sugar until smooth. Add eggs, 1 at a time, beating well after each addition. Stir in vanilla, almond and lemon extracts.
- Combine remaining 3 cups flour, baking powder and salt.
- Alternately add dry ingredients and milk to creamed mixture, blending well. Fold cherries into batter.
- Pour batter into greased and floured 13x9x2-inch baking pan.
- Bake at 325 degrees for 2 hours. Serves 16 to 20.

JERRY ORBACH

Millicent's Trifle

- 1 **loaf pound cake**
- 1 **cup sherry**
- ¼ **cup brandy**
- 1 **(16 ounce) can fruit cocktail, drained and juice reserved**
- 1 **(3 ounce) package raspberry gelatin**
- 1 **cup boiling water**
- 2 **packets Birdseye custard mix**
- 4 **cups milk**
- 1 **to 2 cups whipping cream**
- ¼ **cup plus 2 tablespoons sugar**
- **slivered almonds**

- Remove wrapping from cake and let stand to air dry. Cut in 2-inch slices and place in bottom of glass trifle bowl.
- Pour sherry and brandy over cake and add fruit.
- Dissolve gelatin in boiling water, stir in reserved juice and pour over cake and fruit.
- Chill for about 1 hour or until firm.
- Prepare custard according to package directions but using just 4 cups milk. Pour over trifle. Chill for about 1 hour.
- Whip cream with sugar until stiff. Spread on trifle and sprinkle with almonds. Serves 6 to 8.

BERNICE KORSHAK

Chocolate Chip Cookies

- 1½ **cups all purpose flour**
- ½ **teaspoon baking soda**
- 1 **cup butter, softened**
- ¾ **cup sugar**
- ¾ **cup firmly-packed brown sugar**
- 1 **egg**
- 1 **teaspoon vanilla**
- 1 **(6 ounce) package semi-sweet chocolate chips**
- 1 **cup chopped nuts**

- Sift flour and baking soda together and set aside.
- Cream butter, sugar, brown sugar, egg and vanilla together, beating until smooth.
- Add dry ingredients, chocolate chips and nuts to creamed mixture, mixing well.
- Drop dough by teaspoonfuls onto greased baking sheets.
- Bake at 375 degrees for 6 to 8 minutes.
- Makes 5 dozen.

DOLLY PARTON

Islands in the Stream

     3 **eggs, separated**
    ⅔ **cup sugar**
    2½ **teaspoons all-purpose flour**
     4 **cups milk**
     1 **teaspoon vanilla**
nutmeg

- Cream egg yolks and sugar together, whipping until smooth. Stir in flour.
- Scald milk, being careful not to boil. Add egg yolk mixture to hot milk, stirring constantly and cooking for 20 to 25 minutes or until thickened.
- Remove from heat, add vanilla, pour into serving bowl and set aside.
- Boil a pan of water. Whip egg whites in bowl and then place on top of boiling water. Splash water on them until they set up, remove with spatula and put on top of custard. Sprinkle with nutmeg.
- Serve chilled. Serves 6 to 8.

RESTAURANT PIERRE ORSI, LYON, FRANCE
PIERRE ORSI,
PROPRIETOR AND EXECUTIVE CHEF

Delice Genevieve

     1 **tablespoon plus 1 teaspoon butter**
     1 **tablespoon plus 1 teaspoon sugar**
     4 **yellow Reinette apples, peeled, cored and cut in ¼-inch cubes**
     2 **teaspoons brown rum**
    ½ **cup vanilla-bourbon ice cream**

- Melt butter with sugar, cooking until light caramel color.
- Add apples to sauce, stirring quickly to cook evenly until tender.
- Add rum, ignite to flambé and remove from heat.
- Spoon 2 tablespoons ice cream in individual serving cups. Divide apple mixture among cups and cover with cooking juices.
- Serve immediately. Serves 4.
- If Reinette apples are not available, use tart apple such as a Pippin.

THE HONORABLE WILLIAM PERRY

Lee's Chocolate Cake

CAKE
2½ cups sugar
1 cup vegetable shortening
2 eggs
2½ cups all-purpose flour
½ cup unsweetened cocoa
2 teaspoons baking soda
½ teaspoon salt
1 teaspoon vanilla
1 cup buttermilk
⅞ cup boiling water

- Cream sugar and shortening together until smooth. Add eggs, 1 at a time, beating well after each addition.
- Combine flour, cocoa, baking soda and salt. Add dry ingredients to creamed mixture, beating thoroughly. Stir in vanilla.
- Gradually add buttermilk and boiling water to batter, blending gently.
- Pour batter into 14x10x2-inch baking pan.
- Bake at 350 degrees for 35 to 40 minutes.
- While cake is baking, prepare frosting.
- Cool cake slightly in pan. Spread frosting on cake and cool completely before cutting.
- Serves 20 to 24.

FROSTING
1 (16 ounce) package powdered sugar
½ cup margarine, softened
½ cup unsweetened cocoa
dash of salt
1 teaspoon vanilla
hot water

- Cream powdered sugar with margarine until smooth.
- Add cocoa, salt and vanilla, mixing well.
- Stir in small amounts of hot water until frosting is of spreading consistency.

DON RICKLES
"Mandel Bread is the greatest, especially for the diet!"

Mandel Bread

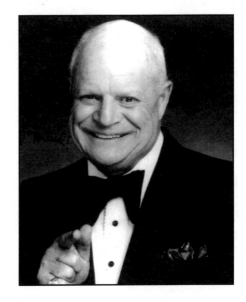

¾ **cup sugar**
3 **eggs**
1 **teaspoon vanilla**
3 **cups all-purpose flour**
1 **teaspoon baking powder**
1 **cup vegetable oil**
¾ **cup chopped walnuts**
cinnamon sugar

- Beat sugar and eggs together until smooth. Blend in vanilla.
- Combine flour and baking powder. Alternately add dry ingredients and oil to egg mixture, mixing well. Add nuts.
- Chill overnight or freeze for 3 hours.
- Shape dough into 3 long loaves and place on baking sheet.
- Bake at 350 degrees for 25 to 30 minutes.
- Cut hot loaves into slices, sprinkle with cinnamon sugar and place on baking sheet.
- Bake at 350 degrees for additional 10 to 15 minutes.
- Makes 2½ to 3 dozen.

Rickles can be tough on stage but he turned into a little boy around his mother. So did I. That's probably because our mothers could talk louder and hit harder than either of us. But our mamas were always after their boys to get more sleep. I've never been a fan of sleep. I'm afraid I'll miss something.
— *Frank Sinatra*

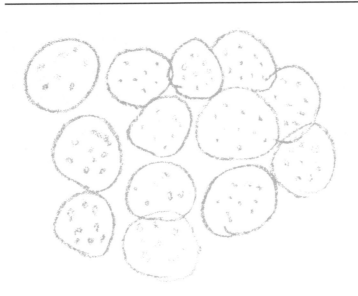

ROSEANNE

The Elvis

2 slices white bread
creamy peanut butter
6 thin banana slices
6 squares milk chocolate candy bar
ice cream (optional)

- Spread peanut butter on both slices of bread. Place banana slices on peanut butter on 1 slice, add chocolate pieces and top with second slice, peanut butter side down.
- Grill on griddle until golden brown, turning once.
- Cut in quarters. Serve with ice cream.
- Serves 4.

GEORGE SHEARING
"Although I have made my living in this country for over forty years as a pianist, I must confess I am still British to the bone...especially when it comes to having tea promptly at 4:00 each afternoon!"

Poppy Seed Cake

2 eggs
⅔ cup vegetable oil
1 teaspoon vanilla
2 cups sifted self-rising flour
1½ cups sifted sugar
¼ cup poppy seeds
1 cup evaporated milk

- Beat eggs, oil and vanilla together until smooth.
- Combine flour, sugar and poppy seeds. Alternately add dry ingredients and milk to egg mixture, blending thoroughly after each addition.
- Pour batter into greased and floured 9x5x3-inch loaf pan.
- Bake at 350 degrees for 30 minutes, reduce oven temperature to 300 degrees and bake for 1 hour.
- Cool in pan for 10 minutes, then invert on wire rack to complete cooling.
- Serves 10 to 12.

JOE SIROLA
"Dobar tek" (Croatian for bon appetit!)

Palacinke (Sweet Crepes)

2 **cups milk**
2 **eggs**
2 **cups all-purpose flour**
¼ **cup sugar**
¼ **teaspoon salt**
1 **drop vegetable oil**
½ **cup club soda**
vegetable oil

- Whisk milk and eggs together until smooth.
- Gradually blend in flour, then sugar and salt. Add 1 drop of vegetable oil.
- Chill batter for 1 hour
- Add club soda just before cooking crepes.
- Pour small amount of batter on hot oiled 6 or 7-inch crepe pan or in non-stick skillet, spreading batter evenly and thinly. Cook until browned, turn and brown other side.
- Serve with sprinkle of sugar and few drops lemon juice or spread with fruit preserve, roll and sprinkle with sugar.
- Serves 4 to 6.

ALAN THICKE
"This makes a delicious and refreshing treat on a hot summer day for all ages!"

Tutti Frutti Ice Cream

2 **liters orange carbonated soft drink**
1 **(14 ounce) can sweetened condensed milk**
1 **(20 ounce) can crushed pineapple**
1 **(3 ounce) jar maraschino cherries, drained and chopped**
whole milk

- Combine orange drink, milk, pineapple and cherries. Pour into ice cream freezer container and add milk to fill line, mixing well.
- Process according to freezer manufacturer's directions, using sufficient ice and rock salt.
- Makes 1 gallon.

BILL SMITROVICH
"Grandma Shaw was from Glassport, Pennsylvania. She was a steelworker and this was her favorite holiday recipe."

Grandma Shaw's Holiday Tarts

1½ **cups sugar**
 ½ **cup butter, softened**
  3 **eggs**
  1 **teaspoon vanilla**
  1 **cup crushed walnuts**
  1 **cup raisins**
pastry for 2 double crust pies
 36 **maraschino cherries**
vanilla ice cream

- Cream sugar and butter together until smooth. Add eggs and vanilla.
- Stir walnuts and raisins into filling.
- On lightly floured surface, roll pastry to thickness for tart shells. Cut in circles, place in greased miniature muffin pans, pressing lightly to fit within cups.
- Bake at 350 degrees for 5 to 8 minutes.
- Spoon filling into partially baked shells, filling each ⅔ full. Top each with cherry.
- Bake at 350 degrees until tart shells are browned.
- Serve warm or cold with ice cream. Makes 3 dozen.

SHARON STONE

Pomme du Jour

- Walk to the refrigerator.
- Open the door.
- Open the fruit drawer.
- Take out an apple.
- Eat it.

THE HONORABLE ARLEN SPECTER

Joan Specter's Chocolate Pecan Cake

½ cup butter, divided
½ cup firmly-packed dark brown sugar
½ cup shredded coconut
⅔ cup chopped pecans
½ cup semi-sweet chocolate chips
1 tablespoon milk
1 cup all-purpose flour
½ cup sugar
1½ teaspoons baking powder
¼ teaspoon salt
½ teaspoon vanilla
⅓ cup water
1 egg
vanilla ice cream

- Melt ¼ cup butter in saucepan. Remove from heat and stir in brown sugar, coconut, pecans, chocolate chips and milk, blending well.
- Spread mixture in bottom of 9-inch round baking pan and set aside.
- Combine flour, sugar, baking powder and salt.
- Add remaining ¼ cup butter, vanilla, water and egg to dry ingredients and mix thoroughly. Pour batter over coconut pecan mixture.
- Bake at 350 degrees for about 30 minutes or until wooden pick inserted near center of cake comes out clean.
- Cool cake in pan for 5 minutes, then invert on serving plate. If coconut-pecan mixture does not separate from pan easily, use spoon or spatula to remove and spread on cake.
- Serve warm or cold with ice cream.
- Serves 6 to 8.

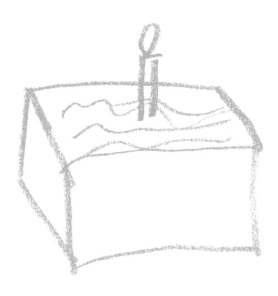

JILL ST. JOHN

Filled Fudge Cupcakes

CUPCAKES
⅔ **cup semi-sweet chocolate chips**
¾ **cup unsalted butter**
1¼ **teaspoons vanilla**
4 **eggs**
1½ **cups sugar**
1 **cup all-purpose flour**

- Melt chocolate, butter and vanilla together in top of double boiler, stirring until blended.
- Using electric mixer, beat eggs until frothy. Gradually add sugar, beating until it is dissolved. Gradually add flour.
- Fold chocolate liquid into egg mixture.
- Spoon batter into paper-lined muffin pans, filling cups ½ full.
- Prepare filling. Add 1 teaspoon filling to batter in each muffin cup.
- Bake at 350 degrees for 25 to 30 minutes.
- Cool cupcakes on wire rack. Makes 2 dozen.

FILLING
1 **(8 ounce) package cream cheese, softened**
¼ **cup sugar**
1 **egg, beaten**
½ **cup semi-sweet chocolate chips, coarsely chopped**

- Combine cream cheese, sugar and egg, beating well. Stir in chocolate chips.

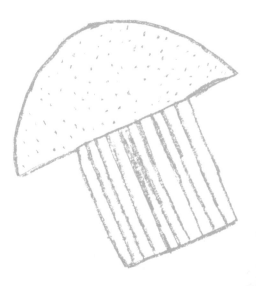

MARLO THOMAS

Chocolate Soufflé

2 **tablespoons butter**
2 **tablespoons all-purpose flour**
¾ **cup milk**
pinch of salt
2 **(1 ounce) squares unsweetened chocolate**
⅓ **cup sugar**
2 **tablespoons cold coffee**
½ **teaspoon vanilla**
4 **eggs, separated**
whipped cream

- Melt butter in saucepan. Whisk in flour, blending well.
- Bring milk to a boil in separate saucepan, add to butter-flour mixture and whisk vigorously. Stir in salt.
- Melt chocolate with sugar and coffee in top of double boiler. Stir chocolate mixture into sauce, then add vanilla. Add 3 egg yolks, 1 at a time, beating well after each addition. Let stand until cool.
- Beat 4 egg whites until stiff. Fold into cooled chocolate mixture.
- Spread batter in buttered 2-quart casserole sprinkled with sugar.
- Bake at 375 degrees for 35 to 45 minutes or until puffed and browned.
- Serve immediately with whipped cream. Serves 6.

ROBERT TOWNSEND

Mom's Jello Cake Recipe

CAKE
1 (3 ounce) package lime gelatin
1 cup boiling water
4 eggs
1 cup vegetable oil
1 (18½ ounce) package yellow cake mix

- Dissolve gelatin in boiling water and set aside to cool.
- Beat eggs and oil together until smooth.
- Add gelatin to egg liquid and beat for 2 minutes.
- Gradually add cake mix to gelatin mixture, blending until smooth.
- Pour batter into greased and lightly floured 10-inch fluted tube pan or 13x9x2-inch baking pan.
- Bake at 350 degrees for 45 to 50 minutes or until wooden pick inserted near center comes out clean.
- Pour glaze on hot cake. Serves 12 to 16.

GLAZE
powdered sugar
concentrated lemon juice

- Blend powdered sugar with lemon juice to form glaze consistency.

DANIEL TRAVANTI

Fool Proof Apple Cake

1 cup whole wheat or unbleached flour
½ cup oat bran
3 tablespoons baking powder
1 tablespoon cinnamon
1 teaspoon allspice
1 cup date sugar or brown sugar
½ cup fat-free yogurt
1 cup skim milk
1 tablespoon vanilla
4 egg whites, whipped until frothy
2 cups peeled or unpeeled diced apples

- Combine flour, bran, baking powder, cinnamon, allspice and sugar.
- Add yogurt, milk and vanilla to dry ingredients, mixing well.
- Blend egg whites into batter and fold in apples.
- Pour batter into 9x9x2-inch baking pan or dish.
- Bake at 350 degrees for 40 minutes.
- Cool in pan on wire rack. Serves 9.

JIM TUNNEY

"I am delighted to enclose one of my favorites — the recipe for my mom's brownies. These were a delight as a child and STILL."

Mom's Terrific Brownies

2 (1 ounce) squares unsweetened chocolate
¼ cup butter
2 eggs
dash of salt
1 teaspoon vanilla
¼ teaspoon almond extract
2 scant cups sugar
1 cup all-purpose flour
½ cup chopped walnuts

- Melt chocolate and butter together in saucepan over very low heat. Cool slightly.
- Blend in eggs, salt, vanilla and almond extract, beating until well mixed.
- Add sugar, 1 cup at a time, flour and walnuts, mixing well after each addition.
- Pour batter into buttered 8x8x2-inch or 9x9x2-inch baking pan.
- Bake at 400 degrees for 20 minutes.
- Cool before cutting into squares.
- Serves 9.

ANDY WILLIAMS

Mama's Rhubarb Short Cake

1½ **pounds strawberry rhubarb or regular rhubarb**
  2 **cups firmly-packed brown sugar**
cinnamon
  1 **cup sugar**
  ¼ **cup butter**
  1 **egg, beaten**
  1 **cup milk**
  2 **cups all-purpose flour**
  2 **teaspoons baking powder**

- Cut strawberry rhubarb in 1-inch pieces or regular rhubarb in strips, then in ½-inch pieces. Divide between two 9x5x3-inch loaf pans. Sprinkle 1 cup brown sugar over rhubarb in each pan and season with cinnamon.
- Combine sugar, butter and egg, beating until smooth.
- Add milk, flour and baking powder to creamed mixture. Divide batter evenly between 2 pans.
- Bake at 350 degrees for 1 hour. Invert pans to cool. Serve fruit side up. Serves 12.

LORETTA YOUNG
"My mother, who was a fabulous cook as well as a fabulous interior designer, enticed all her children with this very special dessert for years. She too must have enjoyed it very much because she gave the recipe to each of us on our wedding day."

Caramel Delight

  1 **(14 ounce) can sweetened condensed milk**
water
whipped cream

- Place unopened can of milk in saucepan and fill pan with water.
- Low boil for 4 to 5 hours, adding water if necessary to maintain depth. (If water level gets low, the danger is that the can may explode.)
- Remove from water and chill for several hours or overnight.
- Open and discard both top and bottom lid of can and slide caramel roll onto chilled plate.
- Using sharp knife and rinsing after each slice, cut roll into thin slices.
- Place slice on individual dessert plate and top with whipped cream. Serves 4 to 6.

CHRISTY TURLINGTON
"A favorite of mine from the Up & Down Club in San Francisco, California."

Up & Down Raspberry Ricotta Cheese Pie

PASTRY
2 cups all-purpose flour
1½ teaspoons sugar
¼ teaspoon salt
⅔ cup chilled butter
5 tablespoons cold milk

- Combine flour, sugar, salt and butter in food processor. Pulse 4 or 5 times to combine.
- Place in bowl, add milk and mix to form pastry.
- Roll pastry on lightly-floured surface to fit 10-inch pie plate. Place in plate.

FILLING
2 cups raspberries
2 tablespoons all-purpose flour
½ cup sugar, divided
1 tablespoon Grand Marnier liqueur
2 cups Ricotta cheese
2 eggs
1 teaspoon vanilla

- Combine raspberries, flour, ¼ cup sugar and liqueur. Spread mixture in pastry-lined pie plate.
- Blend cheese, eggs, vanilla and remaining ¼ cup sugar until smooth. Pour over raspberry layer.
- Bake at 350 degrees for 40 to 45 minutes. Serves 8.

BUD YORKIN

"An interesting dilemma with this recipe is that it's hard to keep your ripe bananas from being thrown out — you must guard them carefully. I finally had to put a sign on them: 'They're brown for a reason!' "

Banana Nut Cake

CAKE
  2 **eggs, separated**
1½ **cups sugar**
  ½ **cup butter, softened**
  ½ **cup sour milk**
  2 **cups all-purpose flour**
  1 **teaspoon baking powder**
  1 **teaspoon baking soda**
  ½ **teaspoon salt**
  3 **ripe bananas**
  1 **teaspoon vanilla**
  ½ **cup finely chopped nuts**

- Using electric mixer, beat egg whites until stiff and set aside.
- Cream sugar, egg yolks and butter together until smooth. Add sour milk and mix well.
- Combine flour, baking powder, baking soda and salt. Blend into creamed mixture.
- Mash bananas with fork, working in vanilla. Add to batter and beat well.
- Fold nuts, then egg whites into batter. Pour into greased and floured 13x9x2-inch baking pan or two 9-inch round baking pans for layer cake.
- Bake at 375 degrees for 30 to 45 minutes.
- While cake is baking, prepare glaze. Pour over hot cake in pan. Serves 20.

FROSTING
  ¼ **cup butter**
  1 **tablespoon lemon juice**
  1 **ripe banana, mashed**
powdered sugar, sifted

- Melt butter in saucepan. Blend in lemon juice and banana. Remove from heat.
- Add powdered sugar to form glaze consistency.

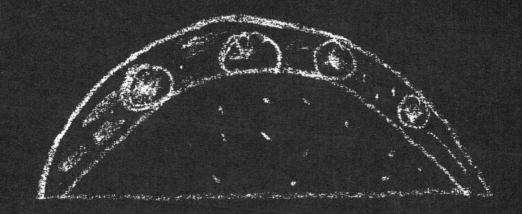

Mexican Favorites

Patty, age 9

PHYLLIS DILLER

Tamale Pie Deluxe

FILLING

 1 onion, chopped
 1 green bell pepper, chopped
 1 clove garlic, minced
 2 tablespoons vegetable oil
 1 pound ground beef
 2 (8 ounce) cans tomato sauce
 ¼ cup dry red wine
 1 teaspoon salt
 ¼ teaspoon black pepper
 1½ tablespoons chili powder
 1 (12 ounce) can corn, drained
 ¼ cup (1 ounce) grated Parmesan cheese

• Sauté onion, bell pepper and garlic in oil in large skillet until tender but not browned.
• Add beef and cook, stirring to crumble, until lightly browned. Drain excess fat.
• Stir tomato sauce, wine, salt, black pepper and chili powder into meat mixture. Simmer, covered, for 20 minutes.
• While sauce is cooking, prepare crust.
• Add corn to sauce and bring to a boil.
• Spread about ½ crust mixture in 12x8x2-inch baking dish. Add about ½ cup crust mixture to meat sauce, pour sauce over crust in dish and spoon remaining crust mixture over sauce.
• Bake at 350 degrees for 45 minutes, sprinkle with cheese and bake for additional 15 minutes. Serves 6 to 8.

CRUST

 1 cup yellow corn meal
 1 teaspoon salt
 3 cups cold water
 2 tablespoons butter or margarine
 ½ cup (2 ounces) grated Parmesan cheese

• Stir corn meal and salt into water in saucepan. Bring to a boil and cook, stirring often, until thin gruel consistency. Reduce heat and simmer for 20 minutes.
• Stir butter or margarine and cheese into corn meal mixture.

When I was a kid I didn't know much beyond the ethnic foods of Hoboken. Jewish, Polish, Irish, and Italian mamas made sure all of us neighborhood kids were well fed. Often we were told to "mangia" in seven languages. — Frank Sinatra

EDDIE ALBERT

"This is such a colorful and attractive dish with the green squash and yellow corn topped with the tomato sauce."

Calabacitas Rellenas de Elote

Zucchini Stuffed with Fresh Corn

ZUCCHINI

6	plump zucchini
2	cups fresh corn
2	medium eggs
2	tablespoons milk
¼	teaspoon salt or to taste
1½	cups (6 ounces) grated mild Cheddar or Muenster cheese, divided

- Cut zucchini in halves lengthwise and scoop out pulp, leaving shell about ½-inch thick. Discard pulp or reserve for another recipe. Place squash in single layer in baking dish.
- Blend corn, egg, milk and salt to form coarse purée; do not add more liquid unless absolutely necessary.
- Add 1 cup cheese to purée. Spoon filling into zucchini shells and sprinkle with remaining ½ cup cheese. Filling will be soup consistency.
- Bake, covered with aluminum foil, at 350 degrees for about 50 minutes or until tender.
- While zucchini is baking, prepare tomato sauce, or sauce can be prepared in advance.
- Serves 6.

SALSA DE JITOMATE COCIDA

Tomato Sauce

3	medium tomatoes
¼	onion, coarsely chopped
1	small clove garlic, coarsely chopped
2	tablespoons peanut or safflower oil
salt to taste	

- Blend tomatoes, onion and garlic together until coarse purée.
- Heat oil in saucepan, add sauce and cook over medium heat for about 8 minutes until thickened. Season with salt.

FOSTER BROOKS

Chili

    4 pounds lean ground beef
    1 (28 ounce) can tomatoes, cored and crushed
    1 large onion, diced
salt and black pepper to taste
    2 (4 ounce) cans green chiles, diced
    2 (6 ounce) cans tomato paste
    1 (28 ounce) can tomato purée
water
    ¼ cup chili powder
    2 tablespoons chili con carne seasoning
    2 tablespoons ground cumin
    1½ tablespoons sugar
    1 to 4 (16 ounce) cans small red beans or pinto
       or kidney beans
    5 or 6 chili pequins, crushed

- Cook beef in stock pot, stirring to crumble, until browned. Discard excess fat.
- Add tomatoes and onion to beef. Season with salt and black pepper.
- Stir in chiles and small amount of water. Simmer, covered, to cook onions.
- Add tomato paste and purée. Fill each can with water and add to mixture. Blend in chili powder, chili con carne seasoning, cumin, sugar, beans and chili pequins. Check seasoning and add salt if needed.
- Simmer until thickened to desired consistency. Serves 16.

PRESIDENT AND MRS. GEORGE BUSH

Mexican Mound

    2 pounds ground meat
    2 packets taco seasoning mix
    1 (6 ounce) package corn chips
    1 cup (4 ounces) grated Cheddar cheese
    1 or 2 small onions, chopped
   10 black olives, chopped
    1 tomato, chopped
    1 cup sour cream
    1 cup shredded lettuce
    1 (4 ounce) can frozen avocado dip, thawed

- Brown beef according to directions on taco seasoning mix. Drain excess fat. Blend seasoning as directed. Simmer until ready to serve.
- Pour corn chips in large bowl. Place cheese, onion, olives, tomato, sour cream, lettuce and avocado dip in separate bowls.
- To assemble, individuals place layer of corn chips on plate, add spoon of hot beef mixture and top with ingredients of choice. Serves 8 to 10.

JOHNNY CASH

"This chili will be better tomorrow than today if properly taken care of overnight. I have also been known to substitute things, such as snake meat, for the steak."

Johnny's "Old Iron Pot" Family Style Chili

  5 **pounds sirloin steak, chopped**
vegetable shortening
  3 **packets chili seasoning mix**
  3 **to 4 (16 ounce) cans red kidney beans**
  3 **to 4 (14½ ounce) cans whole tomatoes**
chili powder to taste
chili con carne seasoning to taste
cumin to taste
thyme to taste
sage leaves to taste
chopped onion
chopped chili peppers
garlic powder to taste
onion powder to taste
  2 **tablespoons sugar**
salt to taste
  1 **(6 ounce) can tomato paste**

- Brown steak in small amount of shortening in stock pot. Drain excess fat.
- Add chili seasoning mix and simmer for 5 minutes.
- Stir in beans, tomatoes, chili powder, chili con carne seasoning, cumin, thyme, sage, onion, chili peppers, garlic powder, onion powder, sugar and salt. Check seasoning. If too spicy, add 1 or 2 more cans of tomatoes.
- Add tomato paste. If chili is too thick, stir in water. Simmer for 20 minutes.
- Serve with saltines and cola soft drink.
- This will serve 12 people, three helpings each! Adapted from a recipe previously published in "Recipes and Memories from Mama Cash's Kitchen."

PRESIDENT AND MRS. BILL CLINTON

Chicken Enchiladas

2 (4 ounce) cans green chiles, drained and chopped
1 large clove garlic, minced
vegetable oil
1 (28 ounce) can tomatoes
2 cups chopped onion
2 teaspoons salt, divided
½ teaspoon oregano
3 cups shredded cooked chicken
3 cups sour cream
2 cups (8 ounces) grated Cheddar cheese
15 corn or flour tortillas

- Sauté chiles and garlic in oil in large skillet until garlic is tender.
- Drain tomatoes, reserving ½ cup juice. Break up tomatoes and add with reserved juice, onion, 1 teaspoon salt and oregano to chiles and garlic. Simmer, uncovered, for about 30 minutes or until thickened.
- Combine chicken, sour cream, cheese and remaining 1 teaspoon salt.
- Heat ⅓ cup oil in skillet. Dip tortillas in oil to soften and drain well on paper towel.
- Spoon chicken filling into tortillas, roll and arrange, seam side down, in 13x9x2-inch baking dish.
- Pour tomato sauce over tortilla rolls.
- Bake at 250 degrees for about 20 minutes or until thoroughly heated. Serves 15.

GLENN DAVIS

"This is not a bread. It's a good casserole to serve with beef, pork, chicken or lamb, a green vegetable and a salad."

Mexican Corn Bread Casserole

- 2 **eggs**
- 1 **cup buttermilk**
- ½ **cup olive oil**
- 1 **(16 ounce) can cream style corn**
- 1 **(4 ounce) can green chiles, drained and diced**
- 2 or 3 **tablespoons finely chopped green bell pepper**
- 3 or 4 **dashes hot pepper sauce**
- ½ **cup yellow corn meal**
- 1 **teaspoon salt**
- 1 **tablespoon baking powder**

- Combine eggs, buttermilk, oil, corn, chiles, bell pepper and hot pepper sauce, mixing well.
- Blend corn meal, salt and baking powder. Add dry ingredients to liquid mixture and blend.
- Pour into greased 8x8x2-inch baking dish.
- Bake at 375 degrees for about 45 minutes. Serves 6.

JAN MURRAY

Chili

- 1 **pound lean ground beef**
- 1 **green bell pepper, chopped**
- 1 **large onion, chopped**
- 2 **stalks celery, chopped**
- 1 **(16 ounce) can red kidney beans, undrained**
- 1 **(16 ounce) can white beans, undrained**
- 1 **(16 ounce) can tomato purée**
- 1 **teaspoon black pepper**
- 2 **tablespoons chili powder**
- 1 **teaspoon cumin**
- ½ **teaspoon garlic powder**
- 1 **teaspoon dry mustard**
- 2 **teaspoons oregano**
- 2 **teaspoons paprika**
- 2 **large fresh tomatoes, chopped**

- Lightly brown beef in Dutch oven, stirring to crumble. Drain excess fat.
- Add bell pepper, onion, celery, kidney beans, white beans, tomato purée, black pepper, chili powder, cumin, garlic powder, mustard, oregano, paprika and tomatoes to beef.
- Simmer for 25 minutes; do not overcook. Celery should retain some crispness.
- Serves 8 to 10.

TOM FLORES

Tom's Mexican Beans

  1 (16 ounce) package pinto beans
water
  1 small onion, chopped
  ½ green bell pepper, chopped
  4 green onions, chopped
  2 stalks celery, chopped
salt and black pepper to taste
pinch of oregano
pinch of cilantro
  6 ounces chorizo sausage
  1 pound lean ground beef

- Pour beans into 4-quart pan. Add water to cover, bring to a boil and cook for 2 minutes. Turn heat off and let stand for 1 hour.
- Rinse beans with cold water. Cover with cold water, bring to a boil, reduce heat and simmer, covered, for 1 hour.
- Add onion, bell pepper, green onion, celery, salt, black pepper, oregano and cilantro to beans. Cook for 45 minutes.
- Cook sausage in skillet. Drain excess fat and add sausage to beans.
- Brown beef in clean skillet, stirring to crumble. Drain excess fat and add to bean mixture. Simmer, covered, for 1 hour.
- Serve with tortillas. Serves 8 to 10.

JOANNA KERNS

My Brother's Salsa

  1 to 5 jalapeño peppers
vegetable oil
  1 (14½ ounce) can peeled tomatoes, undrained
  1 clove garlic, crushed
juice of ½ lime
  ¼ teaspoon salt
  1 ripe avocado, peeled and diced
  1 bunch cilantro, chopped
  1 bunch green onions, chopped

- Blacken jalapeño peppers (number according to intensity of flavor desired) in oil.
- Dampen inside of plastic bag with water, draining excess. Place peppers in bag and freeze for 5 to 10 minutes. Remove from freezer and pull skins from peppers.
- Combine tomatoes, garlic, lime juice, salt and jalapeño peppers in blender. Blend to salsa consistency.
- Place avocado, cilantro and green onion in bowl. Add tomato mixture and stir well.
- Makes 3 cups.

HENRY WINKLER

Henry's Mexican Salad

SALAD
2 heads romaine lettuce, broken in ½-inch
    pieces
2 (6 ounce) cans sliced black olives, drained
2 or 3 large tomatoes, diced
1 large red onion, diced
2 cups (8 ounces) grated sharp Cheddar cheese
1 (4 ounce) can green chiles, drained and diced
1 or 2 (6 ounce) packages tortilla chips,
    crumbled
2 avocados, peeled and diced

- Prepare dressing and chill until ready to use.
- Toss lettuce, olives, tomatoes, onion, cheese and chiles together.
- Drizzle dressing over salad and toss. Sprinkle chips and avocado on top of salad.
- Serves 8 to 10.

DRESSING
1½ cups mayonnaise
  1 (7 ounce) can green chile salsa
  ⅓ cup ketchup
  ½ teaspoon chili powder

- Combine mayonnaise, salsa, ketchup and chili powder. Chill.

KIRK DOUGLAS

Concha's Hot Sauce

3 medium to large firm tomatoes
6 to 8 serrano peppers
salt

- Place tomatoes on tray in toaster oven or broiler. Toast or broil at 350 degrees for 10 to 15 minutes or until skin begins to brown.
- While tomatoes are toasting, cook peppers in iron skillet until browned and skin loosens.
- Peel tomatoes, dice and place in blender. Peel peppers, discarding stems, chop and add to tomatoes.
- Blend at high speed for about 2 minutes. Season with salt.
- Makes 2 to 2½ cups.

I'm one of those people who likes plenty of Tabasco and hot peppers with almost anything, but this recipe for hot sauce should come with a caution label! Frank and I have spent many wonderful times with Anne and Kirk through the years... black tie galas and informal dinners, barbecues, snacks at card parties; with our children and without... and every get-together is special because of the most important ingredient of all — the extraordinary friendship our two families have had for many years.
— Barbara Sinatra

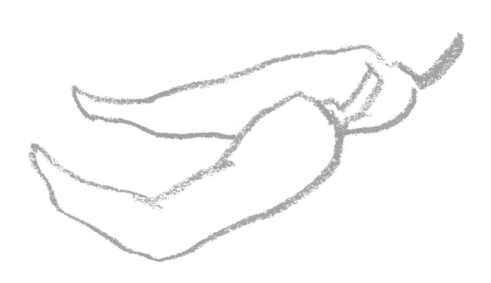

Index

A Little Cry In The Dark

She's a beautiful girl,
so who would believe
the nightmare that she'll live tonight?
No one should ever dream.
She wants to tell her mama,
but she couldn't break her heart;
so nobody hears a little cry in the dark.

Mornin' will come;
her daddy won't speak.
He acts like she's not even there.
She feels too sick to eat
and she pretends there's nothin' wrong;
her smile's a work of art.
Oh, nobody hears her little cry in the dark.

It's a small sound, so it's hard to hear it;
but, if we're still now – a little cry might reach us...

Would the preacher believe?
Who could she tell?
Her prayer tonight will be the same,
"Lord, help me through this hell."
She knows she's gotta stop him,
if she just knew where to start.
Oh, nobody hears her little cry in the dark.

He whispers, "Hon, if you love me,
you won't tell a soul.
Who'd believe you, anyway?
Our secret can't be told!
You know your papa loves you;
yeah, I do, with all my heart."
But, nobody hears her little cry in the dark.
Oh, nobody hears her little cry in the dark.

– Dene Hofheinz Anton, BSCC Aunt
– Jennifer Kimball
©1995